ISLAND OF THE BLUE FOXES

ISLAND

—OF THE—

BLUE FOXES

DISASTER *and* TRIUMPH
on the WORLD'S GREATEST
SCIENTIFIC EXPEDITION

STEPHEN R. BOWN

A Merloyd Lawrence Book
DA CAPO PRESS

Merloyd Lawrence Book by Da Capo Press
Hachette Book Group
1290 Avenue of the Americas, New York, NY 10104
www.dacapopress.com
@DaCapoPress

Printed in the United States of America

First Edition: November 2017

Published as a Merloyd Lawrence Book by Da Capo Press, an imprint of Perseus Books, LLC, a subsidiary of Hachette Book Group, Inc.

The publisher is not responsible for websites (or their content) that are not owned by the publisher.

Print book interior design by Trish Wilkinson

Library of Congress Cataloging-in-Publication Data has been applied for.
ISBNs: 978-0-306-82519-4 (hardcover), 978-0-306-82520-0 (ebook)

LSC-C

10 9 8 7 6 5 4 3 2 1

Contents

PART FOUR. NOWHERE

Timeline

1580s Russian Cossacks begin the conquest of Siberia.

1587 Founding of Tobolsk.

1632 Founding of Yakutsk.

1648 Russian explorer Semyon Dezhnev first navigates the Bering Strait.

1689 Peter the Great becomes co-czar of Russia with Ivan, his disabled stepbrother. Under the Treaty of Nerchinsk, Russia is denied access to the Pacific Ocean along the Amur River.

1696 Vitus Bering first goes to sea as a ship's boy on a voyage to India.

1703 Founding of St. Petersburg.

1724 Vitus Bering is promoted to be commander of the First Kamchatka Expedition.

1725 Death of Peter the Great. He is succeeded by his wife, Catherine I, who continues to carry out his policies and priorities, including the plan to explore Siberia.

1727 Catherine I dies, and Peter II becomes emperor. Bering sails the *Archangel Gabriel* north along the Pacific coast of Kamchatka.

1729 Death of Peter II, succeeded by Peter the Great's niece Empress Anna Ivanovna, who continues his vision of imperial exploration.

1730 First Kamchatka Expedition returns to St. Petersburg. Bering forwards plans for a second expedition.

1732   Empress Anna Ivanovna approves plans for a second expedition to be led by Vitus Bering.

1733   **April**   Contingents of the Second Kamchatka Expedition, also known as the Great Northern Expedition, depart St. Petersburg.

1734   **October**   Vitus Bering arrives in Yakutsk, headquarters for the expedition.

1737   **Fall**   Advance parties of the expedition arrive in Okhotsk.

1738–1739   Martin Spangberg sails to northern Japan in three ships.

1740   **June**   The *St. Peter* and *St. Paul* are completed at Okhotsk and sail around Kamchatka to Avacha Bay. Georg Steller arrives at Okhotsk. Anna Bering and the wives and families of the expedition officers return west to St. Petersburg.

October 28   Empress Anna Ivanovna dies.

1741 May 4   Sea council of officers decides to sail southeast in search of Gama Land.

June 4   The *St. Peter* and *St. Paul* depart Kamchatka for the coast of North America.

June 20   The *St. Peter* and *St. Paul* are separated in a storm, head east independently.

July 15   Aleksei Chirikov on the *St. Paul* sights the coast of North America.

July 16   Bering and Steller on the *St. Peter* sight the coast of North America near Mount St. Elias.

July 18   Chirikov sends eleven men ashore in the longboat for freshwater.

July 20   Bering in the *St. Peter* approaches Kayak Island and sends crews ashore for water. Steller collects plants and animals.

July 24   Chirikov sends four more men ashore to search for the missing shore excursion.

July 27   Chirikov abandons shore crews as dead or captured and sets sail for Kamchatka without obtaining freshwater.

August   Scurvy spreads through the crew of the *St. Peter*, including Bering, who seldom emerges from his cabin.

August 30   The *St. Peter* stops in the Shumagin Islands for freshwater. Nikita Shumagin is the first member of the expedition to die of scurvy.

September 4–9   Crew of the *St. Peter* meet Aleuts, in first encounter with native Americans.

September 9   The *St. Paul* crew encounter Aleuts at Adak Island but are unable to trade for freshwater. Scurvy is showing in the crew.

Late September and October   Scurvy epidemic and storms ravage the *St. Peter*.

October 10   The *St. Paul* returns to Avacha Bay. Fifteen men are abandoned in Alaska, and six are dead from scurvy.

November 6   The *St. Peter* is driven into Commander Bay on Bering Island. Men die of scurvy daily. Feral blue foxes attack.

December 8   Bering dies. Lieutenant Sven Waxell becomes new leader of the shore camp.

1742   January 8   Last scurvy death. With hunting and Steller's medicinal plants, conditions on Bering Island improve.

April 25   Peter the Great's daughter Elizabeth crowned empress after a coup the previous November.

May 2   Work begins to dismantle the wrecked vessel and build a new, smaller *St. Peter*.

August 13   Departure from Bering Island.

August 26   Arrival of survivors in Avacha Bay.

1743   Russian Senate officially disbands the Second Kamchatka Expedition.

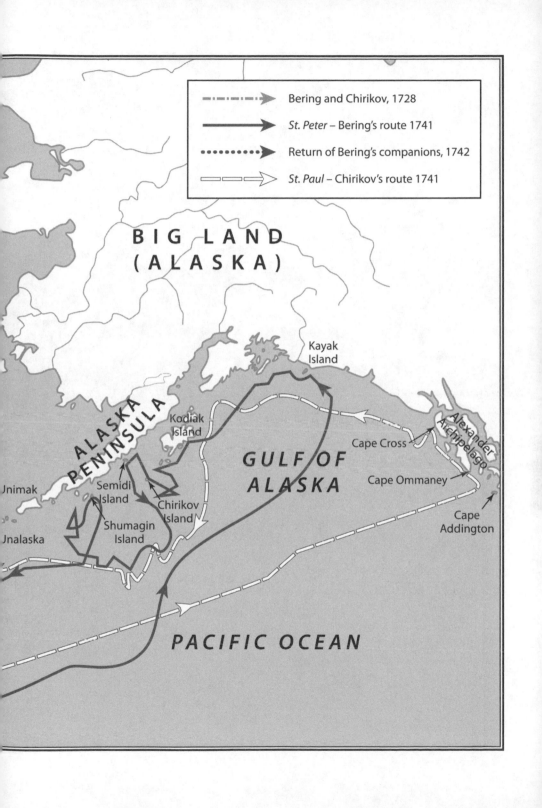

Bering and Chirikov, 1728
St. Peter – Bering's route 1741
Return of Bering's companions, 1742
St. Paul – Chirikov's route 1741

BIG LAND
(ALASKA)

Kayak
Island

ALASKA
PENINSULA

Kodiak
Island

GULF OF
ALASKA

Cape Cross

Alexander
Archipelago

Jnimak

Semidi
Island

Chirikov
Island

Cape Ommaney

Jnalaska

Shumagin
Island

Cape
Addington

PACIFIC OCEAN

PROLOGUE:
THE EDGE OF THE WORLD

I N THE FALL OF 1741, the Russian vessel *St. Peter*, more a wreck than ship, with tattered sails and snapped masts, limped west across the stormy North Pacific Ocean. A chill descended from the north, turning the rain to snow. Ice crusted the rigging and the railings. But the deck was curiously free from activity, as most of the men were lying below in their hammocks, despondent and immobilized from scurvy.

When the waves subsided and the skies cleared from the latest squall, a handful of mariners came on deck and stared at a distant outcropping of land that one of the officers assured them was Kamchatka. The vessel floated quietly into a harbor and dropped anchor as night fell. When the tide changed, however, a great current spun the ship about, snapped the anchor cable, and dragged the helpless vessel toward a concealed reef. Panic-stricken men dashed about, crying out questions as the hull ground sickeningly on the jagged rocks. If it were sundered, they all knew they would be sucked to their doom in the frigid waters. At the last moment, however, a large wave lifted the battered ship over the reef and deposited it in a shallow lagoon near the shore. Scarcely believing their deliverance, the few reasonably able-bodied men began ferrying the sick, the dead, and supplies to the stony beach, a task that consumed many days because of winds and snow flurries.

The sight that greeted them was bleak. Wind-lashed grassy dunes stretched back to a base of low snow-covered mountains. No sooner had the mariners shambled up the beach than a pack of snarling blue foxes swarmed toward them, began tearing at their pant legs, and had to be driven away with kicks and shouts. A small band of mariners, still strong enough to walk, set out to survey the coast and discovered they were on a treeless, uninhabited, and uncharted island. They had not, in fact, reached Kamchatka, their home base, but, as they later learned, were somewhere between America and Asia at the end of the Aleutian chain. The men immediately set about searching for shelter against the rapidly approaching winter and decided to enlarge a series of burrows they found near the dunes and a creek. They collected a rude framework of driftwood, to which they affixed fox hides and the tattered remnants of the sails.

Hordes of starving foxes swarmed about the makeshift camp, drawn from the barren hills by the scent of food. They stole clothing and blankets, dragged away tools and utensils, and became increasingly aggressive. Scratching at shallow graves, the foxes dragged away corpses and gnawed on them within sight of the enfeebled mariners. For the several dozen men who had scrambled ashore from the ship, things could not have seemed bleaker. The pitiable survivors were to spend the dark winter huddled in a collection of primitive shelters on this stony beachhead, subsisting on whatever animals they could hunt, sucking nourishment from withered roots and grasses, while their numbers dwindled. They had no proper clothing and only meager provisions and supplies from the ship. As winter wore on, they endured relentless Arctic winds, waist-deep snow, the ravages of scurvy, and continuous assaults by the feral blue foxes.

THE *ST. PETER* WAS ONE of two ships commissioned for the Great Northern Expedition (1733–1743), also known as the Second Kamchatka Expedition. It was the most ambitious and well-financed scientific voyage in history. Lasting nearly ten years and spanning three continents, its geographic, cartographic, and natural history accomplishments are on par with James Cook's famous voyages, the scientific circumnavigations of Alessandro Malaspina and Louis Antoine de Bougainville, and Lewis and Clark's cross-continental trek. The observations of the expedition's naturalist, German Georg Steller, gave Europe its first scientific description of Pacific America's flora and fauna, including the Steller's sea lion, Steller's sea cow, and Steller's jay. Conceived by Russia's Peter the Great in the early 1720s and led by Danish mariner Vitus Bering, the cost of this incredible enterprise was about 1.5 million rubles, an astonishing one-sixth of the annual income of the Russian state. Yet despite the lavish financing and lofty goals, the Great Northern Expedition is also one of the Age of Sail's darkest tales of shipwreck, suffering, and survival.

The Great Northern Expedition was intended to show Europe the grandeur and sophistication of Russia, while extending its imperial boundaries throughout northern Asia and across the Pacific Ocean to America. The scientific goals, though tethered to the interests of the state, were staggering in their scope. Russia had only recently been transformed, in the estimation of western European nations, from a barbarous backwater to a somewhat civilized state. The politics in Russia at the time were dangerous, corrupt, and fickle, as many of the expedition members found out during and after their years on the frontier.

Bering's original proposal for a voyage of exploration was modest, but when he saw his final instructions from Empress Anna, they had swollen to grandiose proportions. He would be at the head of a huge troop of nearly three thousand scientists, secretaries, students, interpreters, artists, surveyors, naval officers, mariners, soldiers, and skilled laborers, all of whom had first to cross through Siberia and many of whom had to travel as far as the eastern coast of Kamchatka. They had to trek across five thousand miles of roadless forests, swamps, and tundra, along with a supply of tools, iron, canvas, food and medicine, libraries, and scientific implements. Bering's second in command would be the impetuous and proud Russian officer Aleksei Chirikov, both men veterans of a previous major expedition. The scientific objectives were equally vast and included investigating the flora, fauna, and minerals of Siberia as well as settling outlandish rumors about the Siberian peoples. Most important, the expedition was intended to consolidate Russian political control over the entire region and somehow promote the Russian settlement of Okhotsk and Kamchatka, found schools, introduce cattle raising, discover and operate iron mines and a smelter, and construct a dockyard for deepwater ships. Once the weary cavalcade arrived in Okhotsk, Bering was supposed to build ships and sail south to survey the northern coast of Japan and the Kuril Islands. Then he was ordered to build two more ships and sail to Kamchatka, found an outpost, and then sail east to Pacific America, where it was hoped the group would explore the coastline as far south as California.

It was a wildly ambitious project that an absolute dictator with unlimited resources might possibly have accomplished. But Bering had to contend with both limited supplies and an awkward hierarchy. At any time, Bering's commands could be, and sometimes were, unexpectedly countermanded by additional directives from St. Petersburg, usually a result of slanderous letters dispatched by those under his command who didn't agree with his decisions. The expedition was a venomous circle of striving, conniving, and self-interest.

Ill fortune plagued the expedition. In June 1741, after years spent crossing Siberia and just as shipwrights had finally built and outfitted the *St. Peter* and the *St. Paul*, a supply ship carrying most of the provisions for the voyage ran aground on a sandbar. When the two ships sailed to America, they did so with food for only one summer, not the period of two years that was originally planned. Disagreements between the officers began as soon as the shore receded from sight and the sister ships headed east with no clear directive. The approximately 150 men on board were destined for one of the most tragic and ghastly trials of suffering in the annals of maritime and Arctic history.

PART ONE

EUROPE

Peter I, the Great, emperor of Russia, 1672–1725, modernized the Russian state and conceived of the First Kamchatka Expedition as a way of consolidating Russian dominance of Siberia and exploring the farthest reaches of his empire.

Empress Catherine I, shown here in an eighteenth-century painting, was a Lithuanian domestic servant who became Peter the Great's second wife and succeeded him as empress of Russia in 1725, where she proved a surprisingly competent and adept ruler.

Empress Anna Ivanovna ruled Russia between 1730 and 1740, continuing with the progressive reforms of her uncle Peter the Great and approving the overarching plan for the Great Northern Expedition.

The Kremlin, the seat of Russia's government before Peter the Great founded St. Petersburg, shown in this eighteenth-century engraving, was the scene of Peter's dramatic beard-trimming incident in 1698.

Peter the Great ordered the creation of St. Petersburg, shown here thirteen years after its founding in 1703, and made it the new capital of imperial Russia and Russia's first Baltic Sea port.

CHAPTER I

THE GREAT EMBASSY

O N THE MORNING OF September 5, 1698, Peter Alexeyevich Romanov awoke in the chambers of his wooden house near the Kremlin with purpose and determination. He had just returned from eighteen months of travel in western Europe, full of new ideas to modernize the traditions of the Russian state and eager to begin implementing them. Soon a crowd of boyars, the most senior aristocrats, and prominent officials had gathered on the street to welcome him home and to publicly demonstrate their loyalty, for a rebellion had only recently been suppressed. Several of the closest courtiers prostrated themselves, groveling before him in the traditional manner. A few murmurs spread through the crowd when, instead of accepting as his due "the promptitude of their obsequiousness," he instead "lifted [them] up graciously from their grovelling posture and embraced them with a kiss, such as is due only among private friends." This breach of protocol was mildly disturbing, but Peter had set his mind on a course of action, and it was merely the first departure of the day from Muscovite propriety.

The young czar, then twenty-six years old, moved among the crowd, embracing his officials and nodding at their welcomes. He then reached into his coat, produced a razor, and without warning grabbed the long beard of the commander of his armed forces, Alexis Shein. He cut through the dense strands, letting them fall to the ground. Too astonished to do anything, Shein stood immobile while Peter finished a rough shave of his beard. Peter then reached for the next closest boyar and rudely trimmed that man's beard. He worked his way through nearly all of those present, his most loyal and senior inner circle of advisers, until they had been shorn of their beards. Each one stood silent, none daring to voice opposition to the power of the czar, and in particular Peter, who had already earned a reputation for ruthlessness and an unpredictable temper.

Only three men were spared the indignity: an older man who Peter felt had earned the right to a beard, the patriarch of the Orthodox Church, and the personal bodyguard of his estranged wife, Eudoxia Lopukhina, whom he was about to force into a convent. Astonished and speechless, many of the highest-ranking social, political, and military men in the nation now sported new faces. There were a few bouts of nervous laughter. To some, the shaving of a beard was a direct assault on their religion. Under Peter's reign, it would be not only foreign merchants, engineers, and military personnel who strode the streets of Moscow beardless in the later seventeenth century, but Peter himself wore no beard, in defiance of convention, and others soon followed.

Peter's grand tour of western Europe, sometimes called his "Great Embassy," had convinced him that Russia was a backward country in serious need of reforms on many levels of society and that it had failed to benefit from the technological advances then sweeping nations like Germany, the Netherlands, and England. He was saddened to discover that these nations considered Russia not quite part of Europe, a semi-Oriental backwater with its onion-dome architecture, rigid Orthodox Church, and medieval political institutions. Russia had not yet felt the touch of the Enlightenment.

People's minds, in Peter's estimation, were still shackled to out-moded social belief systems, and he was determined to haul his country by whatever means into the orbit of Europe and into an era of what he considered modern thinking. The elaborate and ornate robes that impeded walking and physical work and the long coiffed beards made Russia a laughingstock in western Europe, and Peter was determined to put an end to these symbols of backwardness.

Peter saw these customs as a hindrance to the nation's chances of modernizing. He issued decrees that regulated what was deemed acceptable clothing at official ceremonies or functions and what all government officials should wear while performing their duties—waistcoats, breeches, gaiters, low boots, and stylish hats for men; women could don petticoats, skirts, and bonnets. He also banned the practice of wearing long curved knives at the waist. Anyone wearing old-style dress had to pay a special fee to enter the city, and in time Peter ordered guards at the city gates to cut off the robes of anyone, no matter their status, as a requirement for entering the city.

While Peter was enacting his dress and personal-grooming re-forms, he was also punishing the conspirators who had sought to place his elder half-sister Sophia on the throne during his absence—a rebellion by elements of the Streltsy, Russia's elite military corps. This no doubt added an undercurrent of fear to his beard and cloth-ing declarations. Although the rebellion was short and easily re-pressed by loyalists, Peter had already endured other uprisings by the Streltsy and by his half sister while he was still a child. This time his patience was short: Sophia was forced to become a nun and renounce her name and position in the aristocracy, he disbanded the Streltsy, and more than seventeen hundred of the surviving con-spirators were tortured in specially converted cells in Moscow in an effort to uncover the leaders of the conspiracy. Peter occasionally took a personal role as inquisitor, growling "Confess, beast, con-fess!" while flesh was flayed, beaten, and burned. In the great purge around twelve hundred were killed by hanging or beheading, many hundreds of bodies left on public display, while many hundreds of others were maimed and exiled to Siberia or other remote rural areas, their widows and children driven from Moscow. It served amply as a warning to any would-be rebels—or anyone else who might think of challenging his decrees. Peter eventually disbanded the regiments of the Streltsy in favor of his newly formed Imperial Guards.

In the violent context of the eighteenth century, Peter's actions appear to have been done not to satisfy his sadistic urges but rather for reasons of state, to eliminate treason and provide political stability. He berated a church official who appeared before him to beg for leniency for the traitors: "It is the duty of my sovereign office, and a duty that I owe to God, to save my people from harm and to prosecute with public vengeance crimes that lead to the common ruin." The purge solidified his power through fear and example, so now none would rise to challenge the European reforms that he planned for his country.

IN A FAMOUS PAINTING created during his visit to England, Peter looks resplendent in polished armor and a heavy gilded ermine cape. His stance is bold: one arm grips a rod, while the other is defiantly placed on his hip. Warships with billowed sails can be seen in the background through a window over his shoulder. His eyes are wide and his lips full, his hair curled and artfully ruffled. His head seems disproportionately small for his body, which is encased in its finery and steel. Peter was an unusually tall and striking individual; at more than six foot seven, he towered over most of his contemporaries. But he was also narrow shouldered, and his hands and feet were notably small in relation to his long body. While vigorous and stubborn, he suffered a mild form of epilepsy and had obvious facial tics. Sophia, the widowed electress, or ruler, of Hanover, provided a detailed description of her meeting with Peter in the summer of

1697 and pronounced that he "is a prince at once very good and very bad; his character is exactly that of his country."

At the time of Peter's Great Embassy to Europe in the spring of 1697, no Russian czar had ever traveled abroad—at least not without an invading army—particularly into such distant territory. But Peter had already embarked on schemes to break this isolation. He began by expanding his fleet so that Russia wouldn't be essentially landlocked, with only a remote port at Arkhangelsk on the White Sea in the Far North. The Baltic was controlled by Sweden, while the Caspian and the Black Seas were under the sway of the Safavid and Ottoman Empires. Peter had attacked the Ottoman fortress of Azov, at the outlet of the Don River, and seized the fortress in 1696. To defend his new territory, he began building a stronger navy, sending dozens of young men to western Europe to learn seamanship and naval strategy. Peter had then announced that he would be organizing a journey of more than 250 high-ranking Russians to the capitals of western Europe. Even more shocking was the rumor that he planned to go himself, to see the world and form his own opinions, to help set Russia on the path to greatness and prosperity. Only three years after the death of his mother, when he had assumed full authority as czar, the young autocrat wanted to travel in disguise, as a mere member of an ambassador's entourage.

To understand how this greater world worked, how best to achieve his ambitious goals, Peter planned to avoid pompous ceremony and political displays of honor. Ambassadors to his court reported to their respective countries and speculated that Peter's most likely reasons were for personal amusement, a little diversion and holiday, to see how regular people lived their lives, and to make himself a better ruler. Peter also knew he needed allies in his struggle against the Ottoman Turks. The Great Embassy made plans to visit the capitals of Warsaw, Vienna, and Venice as well as Amsterdam and London. He would not travel to France to see the famous Sun King, Louis XIV, as France was then allied with the Ottomans.

While Peter undoubtedly had a healthy ego, being raised a prince, he was also humble and insightful enough to realize that he, and Russia, had a lot to learn if he was to take advantage of the new technology and knowledge of the age. Writing later in life, Peter observed that he

> turned his whole mind to the construction of a fleet. . . . [A] suitable place for shipbuilding was found on the River Voronezh. . . . [S]killful shipwrights were called from England and Holland, and in 1696 there began a new work in Russia—the construction of great warships, galleys and other vessels. . . . [A]nd that the monarch might not be shamefully behind his subjects in that trade, he himself undertook a journey to Holland; and in Amsterdam at the East India wharf, giving himself up, with other volunteers, to the learning of naval architecture, he got what was necessary for a good carpenter to know, and, by his own work and skill, constructed and launched a new ship.

Peter Mikhailov, as he would be known, also craved freedom, to see and hear and observe for himself the state of the world and not be hidden behind a facade of luxury and ceremony. He didn't care to spend his days just swanning with royalty; rather, he preferred to have the freedom to come and go anonymously. He wanted Russia to become part of the exciting world of western Europe—and the new lands that its mariners had been exploring and were continuing to explore with their fleets. The world was becoming globalized in the late seventeenth and early eighteenth centuries, and western Europe was the technological and inspirational epicenter of this endeavor. New technologies, such as clocks or chronometers, compasses, thermometers, telescopes, barometers, and instruments for accurate cartography, supported navigation and exploration. The enterprising mariners and financiers of the Dutch and English East India Companies as well as the Dutch West India Company were bringing coffee, tea, sugar, and spices such as cinnamon, cloves, and nutmeg to European markets. Exotic plants and animals were in everyday use. Freed to a certain extent from religious dogma, scientists such as Descartes, Leibniz, Leeuwenhoek, and Newton were actively experimenting and exploring the natural environment and the properties and principles that governed the world. This new science was changing the European worldview, and Peter didn't want to miss out personally or let Russia be left behind. He also had more prosaic designs. He purchased new ship cannons, rigging, anchors, sails, and the latest instruments of navigation so that they could be better understood and replicated in Russia to improve the economy.

Most people in the seventeenth and eighteenth centuries lived in rural environments, engaged in some activity directly related to farming with animals. Waterwheels and windmills provided the only energy beyond sheer muscle power. People seldom traveled, as the roads were poor and surplus food or time was scarce. Daily life began with the rising of the sun and ended after dark. Wood was the only source of light and heat. Russia, being on the geographical fringe of Europe, was not part of the transfer of new ideas and knowledge then sweeping the continent, and Peter wanted that to change—to bring about a new way of life for his people.

The thought of a Russian Great Embassy did not bring joy to the courts of the countries that were to receive the group. The Russian ambassadors of the time knew little of the customs of other nations and consequently had difficulty communicating their ideas. They were usually seen as rude and uncouth, bumpkins who refused to follow the protocols of courtly behavior common in western Europe.

The Russian court itself was seen as beyond the pale. According to the Austrian ambassador's secretary Johann Georg Korb, meals at the Russian court were frequently unscheduled and abruptly preceded by the announcement that "the Tsar wants to eat!" Servants would promptly arrive with platters of food and place them on the huge table, seemingly at random, while people grabbed for them, perhaps hitting each other jokingly with long loaves of bread or squabbling over the great bowls of wine, mead, beer, and brandy. Heavy drinking was common along with heated arguments, lively dancing, and even wrestling. Trained bears sometimes roamed the dining hall, proffering cups of pepper brandy and knocking off hats and wigs to much merriment. These antics, while no doubt amusing to the Muscovites in Peter's court, were not much appreciated by European dignitaries preoccupied with the order and timing of entering rooms and table seating, with which long-winded title each person was to be addressed, with which cup to drink from, and in which order to eat the varied dishes. Peter particularly disliked official or formal functions, considering them to be "barbarous and inhumane," preventing monarchs "from enjoying the society of mankind." He wanted to talk and dine, drink, and joke with people of all ranks, while being the first among equals naturally. Peter was proud of his calluses, of laboring with shipwrights, of marching with his soldiers, of working the ropes on a ship, of drinking beer with craftsmen. He was eager to meet with men who had risen to respect out of merit rather than birth or influence.

PETER PERSONALLY CHOSE THE members of his Great Embassy, and the sprawling cavalcade included not only his three principal ambassadors, senior members of Peter's nobility, but also twenty other aristocrats and thirty-five skilled artisans. They would all travel together in addition to priests, musicians, interpreters, cooks, horsemen, soldiers, and other servants. "Peter Mikhailov," a nondescript brown-haired, blue-eyed jack-of-all-trades noteworthy only for his height, joined the ranks. It would be an open secret that he was traveling with the embassy, but it was not to be officially acknowledged, which created unusual dilemmas with protocol. Peter left Russia in the hands of three older trustworthy men, a regency council that included one of his uncles.

The Great Embassy set off overland through the Swedish-controlled territory that bordered the eastern Baltic, which included Finland, Estonia, and Latvia. Here Peter paid particular attention to the fortifications of the city of Riga, a fortress that his father had failed to conquer forty years earlier and that would be a nicely situated place for a Russian port on the Baltic Sea. He considered his reception here to be rude and inhospitable—not fit for a czar. Of course, he was traveling incognito, but he still expected to see the recognition that he was there. Having his entourage ignored and left to fend for themselves and to pay high prices for their food and lodging was not acceptable. Three years later, Peter would use this apparent or perceived ill treatment in Riga as an excuse for starting the war that would consume most of his life and reign, the Great Northern War with Sweden. Riga would eventually be incorporated into the Russian Empire. Certainly, it was convenient that he was treated so poorly there, since there was no other way for him to expand Russia and gain access to the Baltic Sea than by seizing Swedish-held territory. The cavalcade then traveled overland to Mitau in Poland. Growing impatient, Peter boarded a private yacht and sailed ahead to the northern German city of Königsberg, where Frederick III, the elector of Brandenburg, met him to discuss an alliance against Sweden. Like Peter, Frederick also wanted to expand his territory, to become king of a newly formed kingdom of Prussia.

After laying the foundation for future joint military action against Sweden, Peter continued overland to Berlin. By this time, his presence was an open secret, and word traveled throughout northern Europe. People thronged to see the czar of the mysterious eastern land with the outlandishly dressed people and the Oriental customs, known for their hard drinking and barbaric behavior. The Great Embassy became like a traveling circus, and Peter was annoyed at the intrusive scrutiny, as if he were a curiosity, which he was. But he was a charming curiosity, well liked by the gentry of Germany for his good humor, fun-loving displays, and lively conversation. He proved to be nowhere near as uncivilized a bear as had been reported. His many foreign tutors had prepared him well.

In mid-August, Peter and a handful of compatriots, upon reaching the Rhine, boarded a small boat and sailed downstream, leaving the bulk of the Great Embassy to plod along by land. He sailed right through Amsterdam to the Dutch town of Zaandam, where in his quixotic manner he wanted to enlist as a carpenter and learn shipbuilding, as if he were a common laborer. He set himself up in a small wooden house close by the shipyards, purchased some carpentry tools, and signed on to build ships. His anonymity was soon questioned, as rumor spread of foreigners in strange costumes having arrived by ship; crowds were staring at his troupe in their ostentatious Russian dress. Peter also stood out because of his unusual height and distinctive facial tics, and within days he was politely declining offers to dine with the leading officials and merchants of the town. Soon his presence was causing a sensation throughout the republic; people came from Amsterdam to see if the rumors were true, that the czar of Muscovy was working on ships as a common laborer, and soon fences had to be erected around the work site to keep the crowds of gawkers at bay. The next day he grew impatient and forced his way through the throngs, boarded his small ship, and sailed to Amsterdam, where he went directly to the large inn reserved for the embassy.

In Amsterdam, which was much larger and more accustomed to worldly happenings, he hoped to blend in. Water and thousands of ships surrounded him everywhere in this city of canals, and the hollering of sailors was always in the air. He found work at the walled shipyards of the Dutch East India Company (known as the VOC), where there was a fleet of ships of different shapes and sizes. Some were being constructed, while older ones had been dragged above the tide line and lay like the decaying rib cages of sea monsters, rotted planking being torn away and replaced over the skeleton. Ropes and wood and tar and cloth and iron were being molded into vessels of commerce and war, and it was here that Peter spent months gaining a familiarity with all things nautical. But he no longer strove for anonymity. Instead, he met with the burgomaster and leading city dignitaries. The VOC offered him a small house within the walls of the compound to keep prying eyes at bay. He and ten other Russians would begin work on a new one-hundred-foot frigate, to see and participate in its construction from the ground up, from inspecting the logs and materials to overseeing the design plans. The VOC renamed the ship in his honor, *The Apostles Peter and Paul*.

What was most shocking to the young czar were the density and wealth of the Dutch Republic. With about two million people in a small country, its cities were huge by comparison to those in other lands. The Dutch Republic was at its pinnacle of prestige—from the wealth that flowed from the Dutch East India Company—and it was then the richest, most urbanized, and most sophisticated nation in Europe, renowned for its art and clothing, food, spices, and thinkers. Its teeming shipyards serviced a trade network that was then the largest in the world, with ships that sailed nearly everywhere European ships could navigate—everywhere except for the North Pacific. The mighty commercial enterprise transformed the nation and then Europe. The VOC alone employed more than 50,000 people—sailors, artisans, laborers, stevedores, clerks, carpenters, and soldiers. Other Dutch companies fed off the commercial activities of the VOC, and they collectively controlled vast quantities of the trade in northern Europe. The immense wealth this trade produced helped to stimulate the Dutch Golden Age, an era when the Netherlands was the wealthiest and most scientifically advanced of European nations, with flourishing arts and sciences, from painting, sculpture, architecture, and drama to philosophy, law, mathematics, and publishing. Peter had never before seen anything like it. In Amsterdam forests of ship masts congregated in the protected harbor, smaller ships lined endless wharves, and canals indented the city with heavily laden barges.

All this activity was also spurring the development of new financial structures to control and enable it: credit, insurance, loans, the joint-stock company. People from around Europe came to learn methods of commerce and other skills related to the new global trade that extended from regions as far away as the Pacific Ocean. That ocean, Peter was aware, lay at the terminus of his vast sprawling empire, the little-explored and poorly charted eastern land known as Kamchatka, which at the time was thought possibly to connect to North America.

PETER SPENT FOUR MONTHS working in the Amsterdam shipyards and touring the other cities of the Dutch Republic. On November 16, 1697, the frigate Peter was working on was launched to great ceremony and then presented to him by the VOC as a gift. The ship, which Peter renamed *Amsterdam* in honor of his hosts, was eventually loaded with all of the examples of European industry that the Russian contingent had been buying and set sail for still the only Russian port in Europe, Arkhangelsk, on the White Sea.

In January 1698, Peter and a handful of chosen compatriots set off for England at King William's invitation, leaving most of his embassy in Amsterdam. He was to be presented with a new yacht as a gift from the king, and he wanted to compare English shipbuilding techniques to those of the Dutch. The city of London also amazed him—at around 750,000 people, it was on par with Amsterdam and Paris. The Thames was crowded with vessels of all sizes. England and the Dutch Republic fought three wars during the seventeenth century, grappling for supremacy of the world's trade routes to India and the spice islands. As in Amsterdam, by this time much of

London's wealth was arriving from destinations outside Europe: from America, the Caribbean, India, Indonesia, and even China.

Peter was particularly interested in how the British tax system and economy provided the government with revenues for constructing and maintaining the mighty navies that were bringing the wealth of the world to its shores. He was searching for evidence of how to transform his mostly rural nation with an agrarian economy into something resembling a modern European nation with a skilled urban population. Peter spent months working in and touring the king's shipyards and, along with his Russian cohorts, earned a reputation for rowdy, unrefined behavior. Peter's strong opinions were noted, as were his insatiable curiosity and fiery temper. He also toured the royal mint and later used its example as a foundation for his reforms of the Russian currency. Here and in Amsterdam, he interviewed and hired skilled craftsmen and engineers, physicians, and tradesmen such as stonemasons, locksmiths, and shipwrights as well as mariners and navigators. The wages he offered were good enough to induce many to leave home and move to Russia.

In mid-July, as he was readying to depart Vienna, Peter received news of the Streltsy's uprising and the march on the Kremlin with the support of his half-sister Sophia. He canceled the final destination of his tour, Venice, and rushed back through Poland to Moscow—riding day and night, stopping only to change horses, no doubt thinking about the great beards he was about to shave.

AFTER COUNTERING THE UPRISING on his return to Moscow, Peter began implementing his ideas about how a modern state should be structured and governed. He had dwelled on the institutions lacking in his home that he admired in Holland, Germany, and England. The new beard laws and the beard tax were just the first of many actions that he intended to shake Russia from its somnolence. The next twenty-five years of Peter's long reign would be taken up with two main priorities, the first of which was a series of radical institutional changes to Russian society, remodeling it along European lines.

During the decades after his return from the Great Embassy, he adopted the clothes, style, friends, and habits of foreigners; had many foreign friends and advisers; and strove for many years to stamp out the Orthodox belief that foreigners were a source of heresy and contamination. He trimmed the power of the Orthodox Church, introduced calendrical reform, expanded and restructured the army, standardized the coinage, introduced official stamped paper for legal documents, and created state awards. A lifelong pipe smoker, a habit he picked up from his German and Dutch friends, Peter also legalized tobacco. At one time during his grandfather's reign, smoking had been punishable by death, with the penalty later liberalized to having one's nostrils slit. Since no one was going to be slitting the czar's nostrils, the church put up little fight against decriminalizing tobacco. He founded the Academy of Sciences, staffed chiefly with foreign intellectuals. Peter was also against strict arranged marriages, a tradition that he had personally experienced that was not in evidence in Holland, Germany, or England. He had been married according to this tradition by his mother when he was a teenager and unable to resist. Peter determined to be rid of his then wife, Eudoxia Lopukhina, a mournful and pious woman whom he rarely saw or spoke with; he had not written her a single note during his eighteen-month absence in Europe and did not rush to see her upon his return. He had her put in a nunnery and removed from the palace and public life. In 1703 he met Martha Skavronskaya, a Lithuanian peasant in domestic service who became his mistress, then wife, and finally Empress Catherine.

After the political and social reforms, the second major accomplishment of Peter's reign was to launch the war with Sweden, the Great Northern War, a long string of battles of conquest that secured lands along the eastern Baltic coast and tilted the nation westward toward Europe. In this new territory, in 1703, Peter founded a new city. Situated on the eastern coast of the Gulf of Finland, at one time part of Russia but more recently controlled by Sweden, the city was to be a model for Russia. He named it Saint Petersburg. Peter was so anxious that the city be built on a new modern plan, and be built quickly, that he passed an edict that no stone construction would be permitted elsewhere in Russia; all Russian stonemasons had to work on his new city until it was completed. Here he headquartered the Russian Navy and expanded it, using the host of artisans and tradesmen he had recruited during his Great Embassy. The new city became the center of his government and court. On September 10, 1721, Russia and Sweden ended the twenty-one-year Great Northern War when they signed the Treaty of Nystad, the same year that Peter added the honorific *emperor of all Russia* to his official title. During the war, Russia had conquered much of the eastern Baltic and Finland, and Peter agreed to pay a large sum in silver to Sweden in exchange for keeping Estonia, Livonia, Ingria, and southeastern Finland as part of the Russian Empire.

PETER LED AS ACCOMPLISHED, and colorful, a life to rival that of any grand monarch. He had done more than any other Russian leader to restructure the nation and set it on a modern path, and he still had grand plans. Not for nothing was he called Peter the Great. But in the summer of 1724, after decades in power, he became seriously ill, was perhaps even dying, despite his relative youth. His physicians opened his abdomen and pierced his bladder, releasing four pounds of urine that had been painfully building inside him. He rallied in the fall, but by December he was again bedridden and in daily pain.

Peter could have looked back on a career of unparalleled accomplishment and success—a life of drama and adventure that had seen

Russia transformed from an ignorant medieval backwater to one of Europe's preeminent nations. Yet he was not content to linger on past glories. He was dreaming of one long-desired geographical and scientific ambition, a final act that would elevate even further the Russian state in the estimation of European nations and the scientific community as well as consolidate his grasp on the farthest-flung reaches of his vast and sprawling empire. As he lay in the imperial splendor of his apartments in the palace, grounded by his illness, he was thinking about something new, a final brilliant cap to an illustrious career and life. He scrawled out a set of instructions—a command that would have repercussions for many decades and lead to one of the greatest scientific expeditions in history and the discovery of a sea route to a new land. In his final days, one of Peter's great interests was in geography and determining the extent and resources of the farthest districts of his empire as well as a longtime pet interest: the relationship between Asia and North America. This was a great geographical mystery that lay, in this era before the American Revolution and Captain Cook's voyages, in one of the final uncharted parts of the globe, the North Pacific Ocean.

In the waning days of 1724, Peter spoke to his closest adviser from his deathbed. He outlined his ideas and plans to his attendants and, "concerned that his end was near," was eager to get the expedition under way. Calling the general-admiral Count Apraxin (Fedor Matveevich) to his bedside, he said:

> Bad health has obliged me to remain home. Recently I have been thinking over a matter which has been on my mind for many years but other affairs have prevented me from carrying it out. I have reference to the finding of a passage to China and India through the Arctic Sea. On the map before me there is indicated such a passage bearing the name of Anian. There must be some reason for that. In my last travels I discussed the subject with learned men and they were of opinion that such a passage could be found. Now that the

country is in no danger from enemies we should strive to win for her glory along the lines of the Arts and Sciences. In seeking such a passage who knows but perhaps we may be more successful than the Dutch and English who have made many attempts along the American coast.

He handed over to the count the instructions written in his own hand, on December 23, 1724, although he did not sign the official document for another month, on January 26, 1725. Peter's instructions were concise, considering their long-term impact on world history:

I. To build in Kamchatka or in some other place one or two decked boats.

II. To sail on these boats along the shore which runs to the north and which (since its limits are unknown) seems to be a part of the American coast.

III. To determine where it joins America. To sail to some settlement under European jurisdiction, and if a European ship should be met with learn from her the name of the coast and take it down in writing, make a landing, obtain information, draw a chart and bring it here.

One month after drawing up these plans for the first major Russian exploration, later to be called the First Kamchatka Expedition, one that would fill the geographical gaps left by other European nations and become a symbol of the awakening of the Russian Empire, Peter the Great died on February 8, 1725, at age fifty-two. His widow, Catherine, became the new empress, and she continued to support her husband's dream. Peter had chosen a twenty-year veteran of his navy and the Great Northern War to lead the expedition, a mature and respected Danish commander named Vitus Bering.

CHAPTER 2

THE FIRST
KAMCHATKA EXPEDITION

A PAINTING LONG THOUGHT to be of Vitus Jonassen Bering depicts a jowly man with friendly eyes and a curious disposition. The portrait seems at odds with the life and deeds of the famous commander, who spent most of his life at sea or exploring Siberia, and is now thought to be a portrait of his great-uncle Vitus Pedersen Bering, a famous Danish historian and poet. Facial reconstruction of Vitus's exhumed remains by a Danish-Russian archaeological team in 1991 revealed he was a heavily muscled man of about five feet, six inches in height, weighing 168 pounds. He stood out for his rugged appearance, with prominent cheekbones and long wavy hair. He was a handsome man in good health throughout his life.

Bering was one of the many talented foreigners attracted to Russian service by Peter the Great's expansion of the Russian Navy. He was born on August 5, 1681, in the town of Horsens, a Baltic port on the east side of Jutland whose fortunes had faded along with military losses to Sweden throughout the seventeenth century. His father was a customs officer and church warden, respectably middle class. But there was little future for a young, ambitious man in the town. Love of ships and the sea led him to sail as a fifteen-year-old ship's boy, along with his older brother, on a voyage one year before Peter the Great set off on the Great Embassy. For eight years Bering sailed on Dutch and Danish merchant ships on voyages as far as India, Indonesia, North America, and the Caribbean. He learned navigation, cartography, and command and spent time at an officers' training institute in Amsterdam. In 1704 the young Bering met Cornelius Ivanovich Cruys, a Norwegian who had been hired by Peter the Great in 1697 to help create a new Russian navy. Bering was fortunate and probably pleased when Cruys offered him a position in the Russian Imperial Navy at the start of the Great Northern War between Russia (joined at times by Denmark, Saxony-Poland, and Prussia) and the Swedish Empire, at the time Denmark's archenemy. It was an auspicious time to be a skilled and intelligent mariner. Bering was later fond of claiming "with praise how from his youth, everything had come his way." He enjoyed a successful career in the Russian Navy, ascending through the ranks, from sublieutenant to lieutenant in 1707, to captain lieutenant in 1710, to captain fourth rank in 1715, and finally to captain second rank in 1720. Then his luck ran dry for a short spell.

Bering, whom a later companion described as "by faith a righteous and devout Christian, whose conduct was that of a man of good manners, kind, quiet" and who was "universally liked by the whole command, both high and low," never distinguished himself in any sea battles. He was competent and trustworthy, and his most significant act of distinction came in 1711 when, during a failed campaign against the Turks, he ran his ship, *Munker*, through the Sea of Azov, across the Black Sea, through the Bosporus Strait to the Mediterranean, and all the way north to the Baltic Sea, where he remained stationed throughout the war. The strenuous and dangerous voyage demonstrated leadership, daring, and initiative—traits that would serve him well as commander of two of history's longest and most complicated land and sea expeditions.

Through mutual friends in the Lutheran community predominant along the Baltic coast, he met Anna Christina Piilse in Viborg, and they were married in 1713. She was twenty-one years old, eleven years younger than Bering, the eldest daughter of a wealthy German-speaking merchant family who lived along the Neva River, near the new city of St. Petersburg. They would eventually have nine children, four of whom survived to adulthood. They did not see each other frequently during the war when Bering was at sea, preparing Anna Christina for the many years Bering would be away leading expeditions to the Pacific Ocean. They were an upwardly mobile couple concerned with their position in society; Bering's career was important. All was well during the war while Bering was rising in the ranks, but when he failed to gain a promotion in recognition of his war service, he slipped behind many of his colleagues. Worse was to come. Anna's younger sister Eufemia became engaged to Thomas Saunders, an officer originally from Britain who was a rear admiral in the Russian Navy, a rank superior to the one Bering had attained and one that came with a noble title. Soon the older sister would be of obviously inferior social status to the younger, and her husband would be of lower rank than his brother-in-law. This was not good for family harmony and was a real setback for Vitus and Anna. They pondered the distressing turn of events and decided that the only way to preserve their honor and save face was for Bering to resign from the navy. Bering sent off an official request for retirement to be effective before Eufemia's marriage. He was bestowed the rank of captain first class in retirement in February 1724, and he and Anna moved from St. Petersburg back to Viborg with their two children. However, since he had no pension and now no income and had a family to support, the retirement didn't last long, and within six months he asked to be reinstated. Since Eufemia was in St. Petersburg, Anna decided to remain in Viborg, where she would be spared the humiliation of accidentally encountering her higher-ranked younger sister. Bering reported to duty, commanding a ninety-gun ship in the Baltic fleet. But Peter the Great and his advisers had plans afoot that would change Bering's life.

With the war officially ended in 1721, Peter could devote some attention to the vast and sprawling but little-documented province east of the Urals. He was worried that other European powers would begin exploring Siberia and undermine Russia's claim. He was particularly concerned when the French Academy of Sciences approached him in 1717 and asked for permission to explore Siberia. He turned them down, much as he would have wanted more knowledge of this little-known region of his domain; it would have been an intolerable blow to his and Russia's pride if the exploration of their own territory had to be entrusted to foreigners.

SPANISH CONQUISTADORES HAD DEFEATED mighty nations in Central and South America—the Aztec, the Maya, and the Inca—and incorporated those lands into an enormous global empire that eventually stretched both east and west, from Europe to the Philippines. The French had colonized eastern North America. The English had founded colonies in North America and had a global trading empire. The Dutch had founded New Netherlands and conquered the Portuguese seaborne empire in Indonesia. The Dutch and English East India Companies were warring to control Indonesia and the Indian Ocean trade; the British were on their way to conquering India. Spanish ships had explored north along the western North American coast from Mexico as far as present-day British Columbia. But the interior of North America and its Pacific and northern coasts were mostly a giant terra incognita, as was the northeastern coast of Asia. Peter felt that Russia could make a mark for itself there, perhaps not only conquering new territory or establishing valuable trade routes and consolidating his empire, but also in the realm of science and geography. He sought to claim for Russia some part of the international prestige that would be reflected or bestowed for contributing to global knowledge—to be acknowledged not merely as a user but a contributor to knowledge through the creation of a detailed map of Siberia.

While gaining respect from other nations, at the same time Peter wanted to establish a profitable trade relationship with China that would help develop the vast province of Siberia. Peter had repeatedly attempted to improve Russia's trade relationship with China and had met with little success. He knew from his youthful journey to Amsterdam and London that the key to wealth was a strong economy and that the way to achieve this, in addition to currency reforms and a stable legal system, was through trade and commerce. These improvements would also incidentally provide increased government revenues. His attempts to open a dialogue with the Chinese government to enable Russian caravans to enter China and for Russian consulates to be established in some Chinese towns were rudely rebuffed. His envoy, Captain Lev Ismailov, offered elaborate gifts but overplayed his hand when he asked to establish a Russian church in Beijing as a component of a trade deal. The official response was condescending and arrogant: "Our Emperor does not trade and has no bazaars. You value your merchants very highly. We scorn commerce. Only poor people and servants occupy themselves in that way with us, and there is no profit at all to us from your trade. We have enough of Russian goods even if your people did not bring them." In the later years of Peter's reign, in spite of his efforts, trade in the eastern empire was declining, and the Chinese government refused him access to the Amur River, on the border of Russia and China, that would have provided access to the Pacific.

The only way to circumvent this blockade of Russian commercial, and hence political, interests was to look north. Peter cast his eyes on the ill-charted eastern regions of Siberia that Russia had rudimentarily explored and conquered from various Tatar chieftains beginning in the later sixteenth century. Far to the east along the windswept rugged shores of the Sea of Okhotsk, where a Russian outpost was established in 1648 at the very edge of Russian territory, there was no one to block Russia's advance. It was only a matter of time before English, French, Spanish, or Dutch mariners would begin exploring the North Pacific, as they had everywhere else in the world. Peter wanted that distinction for Russia. When Peter the Great became ill late in 1724, with the urinary tract infection that would kill him several months later, the planning for this long-dreamed-of expedition took on a new urgency. In December he tasked senior members of the Admiralty College to prepare lists of people who could take senior positions in the ambitious enterprise: surveyors, shipwrights, cartographers, and commanders. Bering's name topped the list for commanders, and he was recommended by Vice Admiral Peter von Sievers and Rear Admiral Naum Senavin: "Bering has been in East India and knows the conditions." His two-decade service in the Russian Imperial Navy combined with voyages that took him to North America and Indonesia made him the obvious choice to command an expedition that would sail uncharted waters in the Pacific. The expedition would encounter new peoples and cultures, and Bering possessed at least some experience in overseas foreign countries. Peter the Great wrote, "It is very necessary to have a navigator and assistant navigator who have been to North America."

BERING'S PRINCIPAL DISTINGUISHING SKILL as a commander during the Great Northern War had been in logistics, the organization and shipment of supplies, and this talent may have been one of the reasons he was selected to lead the First Kamchatka Expedition. Nothing like this expedition had ever been attempted before. To reach the Pacific Ocean, where the "real" expedition along the coast was to begin, Bering and his comrades would have to traverse all of Siberia, which consisted of several-level broad watersheds that flowed north from the mountainous regions of Central Asia to the icy sea in the North. The trip would, in essence, be a series of mighty portages between river systems stretched out over many thousands of miles. Although it was a well-established route, with numerous fortified outposts, situated on the major river junctions, it was used by small troupes of merchants, not by large expeditions carrying vast quantities of supplies and equipment. In the public mind today, Siberia has a reputation for harsh winters, howling winds, and sparse population—a convenient near wasteland for political dissidents and other Russian exiles. In the seventeenth century, it had the same reputation and was beginning to serve the same political purpose.

Siberia was nominally just one of ten provinces of the Russian Empire, as established by Peter the Great in 1708. But it was a province like no other. Sprawling from the Ural Mountains to the Pacific Ocean, covering most of Asia north of Mongolia and China, it was twice the size of the other nine Russian provinces combined and represented three-quarters of Russia's landmass. Siberia encompassed an incredible 5.1 million square miles, 10 percent of the world's surface, with terrain as varied as its size would suggest: windswept tundra, vast plains, enormous coniferous forests (or taiga), and multiple mountain ranges, including the Urals, Altai, and Verkhoyansk. It was, and remains, one of the world's most sparsely populated regions. Peter had never traveled there, nor had anyone else from the Russian political elite (at least none that had returned). Barely three hundred thousand people lived in the whole region, which by the eighteenth century consisted mostly of ethnic Russians. Siberia was rich in furs, and the principal revenue from the region was a tax on the valuable pelts of animals such as sable and fox, which were plentiful in the sub-Arctic climate of short hot summers and long cold winters. Today, approximately forty million people live in Siberia, still only 27 percent of the Russian people.

The region and its varied native peoples (primarily the Enets, Nenets, Yakuts, Uyghurs, and others) had been conquered by the Mongols in the early thirteenth century and had been ruled by various local rulers until the sixteenth century, when Russian Cossacks marched east of the Urals and established military outposts, small wooden forts called *ostrogs*, around which towns grew. Although the region was far too huge to administer properly, Russian officials sent out from Moscow used the existing loose political and taxation system of the *khanates* to further their exploration and expansion, essentially imposing a tax on furs (the extremely valuable minerals and oil were not exploited until later). By the early eighteenth century, Russian outposts extended as far as the Pacific in Kamchatka. But while these lands were technically under Russian administration, there were no roads west of Tobolsk, the small Russian city and Siberian administrative center just east of the Urals on the Irtysh River. Tobolsk consisted of a large stone fortress on a hill that served as the government and military capital of Siberia as well as the home of the highest officials of the Siberian Orthodox Church. The government and church buildings were surrounded by around three thousand wooden houses of various sizes and quality on the plains below, which were prone to seasonal flooding. The city had about thirteen thousand inhabitants. The only other supply base for travelers in Siberia was the town of Yakutsk, a fur-trading depot with a Russian official governor and population half that of Tobolsk, situated about halfway across Siberia. Irkutsk was also a growing town, nearly as large as Tobolsk, surviving on trade with China, but it was south of the regions where the First Kamchatka Expedition would be concentrating its efforts. The numerous Siberian ostrogs were small outposts and could not be relied upon for any food or supplies. Between Yakutsk and the tiny settlement Okhotsk, on the western coast of the Sea of Okhotsk, the terrain was rugged and mountainous. In 1716 Russians pioneered a sea route east from Okhotsk to the western coast of Kamchatka at the Bolshaya

River. The obvious and easier route to the Pacific to the south, along the Amur River, had been closed to Russia by the Chinese after the Treaty of Nerchinsk.

The expedition would have to cross one-third of the globe, contending with a hostile climate and no roads. The farther east they traveled, the worse and more unknown the conditions would become, and the possibility of finding people associated with Russia to offer aid to an imperial enterprise would diminish. Bering's small army would have to haul all their equipment and supplies across Siberia, including everything they would need to build their ships once they arrived in Okhotsk. This included all metal goods, including anchors, nails, tools, and weapons, as well as ropes and sails. Even food would be difficult to obtain in large quantities, given the sparse population, the corrupt officials, and an unskilled labor force given to hard drinking. One of the main tasks of the expedition was to make a new map of the route from Tobolsk to Okhotsk, detail the route across the Sea of Okhotsk to Kamchatka, and then chart the Pacific coast north to the so-called Icy Sea. With this detailed, accurate, and verified travel knowledge, others could follow and the territory could become more firmly attached to the empire. It was a daunting and unprecedented undertaking. Peter's instructions were sweeping but vague, as there was no accurate knowledge of how to accomplish the goal or any appreciation of the difficulties that might present themselves. It was clear, however, that the enterprise would take many years.

In January 1725, Bering returned to Viborg "to attend to his affairs," such as arranging for the financial support of his family from his salary during his commission and spending time with his wife and his children, who would be much changed by the time he returned many years later. Bering was also planning some personal business transactions. In addition to his significant salary of 480 rubles per year, his position offered him the opportunity to make his fortune—as commander he was allowed a significant baggage allotment and the right to use expedition resources to transport personal trade goods, which, if he chose and planned wisely, would be worth a fortune when he sold them in distant Siberian outposts. Anna's father, a well-known and successful merchant, no doubt offered advice to his son-in-law, a career naval man with little experience in trade or commerce. Despite the years apart the commission would require, both Bering and Anna embraced the opportunity to enrich themselves and advance Bering's career in the Russian service. Wealth and status were the goals of this couple.

In St. Petersburg, Bering had also by now met the men who would be his junior officers. Lieutenant Martin Spangberg, at age twenty-seven, was a fellow Dane seventeen years younger than Bering. He had served in the Russian Navy for several years, made at least one voyage to the American colonies, and earned a reputation for being tough, decisive, and tenacious, if not highly educated or literate. Aleksei Chirikov, in contrast, was only twenty-two and had served in the Russian Navy for only one year before being promoted to lieutenant for the expedition. A Russian native, he had begun his career at the Moscow School of Mathematics, where he excelled, before transferring to the Naval Academy in St. Petersburg, to which he returned as a teacher only one year after graduation. His technical skills and training in astronomy, cartography, and navigation, all dependent on a solid foundation in mathematics, were key for cartographic exploration. The remaining thirty-four men of the expedition included sailors, skilled artisans, animal handlers, midshipmen, carpenters, mechanics, a surgeon, a chaplain, a geodesist, a quartermaster, a shipbuilder, and general laborers.

AFTER PETER THE GREAT died in February 1725, Empress Catherine I continued with most of her late husband's projects, including the First Kamchatka Expedition. Chirikov had already departed

St. Petersburg on January 24, leading a cavalcade of twenty-six men traveling with twenty-five horse-drawn sledges, loaded with equipment that would be unavailable east of the Urals: six 360-pound anchors, eight cannons, dozens of guns, hourglasses, rigging, canvas for sails, ropes, chests of medicines, and scientific instruments. He followed well-known roads as far as the city of Vologda, where they waited for Bering and Spangberg to finish their meetings at the Admiralty College. They would then receive their official orders and documents from the senate, commanding the governor of Siberia, Prince Vasiliy Lukich Dolgorukov, to provide them with all manner of assistance. The senate's note to the governor was brief but clear: "We have sent to Siberia Navy Captain Vitus Bering with the requisite number of servitors to organize an expedition. He has been given special instructions regarding what he is to do. When the Captain reaches you, you are to render him every possible assistance to enable him to carry out those instructions." On February 6, Bering and Spangberg set off, lightly loaded, with six men on sledges, and met Chirikov before continuing together through the dark days of winter over the snowy low passes of the Urals to Tobolsk. They arrived on March 16, having covered a distance of 1,763 miles, the simplest part of the journey.

During the next two months, while waiting for the river ice to thaw, Bering met the governor, showed his letter from Empress Catherine, and requested an additional fifty-four men to help with the expedition. Skilled men were scarce in Siberia, and only thirty-nine could be found, enough to more than double his contingent. Bering needed more carpenters and blacksmiths, but they were not to be found. He also arranged for the sale of his horses and sledges because east from Tobolsk there were no more roads. The way forward would be by river barge along the Irtysh River to the Ob River—he needed carpenters to build the rafts and laborers to unload the sledges of the thousands of pounds of equipment and repack it into the boats. The four flat-bottomed riverboats were each forty feet long and equipped with a mast and sails. Bering sent a small contingent ahead in smaller boats to announce the arrival of his expedition and to requisition supplies and food, a procedure that he repeated at each fort or settlement along the route. The system of generally north-flowing rivers and their tributaries that cross the Siberian plain formed part of a well-established, if sparse, commercial network, with furs moving either back to Europe or to China and Chinese goods trickling north and east. But nothing on the scale of Bering's expedition had ever crossed the country before. To cross Siberia as far as Yakutsk, they would have to ascend the Ob River, cross a 46-mile portage to the Yenisei River, and then follow smaller tributaries to float down the Lena River to Yakutsk—each river system required a new set of boats, and each offered its own unique set of obstacles and challenges.

In May the expedition took off again, pushing the loaded riverboats into the fast-flowing Irtysh, scattered with small icy bergs, and still in wind and snow they began the long journey east to the confluence with the next river, the mighty Ob. They floated all night in the swift current under the dark skies, occasionally pulling into a tiny village for warmth and shelter. After a week of disagreeably cold and blustery downstream travel, they reached the confluence with the Ob on May 25. They pulled ashore, and the carpenters made large rudders for the mighty boats to augment the barge poles and oars. Periodically, men had to get out and haul the huge boats upstream, exhausting, unrewarding work against headwinds and with clouds of mosquitoes swarming and feasting on them as they dragged the boats along the river. They struggled for nearly a month, into June, to reach the Ket River tributary and continued along this shallow, winding waterway toward the ostrog of Makovsk, where they readied for the interminable portage to the town of Yeniseisk, the commercial center of the Yenisei River system. The Yenisei was the next river system on their eastward sojourn, which they reached on June 20. Their reception was less than cordial now that they had passed into Siberia, and Bering was beginning to note a pattern: local officials appeared to be a power unto themselves and had little respect for imperial decrees from the Far West, a land they themselves may have never seen. On one occasion, when asked for support, a commander of an ostrog spat and threw Bering's official letter on the ground. Here the man refused to get his people to help unload the boats for the portage, claiming, "You are all swindlers and you should be hanged."

Bering could be a domineering man, and he had a lot of men and soldiers in addition to his imperial letter, so he soon got what he wanted: many dozens of horses and carts for the portage. They managed the exhausting trek, but further disappointment awaited them at Yeniseisk. Although the governor provided Bering with additional laborers, Bering complained that "few were suitable, and many were lame, blind, and ridden with disease." It was mid-August by the time they unloaded the tons of equipment and supplies from the carts onto a new batch of riverboats and set off along the Tunguska River to the Ilim River, where they again unloaded and loaded the vast mountains of material into smaller boats and worked through numerous short portages around rapids. The main expedition arrived at the town of Ilimsk on September 29, just before the river froze for the winter. The next portage, to the ostrog of Ust-Kut on the Lena River, would be a farther 80 miles of hard travel. During the winter, Bering divided his men and sent Spangberg and thirty men with dozens of laden horses ahead on the portage to build more riverboats so that in the spring when the ice thawed, they would be ready to float the 1,200 miles down the Lena River northeast to the town of Yakutsk. The expedition was supposed to have reached Yakutsk before winter and was at least half a year behind schedule. They had covered only half the distance to Kamchatka.

Meanwhile, during the winter, Bering made an overland trek south to the town of Irkutsk on Lake Baikal, where he interviewed the governor about the conditions ahead over the mountains from

Yakutsk to Okhotsk. This would be the most challenging part of the journey. There was no official or well-established route or trail to Okhotsk through the mountainous terrain, where the rivers were shallow, circuitous, and riddled with rapids. The transport of thousands of pounds of equipment through this terrain had never been done before and was on Bering's mind as the greatest problem of the entire trek. The locals usually traveled by hauling sleds in the winter, a trip that could take between eight and ten weeks in each direction. "The snow is very deep here, up to seven feet," Bering reported, "and in places even more. When people travel in winter they have to shovel the snow off right down to the ground every evening in order to keep warm during the night."

It wasn't until June 1726 that all contingents of the expedition and all the supplies had floated down the Lena River to Yakutsk, one of the largest towns in the entire region at more than three thousand inhabitants in at least three hundred buildings, with a surrounding population of natives perhaps ten times as large. A quick departure was imperative to make the dangerous and dreaded mountain crossing before winter, but all was not well. In Yakutsk nothing had been organized before their arrival. Bering was incredulous—he had sent men ahead with official requests for hundreds of horses, tons of grain, and dozens of laborers, yet none of it was ready. Bering marched to the governor's office and argued and fought, finally threatening the governor with being blamed for the entire expedition's failure, the imperial wrath that would descend upon him, and the certainty of the loss of his job. Only then did the governor finally secure the men and supplies, sixty-nine men and 660 horses, earning great resentment from the local people, as there really wasn't much to spare here, so far from everything. Perhaps most frustrating, the men's pay was unavailable, and there were grumbling and discontent.

So Bering divided his troupe. Spangberg was the first to depart on barges loaded with about 150 tons of flour and equipment as well as the anchors and cannons—the other equipment that couldn't be transported overland due to the terrain. He took more than two hundred men and a dozen newly constructed boats. Bering sent a smaller second group ahead from Yakutsk to Okhotsk by the overland route, which he soon followed with his own contingent, a pack train of hundreds of horses, dozens of them alone carrying Bering's personal trade goods. Wagons or carts were useless on the rugged, rocky, and steep mountain trails. Chirikov remained in Yakutsk until the following spring, awaiting the final deliveries of more flour and other supplies.

Bering's cavalcade, a dusty snake of burdened beasts enveloped in noise, dust, and dung, wound its way up the treacherous trails through the mountains and down to Okhotsk. Conditions were staggeringly difficult, far worse than what Bering's bland comment conveyed: "I cannot put into words how difficult this route is," he wrote in his report. The journal of Peter Chaplin, one of the junior officers charged with keeping accurate records of daily events, is a litany of problems, a tally of dying horses, food shortages, and deserting men during days that were frequently "gloomy" and mornings that were "icy cold." Horses starved to death because they had no grass to feed on, the men were delayed cutting the stunted trees to build corduroy roads to get the pack train across swampy land, and sometimes they forded freezing rivers six times a day, back and forth up narrow valleys. As fall progressed, snow and deathly cold temperatures moved in. Three men and dozens of horses died, while forty-six deserted with supply-laden horses, disappearing in the night. Mounds of supplies were left by the trailside to be retrieved later. When Bering and a remnant of his cavalcade arrived in Okhotsk on October 1 after forty-five days of hard travel, he was dismayed to find that Okhotsk was smaller than he had anticipated and unprepared for his arrival. Okhotsk was a minor administrative principality for the collection of tribute; it had no amenities other than some local horse ranches, several native huts, and a contingent of Russians in a town of about eleven small houses. So instead of resting and recuperating, he and his men had to quickly begin the construction of winter houses and storage warehouses, no easy task with most of the horses dead and the men conscripted into carrying logs. Then they had to start building the ship they would need to cross the Sea of Okhotsk to Kamchatka the next summer. They also were busy catching fish in the ocean and making salt to preserve the beef from the cattle they would slaughter. Most troubling, by December Bering still had no word from Spangberg, until he and two of his men staggered into Okhotsk to announce a disaster.

THE RIVER ROUTE TAKEN by Spangberg had been much worse than Bering's. Winter came early, in August, and it was the worst winter in the memory of any of the locals. After floating down the Lena River on the barges, Spangberg started on the journey up the Aldan and Maja Rivers. The rivers were filled with rapids, and the men had to march along the shore, hauling the boats with ropes through a tangled mess of overgrown scrub and rocks. The work was so tiring and tedious that they sometimes covered less than a mile in an entire exhausting day. By the end of September, forty-seven men either had been dismissed or deserted, and then the boats became frozen in the ice. Spangberg, a dauntless and resourceful man, set to building winter cabins and sleds, while the men became sulky and surly, restless and mutinous. Spangberg bullied his men into action with threats of flogging, in true naval disciplinary tradition. He had them unpack the boats and load the new sleds and then begin hauling the sleds east through the snow. He carried eighteen tons of equipment on ninety sleds, the men dragging them through waist-deep snow that covered the land by late October. Soon they were worn out from exhaustion and began tossing things from the sleds, such as cannonballs, a cannon and gunpowder, and nautical equipment. Detritus lay strewn along the trail. By December they were starving, eating chunks of dead horses, saddlebags, harnesses, boots, and belts. Spangberg and two strong men dashed ahead to a place called Yudoma Cross, at the height of the land. It was an unremarkable spot, notable only for the crude cross that someone had placed in a clearing. From there, it was downhill to Okhotsk. It was also the place Bering had passed months earlier on the overland trail. They uncovered supplies of flour that had been left for them and rushed back to the others and brought them up to Yudoma Cross. Four men starved or froze to death on the way. Spangberg left some of the weaker men and set off downriver for Okhotsk with about forty sleds and their drivers. They ate frozen dead horses that they came upon on the trail. Finally, Spangberg and two companions rushed ahead, slogging through the snow day and night with light sleds carrying the most vital supplies, until they arrived in Okhotsk on January 6. About sixty others staggered into town ten days later.

Bering dispatched rescue parties to retrace the route and bring food to any survivors, but at first they refused to go because it was dark, snowy, and freezing cold and they feared for their lives. Bering was not to be deterred, so he had some men build a gallows and threatened the men with hanging if they refused their orders. The rescue party of ninety men and seventy-six dog teams led by Spangberg slowly departed on February 14, grumbling and muttering. At Yudoma Cross they found four dead frozen bodies and rescued seven destitute stragglers. The hardship was so great that twelve men recruited from Siberia had grabbed axes and knives and deserted once they had reached Yudoma Cross, declaring, "We do not want to die like the others did, so we are going straight to town [Yakutsk] and you can't stop us." During the remainder of the winter and spring, Bering sent groups back along the route to retrieve the abandoned supplies, while others worked on constructing the ship that would take them across the Sea of Okhotsk to Kamchatka.

By late spring, however, starvation was again their most immediate threat. The spring salmon runs were far lower than usual, and the men were starving by the time Chirikov arrived with a pack train in June, carrying tons of flour and other supplies from Yakutsk.

CARPENTERS HAD BEEN WORKING on the new ship through the winter, and by early June it was ready to be launched. They named it *Fortuna*, in hopes of better things to come. The carpenters had also repaired an older ship, the *Vostok*. While Chirikov returned to Yakutsk to bring a second load of flour and cattle for the expedition (losing 17 out of 140 horses but no men and experiencing no great hardship), Spangberg took command of both ships and transported forty-eight men (blacksmiths, carpenters, and the shipbuilder) 630 nautical miles across the Sea of Okhotsk to the tiny town of Bolsheretsk, a town of fourteen modest houses, upriver from the mouth of the Bolshaya River on the west coast of Kamchatka. Once dropped off, these men were to follow a trail across the peninsula to the Pacific coast and begin work on the larger ship needed for the voyage north. The winds were fair, and Spangberg brought both ships back across the sea to Okhotsk, picked up Bering and the re-maining men on August 22, and sailed again to Bolsheretsk. Since they had no accurate maps of Kamchatka, which had been explored only by Russians coming from the north in the seventeenth century, they were unaware that Kamchatka is a peninsula. They could have sailed around it and dropped the equipment directly on the Pacific coast, saving themselves another arduous overland journey.

For the final leg of the trek to the Pacific, Bering had to trans-fer his equipment from the larger ships to smaller boats to get up-stream on the Bolshaya. The plan was then to portage inland to the headwaters of the Kamchatka River, to another Russian outpost called Upper Kamchatka Post, and then travel by dogsled or boat 15 miles to Lower Kamchatka Post farther north on the Pacific coast. Spangberg again led the way with an advance party, while the others reorganized the equipment, hunted, fished, and got organized for the mountain crossing by sled during the winter and boat in the spring. It was to be a grueling slog, hauling all the equipment upstream and over portages, loading and unloading boats, while it rained and then snowed and winds howled. Bering tried to enlist Kamchadal dogsled drivers, but other than this he had little contact with them. It took eighty-five sleds and weeks of hard travel, crossing the more than 500-mile round trip from the Sea of Okhotsk to the Pacific several times.

The Kamchatka Peninsula is about 750 miles of heavily forested, mountainous terrain divided by a broad central valley. It is known for abundant wildlife, particularly large brown bears; chilly, damp summers; and cold winters. Snow blankets the land from October to May. Arctic winds blow down from the north, and cold sea currents surround it on both coasts. It is much wetter than Siberia, with glaciers on the highest peaks and fog routinely clinging to the coasts. It is also the most volcanic region on the Eurasian continent, with many active volcanoes and innumerable thermal springs issuing steam, and it is prone to earthquakes and tsunamis. The storms are legendary: one British traveler in the nineteenth century wrote, "The poorga [blizzard] raged with redoubled fury; the clouds of sleet rolled like a dark smoke over the moor, and we were all so benumbed with cold that our teeth chattered in our heads. The sleet, driven with such violence, had got into our clothes and penetrated even under our parkas and into our baggage." Describing his own experience, Bering stated, "Each evening we made a camp in the snow and covered the opening. . . . [I]f a storm catches anyone out in the open and he fails to prepare a shelter for himself, then he will be covered by snow and die."

There were only about 150 Russians in all of Kamchatka, mostly soldiers and tax or tribute collectors living near the three ostrogs.

The remainder of the population consisted of the culturally and lin-guistically similar Kamchadals in the North and the Kurils in the South. Although Bering was supposed to make notes about the var-ious native peoples who lived in the disparate regions of Siberia, he was not much of an ethnographer. "The Yakuts have many horses and cattle which supply them with food and clothing. Those who have only a few head of livestock live on fish. They are idolaters and worship the sun, moon and certain birds such as swans, eagles, and ravens. They hold in high esteem their priests, whom they call shamans. They have crudely carved little statues they call shaitans [devils]. . . . [T]he rest have no faith at all and are quite devoid of any good habits." In Kamchatka he wrote, "The Kamchatka people are very superstitious. It is customary to take anyone who is very ill and near death, even one's own father or mother, out into the forest with only enough food for a week, winter or summer, and many die."

These grim but less than revealing observations, nearly always focused on perceived negative aspects of the culture, were partly due to the fact that the expedition had little interaction with any of the non-Russian or Russian-influenced people on this expedition. The near lawlessness that reigned under the loose administration of the ostrogs prior to Bering's arrival had caused much decline in Kamchatka's native population, previously perhaps as high as twenty thousand. By the late eighteenth century, only a few thou-sand remained; many others had blended with the Russians to form a distinct culture. The Kamchatka natives, like those in Siberia, were often compelled to labor and provide service above the offi-cial amount of tribute demanded by St. Petersburg. While this was against regulations, Kamchatka was so far from Russia that there was no one there to keep officials honest. The expedition placed a crushing strain on the Russians and the Kamchatkans.

By the spring of 1727, the expedition had traveled a staggering distance: the air distance in a direct line between St. Petersburg and eastern Kamchatka is more than 4,200 miles. But the expedition covered many times this distance, up and down rivers, weaving across the trackless Siberian plateau, often having to backtrack, and going over rugged mountain ranges without roads, mostly along the sixtieth parallel of longitude. The journey had so far taken close to three years. This distance and the wild terrain were the main obstacles to Peter's ambitious plans for a Russian Pacific empire. Now, at the Pacific coast, Bering had a new objective—to build a large seagoing ship and set out for the Arctic Ocean.

SPANGBERG AND HIS CREW spent the fall and winter of 1727 beneath the mighty 14,580-foot Klyuchevskoy Volcano. They chopped trees near a small native settlement about 100 miles inland from the coast where the largest trees grew and then floated them closer to the coast where the shipbuilders and carpenters were laboring. Others distilled liquor from grass, known as *slatkaya trava*, following a local recipe; boiled seawater for salt; churned fish oil into butter; and caught and dried vast quantities of salmon on wooden flakes. By late April, the skeleton of the ship was taking shape, its ribs and frame were already set, and the planking was well under way. It was 60 feet long and 20 feet wide and stood 7 feet tall from keel to deck. Within weeks the two masts, sails, rigging, and anchors were ready and the ballast, three cannons, and food loaded. They christened the small ship *Archangel Gabriel* and launched it on a warm day, July 9. They had provisions for forty-four men for a year, much of it brought from afar: 15 tons of flour, 3 tons of sea biscuit, and twenty barrels (for freshwater), in addition to local supplies of 12 tons of fish oil and 760 pounds of dried salmon. Four days later, the men climbed aboard, and the ship pushed off and sailed 120 miles to the open ocean and then north along the Pacific coast of Kamchatka to complete the final task of their epic assignment.

Chirikov was calculating latitude and longitude and sketching a rough chart of the coastline. To his surprise, the coast trended northeast. As they kept the course, for weeks land was visible as a giant fog bank to their left. They stopped only twice, to go ashore and search for freshwater, as the mountains "were all very high and equally steep, like a wall, and variable winds blew from the ravines between the mountains." They saw and made note of all prominent land features and the abundance of marine animals such as whales, sea lions, walrus, and porpoises. The weather was generally foggy and drizzly. Near the end of July, the *Gabriel* passed the mouth of the Anadyr River. The weather remained good for sailing, with fine winds and no storms. On August 8, the lookouts spied a large skin boat approaching, with eight men aboard who spoke a language they could not understand very well (probably Chukchi Inuit). Even with his local Kamchatkan interpreter, Bering could obtain no information about the geography farther north or west other than that "they do not know how far the land extends to the east . . . but later he said that there is an island that can be seen from land on a clear day, if one moves not far from here to the east." Nevertheless, they kept sailing north until they reached latitude 65 and were faced with a choppy open sea stretching to the northern horizon: the Icy Sea. Although they did not know it, they were sailing through the strait that British mariner Captain James Cook would name for Bering nearly fifty years later on his third famous voyage of discovery. An earlier Russian explorer first made a voyage along this coast, Cossack merchant Semyon Dezhnev. In 1648 Dezhnev led ninety men in seven small single-masted boats from the mouth of the Kolyma River 1,500 nautical miles along the Siberian coast and south along the Kamchatka coast. Some of the boats were wrecked and many perished, but at least two dozen men made it south along Kamchatka and founded a small trading post. Unfortunately, the scant reports of this voyage were never sent back to Moscow or to any Russian officials east of Yakutsk, and so the story of the daring and deadly voyage was unknown until 1736 and not of help to Bering.

On August 13, Bering felt that they had sailed far enough to meet the orders he had been given. He called the officers, in the Russian tradition, into his cabin for a conference. In the Russian Navy, any major decisions had to be made by a joint council, not just by the captain. He asked them: Had they answered the question of whether Asia and America were connected by land? The opinions varied. Chirikov wanted to sail farther and perhaps overwinter; Spangberg suggested sailing north for three more days before returning, since they had seen nowhere to safely harbor the ship and survive an Arctic winter. Bering pointed out that basically the entire coast as far north as they had sailed was "mountainous, almost as straight as a wall, and covered in snow even in winter." He did not want the ship to be iced in or wrecked on this barren, unknown coast, and he suspected that they would soon encounter sea ice.

After the discussion and the submission of Chirikov's and Spangberg's written arguments, Bering made his choice and wrote his reasons:

> If we remain here any longer, in these northern regions, there will be the danger that on some dark night in the fog we will become beached on some shore from which we will not be able to extricate ourselves because of contrary winds. Considering the condition of the ship, the fact that the leeboards and keel board are broken, it is difficult for us to search in these regions for suitable places to spend the winter. . . . In my judgement it is better to return and search for a harbor on Kamchatka where we will stay through the winter.

Bering was a cautious and informed commander rather than a daring gambler; it was probably these traits that made him stand out to Peter the Great for this assignment, but also held him back in the navy during the war. He was pragmatic and goal oriented, looking for what could be accomplished with safety and the best chance of success. In this case, he was probably correct in his assessment of the risks and rewards: if some accident were to befall them on this coast, no help would be forthcoming, all the information would be lost, and probably there would be no further exploration. Bering evidently saw his job as paving the way for the future of Russia's presence in the Pacific. He did not have the resources to go farther and did not think there was much to be gained. He ordered the ship to sail north for three more days, as Spangberg suggested, but when they saw nothing, they turned around and returned south. Although they were sailing through the Bering Strait, no one aboard spied the Alaska coastline due to continuous clouds and fog.

Much ink has been spilled by historians unsatisfied with Bering's accomplishments, whether Bering was overly timid or too quick to retreat, should have gone farther or searched for land to the east, or relied too much on the opinions of native peoples. But at the time, nothing was known of this land, and he probably did not view discovery as the main purpose of his expedition. He was chiefly sent out to establish the route across Siberia for future better-equipped expeditions and to chart the Kamchatka coastline, not to risk everything on a gamble that land could be found or that they could survive an Arctic winter here.

On the return voyage, they again encountered four large skin boats with about forty Chukchi in them, but, as before, communication was nearly impossible without an interpreter, although they gleaned the idea that there was some sort of big land or island to the east. Nevertheless, the groups did some trading: meat, fish, freshwater, blue-fox furs, and walrus tusks were exchanged for some metal tools and needles.

The *Gabriel* sailed into the mouth of the Kamchatka River on September 2 after a few days of rough weather. The sailors had been fifty days at sea and within a month were iced in. They spent the winter repairing the ship and readying for a return voyage. Bering wanted to sail south around the Kamchatka Peninsula, to test how far south it extended and to see if it was possible to get the *Gabriel* to Okhotsk without another grueling slog across the mountains of Kamchatka. During the winter, Bering talked with Russians who had lived in Kamchatka for many years, and they regaled him with apocryphal tales of mysterious lands to the east, where there were forests and large rivers and the people used large skin boats similar to those used in Kamchatka. These stories had him pondering. When the river ice melted in May, they readied to depart, but Bering decided to sail to the east for four days to test the idea of nearby land. Though storms forced him to retreat without seeing anything, he came very close to the remote island that he would revisit twelve years later under entirely different circumstances.

On July 24, he was back in Okhotsk, along with most of his men. The return journey, without tons of equipment and with a much-reduced number of workers, following a now-known route, was quick and uneventful. They reached Tobolsk on January 11 and reported to the officials. Bering declared the goods that he had traded for and paid the customs. They arrived back in St. Petersburg on February 28, 1730, just over five years after departing. He and Spangberg and Chirikov were all promoted and rewarded and were reunited with their families. But all was not well for everyone. Fifteen men had died, largely from cold and starvation, and most of the approximately 660 horses used by the expedition had perished, seriously damaging the economy around Yakutsk and ruining the horses' owners. The toll the expedition had taken on the local economy contributed to resentment and civil unrest. In Kamchatka, Bering's commandeering of men and dogsled drivers led directly to the uprising in the 1730s that resulted in the burning of Lower Kamchatka Post and the consequent retribution against the native population.

Nevertheless, before sailing from Kamchatka, Bering had charted the southeastern coast of the peninsula and discovered a bay that would be perfect for a future harbor. He called it Avacha Bay, and already knew that he wanted to return and unravel more of the geographic mysteries of this distant region.

CHAPTER 3

THE BEST-LAID PLANS

ONE OF THE MOST notable characteristics of Peter the Great was his insatiable curiosity. It was this curiosity that led him to force the tectonic changes to Russian society that disrupted the old rigid order and ushered in reforms that transformed the nation. Even when traveling by carriage or horse through a small backwater town, he would always ask the locals what was worth seeing, what was different or unusual nearby. If he was told that there was nothing noteworthy, he would reply, "Who knows? If it not be so for you, perhaps it will be for me. Let me see everything." This attitude made him interested not only in European commerce and military strategy and technology, but also in the arts and sciences. He encouraged Russians to go abroad to study at European educational institutions, particularly to attain technical and scientific skills not then available in Russia, and he funded basic schools for mathematics, artillery, engineering, and medicine.

Peter's largest endowment was for the creation of the Russian Academy of Sciences in St. Petersburg, which nearly three centuries later is still Russia's most respected scientific academy. He wanted a Russian institution on par with those elsewhere in Europe so that

Russians could study at home and, he hoped, speed up the process of modernizing the Russian economy. Famous German polymath Gottfried Leibniz, who had earlier founded the Berlin Academy of Sciences, originally proposed the idea to Peter in the early years of his reign, but Peter held off founding the Academy of Sciences until January 28, 1724, a year before his death. As he envisioned it, the institution would function much like a university. Its first professors, all hired from Germany, Switzerland, and France, taught Russian and German students as well as doing their own research. They included historians, lawyers, philosophers, chemists, mathematicians, astronomers, and doctors of medicine. Although Peter died before any of these learned men arrived and began classes, the institution was to have the powerful role Peter envisioned, shaping Russian intellectual life, including the exploration of the unknown eastern hinterland.

The final decree authorizing the academy's founding was signed by Peter's widow, Catherine. Although she reigned for only two years, she oversaw the kernel of the academy with the arrival of sixteen scholars and their families from France, Germany, and Switzerland. The academy's first eight students were likewise from other European countries, but their ranks soon expanded. When the Russian court temporarily moved back to Moscow, the academy was neglected, with many scholars departing over complaints about unpaid salaries. Nonetheless, it was still very much a prized institution and vital to Russia's growing respect in Europe. Soon its many scientists would be put to an altogether new task, something very different from the world of the cloistered academic.

WHEN BERING ARRIVED BACK in St. Petersburg after a five-year absence, the political atmosphere had changed significantly.

Empress Catherine, newly enthroned just as he was departing, had died in 1727 and been succeeded by Peter II, who died of smallpox at the age of fourteen on January 19, 1730, mere months before Bering returned. The new empress was Anna Ivanovna, Peter the Great's niece. Although she returned the Russian court to St. Petersburg and continued with Peter's reforms and the Westernization of Russian institutions, the architectural development of St. Petersburg, and support for the arts and sciences, her reign is often viewed as a "dark era" in Russian history. Her lavish balls and public spending on grand palaces belied the grave suffering in the countryside and an interminable series of wars with Poland and Turkey. But it was her strange and cruel personality that ensured her fame. She would shoot animals from the palace windows and was abusive and rude to people she considered inferior. She would publicly mock and humiliate those with disabilities. Her punishments and favor seemed extreme and arbitrary and contributed to a climate of fear and secrecy. Saxon minister Count Johann Lefort remarked darkly that the Russian court under Anna was "comparable to a storm threatened ship, manned by a pilot and crew who are all drunk or asleep . . . with no considerable future."

Anna Ivanovna had a strong preference for placing foreigners in positions of authority and prestige. In the first months of her reign, she banished to Siberia several Russian aristocrats believed to be antiforeigner. While infuriating and demoralizing to Russians, this preference was good for Bering and for Bering's new proposal that he return to Siberia and Kamchatka, build larger oceangoing ships, and set out to discover and explore the west coast of America. Although some in the academy, the court, and the admiralty muttered that Bering was not daring enough and that he had failed to establish the conclusive truth of Asia's relationship to America— or uncover anything new about the long-rumored land *bolshaya zemlya*—he argued that he had not been properly equipped to do more than he had done and pointed to the rude conditions under which he had labored. He highlighted the excellence of his new map of Siberia and the value of his notes on local conditions.

Both Bering and his wife were very ambitious, and Anna always advocated for her husband through her network of family and friends in St. Petersburg and Moscow. Bering was promoted into the nobility and given an award. They were now quite wealthy, owing to the promotion, his reward, and the profit from his private trading while in Siberia. They settled into a comfortable home in a fashionable district with servants and their surviving children, two boys, who were now six and eight and scarcely remembered their father, and they reveled in their new status. Anna was no longer socially inferior to her younger sister. They were feeling so fortunate and well-off that Bering donated the inheritance he received from his parents to the poor in his hometown of Horsens.

Bering took only a few months, until April 30, 1730, to submit to the Admiralty College his detailed report of the First Kamchatka Expedition and a proposal for a second one. The first expedition, in his view, suffered from too many unknowns and a lack of appreciation for the challenges, so a follow-up expedition was obvious, this time to be better planned, provisioned, and manned. Bering knew that the mission could succeed only if the leadership of the first expedition was reprised in the second. From the government's perspective, he was clearly the favored candidate, and so were his senior officers, Spangberg and Chirikov.

Despite the extreme conditions, the possible starvation, the miserable cold, and the great chance of death on a voyage into the unknown, these commissions were desirable in the troubled times. Siberia also offered freedom and a chance to make a lasting mark in the world, a chance for a limited amount of fame and respect for adding new geographical knowledge. A second expedition would be good for their careers as well as appeal to their adventurous souls.

Bering submitted his plans to the empress:

1. According to my observation the waves of eastern Kamchatka are smaller than in other seas, and I found on Karaginski Island large fir trees that do not grow on Kamchatka. These signs indicate that America, or some other land on this side of it, is not far from Kamchatka—perhaps from 150–200 miles. This could easily be ascertained by building a vessel of about 50 tons and sending it to investigate. If this be so, a trade might be established between the empire and the inhabitants of those regions.

2. Such a ship should be built in Kamchatka, because the necessary timber could be obtained more easily. The same holds true in the matter of food—fish and game are especially cheap there. Then again, more help may be had from the natives of Kamchatka than from those of Okhotsk. One other reason should not be overlooked, the mouth of the Kamchatka River is deeper and offers a better shelter for boats.

3. It would not be without advantage to find a sea route from the Kamchatka or Okhota River to the Amur River or Japan, since it is known that these regions are inhabited. It would be very profitable to open trade relations with these people, particularly the Japanese. And since we have no ships there, we might arrange it with the Japanese that they meet us halfway in their boats. For such an expedition a ship about the size of the one mentioned would be needed, or one somewhat smaller might serve the purpose.

4. The cost of such an expedition—not including salaries, provisions and materials for both boats, which cannot be had there and would have to be taken from here and Siberia—would be from 10,000 to 12,000 rubles.

5. If it should be considered wise to map the northern regions of the coast of Siberia—from the Ob to the Yenisei and from there to the Lena—this could be done by boats or by land, since these regions are under Russian jurisdiction.

This proposal for territorial and commercial expansion at low cost was sure to interest the state. The possibility also existed of establishing naval bases and for the discovery of precious metals. Empress Anna wanted to continue Peter the Great's territorial and commercial expansion of the empire. So began two years of planning.

Bering's initial proposal was straightforward: to build ships and sail to discover America from Kamchatka, but he reluctantly admitted that he would have to include several other items of interest to the Russian state to justify the expense of the expedition. He planned to pioneer and chart a route to Japan through the Kuril Islands and to work toward creating a chart of the northern coast of Siberia. Over the two years of planning, the expedition grew in scope with the contributions and interests of several key planners: Count Nikolai Golovin, the president of the Admiralty College; Ivan Kirilov, the senior secretary of the senate and a keen geographer; and Count Andrey Osterman, a diplomat in Empress Anna's court. Kirilov believed that the second expedition would expand the empire and, despite the costs, eventually result in "inexhaustible wealth" for Russia. He also optimistically believed that Siberia offered great transportation advantages since its many river systems were merely underdeveloped canals. The secondary objectives of the expedition were not geographical but rather political and colonial, designed to secure and expand Russia's governing presence by creating maps, building infrastructure, collecting tribute or taxes, and promoting trade. According to the official instructions from Empress Anna, the senate has "given thorough consideration to the matter so that this expedition will be of genuine benefit to Your Majesty and to the glory of the Russian Empire."

Throughout 1732 Empress Anna and the senate issued a series of *ukases*, or decrees, that established the objectives and structure of the new expedition. There was an April 17, 1732, official order from the senate announcing Bering as the commander; on May 2, a general outline of the expedition; on May 15, an order from the admiralty to begin the preparations and commission Vitus Bering as commander, with Chirikov second in command. On December 28, 1732, Empress Anna sent further detailed instructions and officially signed the order authorizing the Second Kamchatka Expedition. In recognition of the anticipated difficulties and hardships of the undertaking, the three principal commanders, Bering, Chirikov, and Spangberg, were promoted, Bering to captain-commander and the two others to captain, along with eight new lieutenants. They were offered double pay and given two years' pay in advance. Bering was also ordered to "act in mutual agreement with Captain-Lieutenant Chirikov on all matters during the course of this voyage." The instructions did not make clear who was in charge if there were difficulties in reaching mutual agreement.

THE GREAT NORTHERN EXPEDITION, as the Second Kamchatka Expedition was sometimes called, was one of the most ambitious scientific and exploratory expeditions ever undertaken. Based on Bering's modest proposal to follow up on the inconclusive results of his first voyage, the second expedition was designed to demonstrate to Europe the power and sophistication of Russia. As the years of planning wore on and the scope of the expedition swelled, Bering had cause to worry. By the time Bering saw his final instructions in December 1732, they had expanded to a venture far beyond what he had ever envisioned. He would be at the head of a contingent that would number in the thousands: scientists, secretaries, students, interpreters, artists, surveyors, naval officers, mariners, soldiers, and skilled laborers, all of whom had to be brought to the eastern coast of Asia across thousands of miles of roadless forests, swamps, and tundra, again hauling vast quantities of equipment and supplies with them because there would be nowhere to purchase these items in Siberia. As before, the heavy goods they would be carting included tools, iron ingots, canvas, dried and preserved food, books in multiple personal libraries, and scientific implements. They would more or less follow the same rugged route of the First Kamchatka Expedition into eastern Siberia.

The objective of the expedition had also been elaborated. Now there was to be a multipronged assault on the mysteries of Siberia, followed by an ambitious voyage across the uncharted expanse of the North Pacific Ocean. Once he arrived in Okhotsk, Bering was again supposed to build two ships and sail to Kamchatka and then east to America, charting the coastline far to the south. Concurrently, he was also to build another three ships and survey the Kuril Islands, Japan, and other areas of eastern Asia. These were his most reasonable and practical instructions. His orders also called on him to populate Okhotsk with Russian citizens, introduce cattle raising on the Pacific coast, found elementary and nautical schools in the distant outposts, construct a dockyard for deepwater ships, establish astronomical positions throughout Siberia for future mapping, and create mines and ironworks for smelting ore so that the region might become self-sufficient in these activities and avoid the horrendous cost of transportation. Not surprisingly, despite Bering's Herculean efforts, these tasks wouldn't be completed for generations. Bering had imagined his expedition as a glorious footnote to his career that would resonate throughout history, but he grossly underestimated the scope of the undertaking and the seemingly limitless problems that would arise.

Ironically, the western islands of Alaska had recently been sighted by a different Russian mariner, Mikhail S. Gvozdev, in 1732, using Bering's old ship *Archangel Gabriel*. Gvozdev was part of a small military expedition sent out to punish the Chukchi in Kamchatka who had attacked and destroyed Russian outposts and refused to pay the tribute; the rebellion was likely brought on by Bering's demands for food and labor during the First Kamchatka Expedition.

Gvozdev sighted the coast of Alaska in August and met a man in a kayak before sailing back to Kamchatka.

Although organized under the auspices of the Russian Imperial Navy, the Bering expedition was never a standard naval operation, and the leaders would seldom be utilizing their nautical skills, and not for many years. Rather than Bering navigating and running a ship, most of the journey would involve retracing the six thousand miles across Siberia, using management skills: organization, recruitment, the logistics of pack trains and river barges, and diplomacy with regional authorities. Kirilov, the senior secretary of the senate, was a dreamer who imagined Russia as a new emerging world power. He wanted to send a new administrator to Okhotsk to prepare the town for the arrival of the expedition and to begin the construction of ships. The enthusiasm for this job—leaving the known world for the uncivilized regions of Siberia—was not high. The office of administrator in Okhotsk was not a plum position and did not attract a great deal of interest among the civil service. After all, wasn't Siberia where they sent political exiles? The best that Bering and Kirilov could find, perhaps better described as the best of the worst, was Grigory Skornyakov-Pisarev, then an exile living north of Yakutsk in a small village along the Lena River.

Highly educated and with a promising career before him during the reign of Peter the Great, Pisarev had been implicated in a conspiracy, branded a traitor, and sent to Siberia. At one time he had some proven skills, but his appointment as administrator was made without consulting him or anyone who knew him in the intervening fifteen years since his exile. Unbeknownst to Bering and Kirilov, he was now dissolute, unambitious, and lazy—hardly surprising given his fall from grace and the waste of his talents in Siberia. Nevertheless, orders were sent out advising him of his new responsibilities. Pisarev was to move to Okhotsk as the senior official of the to-be-expanded town and also all of Kamchatka and begin transforming the town into a significant port from which a regular commerce could be developed with Kamchatka. He was to begin organizing the construction of a new wharf, a church, barracks, and houses. He was to bring Russians and Tungus to the vicinity of Okhotsk to establish cattle and sheep ranching and other farming. To accomplish these goals, Pisarev was instructed to release hundreds of men from debtors' prison in Yakutsk and bring them to Okhotsk for use as laborers. How were Bering and Kirilov to know that Skornyakov-Pisarev was now difficult to rouse from his torpor and had lost any warm, dutiful inclinations toward his government? In fact, he would prove more an obstacle than an aid, barely even arriving in Okhotsk until 1735, just before Spangberg reached the region with the first contingent of the expedition, anticipating and counting on infrastructure to accommodate him and his entourage.

THE BIGGEST DIFFERENCE BETWEEN the first and second expeditions lay in the hugely expanded scientific goals of the second one. A ukase dated June 2, 1732, addressed to the Academy of Sciences, instructed it to select members for the scientific aspect of the expedition to study, as scientist Gerhard Friedrich Müller wrote, "what might be noteworthy in the manner of plants, animals and minerals." The scientists' job was to expand existing knowledge of Siberia and to make a detailed inventory of what was there—flora, fauna, minerals, trade routes, native peoples, and economic possibilities. It was to be a huge scientific endeavor, but it was science in the service of the state, imperial science rather than disinterested scientific inquiry.

Bering became concerned by the ever-increasing scope of his proposed expedition during the years of planning. It seemed new objectives were constantly added, all of which would no doubt be of great value—of that there was no real dispute—but how would

Bering organize it all and be an effective commanding sea captain on a voyage of discovery? The scientific component, though a source of prestige for the government, meant added complexity for him. His increased pay did not cover the increased responsibility and fantastically complicated logistics. One of Bering's junior officers, Lieutenant Sven Waxell, quoted him as saying, "There is no art in sending people off on a journey, for that is something they were accustomed to manage by themselves, but that to find them subsistence when they reach their destination was a thing that called for considerably more prudence and thought." This observation was no doubt inspired by the vast distances, primitive conditions, sparse population, and harsh climate of Siberia, where procuring good food was a real challenge. Bering knew well what Siberia could throw at an unprepared party.

The scientists were led by three prominent members of the Academy of Sciences: Johann Georg Gmelin, Gerhard Friedrich Müller, and Louis Delisle de la Croyère. Gmelin was a young German naturalist, chemist, and mineralogist from Württemberg who moved to St. Petersburg in 1727 to teach chemistry and natural history. New animals and plants were his academic interest. He had also been asked by colleagues to investigate whether Siberian men produced milk in their breasts, as had been rumored, and whether they could move their ears at will. Müller was a German historian and geographer who had been in St. Petersburg since 1725. Now in his early thirties and a full professor, he was admired for his extensive studies in Russian history. Known for superior airs (he was proud of his academic position and distinction), he frequently locked horns with colleagues whom he saw as inferior. Müller's portrait shows him to be plump and well groomed, surely not ready for the conditions of Siberia. "I also offered my services," he wrote, "to describe the civil history of Siberia, and antiquities, the manners and customs of the people, and the story of the journey." The third leader of the scientific contingent was a French astronomer and geographer, Louis

Delisle de la Croyère, stylish and thoughtful, significantly older than the others in his midforties. He was also the brother of the well-known French cartographer and geographer Joseph-Nicolas Delisle, whose maps erroneously showed a huge island just off the coast of Kamchatka. Croyère had already undertaken a journey to Siberia in the late 1720s during the time of the First Kamchatka Expedition. Some of the others later complained about his unsuitability for the job of geographer and his general incompetence.

Oddly, the three members of the academy were to report directly back to the Academy of Sciences. They were not technically under Bering's authority; in fact, subsequent events made it almost seem that they believed that he should have been under their authority. The scientists and their assistants, entourage, and equipment added significantly to the size of the expedition, which was starting to resemble a resettlement migration—starting a new Russian society in northern and western Asia—more than an expedition of geographical discovery. The core members of the expedition consisted of more than five hundred people—the expedition officers, scientific assistants, artists, surveyors and students, boatmen, carpenters, blacksmiths, laborers, and others. Then there were around five hundred soldiers to keep order and ensure Bering's orders were followed. Bering also planned on calling up to two thousand Siberian laborers at any time, to be recruited, or compelled, into service as needed. The scientists in particular required a great deal of baggage. And many of the scientists and soldiers' officers and the expedition officers such as Bering, Chirikov, Spangberg, and Waxell were bringing their wives and children, which also significantly increased the tonnage of goods that would need to be transported across two continents. This was, of course, along with the same type of equipment that had so burdened and slowed the first expedition—all the shipbuilding materials and tools, clothing, and manufactured goods needed by people for an estimated decade-long journey. Unusual items included twenty-eight iron cannons; geodesic, astronomical, and surveying equipment (usually made of heavy bronze); and other instruments for measuring climate and temperature. There would be thousands of horses and hundreds of dogs. Riverboats were to be constructed at key watersheds. It was, even on paper in St. Petersburg, a staggering proposition.

Bering opposed including the scientists, not exclusively because he didn't want the extra responsibility, but due to the anticipated food shortages and lack of shelter for so many flooding into a region of sparse population and marginal living conditions. Bering remembered the reality of Siberia from his first expedition—the extreme harsh weather, lack of any significant cities, poor and meager agriculture, and low and widely distributed population. Okhotsk, which was where Skornyakov-Pisarev was supposed to focus his attention and create infrastructure for the expedition's arrival, was nothing but a few primitive huts in a wind-lashed plain of harsh grasses and stunted trees, with a great deal of sand and poor stony soil. The members of the first expedition almost starved there awaiting the spring salmon migration. How were all these thousands of people going to find food, and where would they be housed during the winter? The biggest city, Tobolsk, just to the east of the Urals, had only thirteen thousand people, and nothing else in Siberia compared to it; Yakutsk had only around four thousand by this date and a few thousand more in the vicinity. The officers, particularly the three scientists and their assistants, were prickly about securing accommodation suitable to their higher status and would be packing large quantities of goods not strictly necessary for the journey or their scientific endeavors but personal creature comforts: plenty of brandy and wine, table linens and utensils, clothing, libraries, and so on. The situation was ripe for conflict. A chasm existed between what was possible and what was expected, and Bering was being held accountable for these misaligned dreams and expectations.

How could this monstrously complicated octopus of an expedition, with its competing demands, interests, and objectives, snake across two continents without starving, let alone haul all their equipment and survive once they arrived in Okhotsk? Bering was not without resources and important contacts, and he brought up the issue with his brother-in-law Saunders and his commander at the Admiralty College, Count Nikolai Golovin, who was one of the three men responsible for dreaming the expedition into something larger than Bering had ever envisioned. After many meetings in Moscow and St. Petersburg, discussing the options and sketching out numbers, and with Bering's input on Siberian travel conditions, which may have been hard to appreciate by anyone who had never been there, Golovin proposed something radical to the empress. He offered to take command of several ships and sail from St. Petersburg west to the Atlantic Ocean and then south around the Cape of Good Hope before crossing the Indian Ocean and then turning north through the Pacific Ocean and the Sea of Okhotsk to the town of Okhotsk, or Avacha Bay in Kamchatka, to deliver the needed supplies. It would show the world, he argued, Russia's nautical power and ability on a voyage of noteworthy duration and location (this was decades before James Cook led any of his famous voyages of discovery in the South Pacific or North Pacific Ocean). It would provide training for hundreds of young Russian seamen and greatly aid the establishment of new colonies in the Pacific and make Russia stand out as a mighty empire. The expedition could also help construct a naval base and fort to protect the new trade they would establish with Japan, with livestock and agriculture being introduced to Kamchatka as a side bonus. It all looked appealing on paper, and not the least benefit would be that Russia could beat the British to the Pacific Ocean; it was already known that Dutch ships routinely sailed this route and traded with the Japanese at Nagasaki.

Before Golovin got too excited, however, others raised objections: Russian expansion to the Pacific would best proceed if it was a secret from other European powers, lest they foresee Russia preempting them in prestige and geography and attempt to interfere. Kirilov contributed his opinion that crossing Siberia should be easy, even with tons of food and equipment, owing to its numerous "natural canals" with only three portages. He appears not to have believed Bering's report of the earlier expedition's tribulations, near starvation, and deaths along these canals and "easy portages." In any case, the expense of sailing around the world was too great, and Golovin's proposal was turned down. In an official note, the Admiralty College assured the senate that the expedition was thought out, the problems foreseen, and actions taken for "all necessary supplies" to be sent to Siberia. Moreover, all the Siberian authorities in Tobolsk, Irkutsk, and Yakutsk would be officially notified and ready to give Bering all the assistance he needed so that "when Captain Bering arrives, everything will be ready for him."

PART TWO

ASIA

The infamous packhorse trail from Yakutsk to Okhotsk is shown in this engraving from an eighteenth-century atlas. "I cannot put into words how difficult this route is," Bering wrote in a report.

The beautiful natural harbor in Avacha Bay. Illustration from Stephen Krasheninnikov's *Account of the Land of Kamchatka* from 1755.

Yakut woman and child astride an oxen, from an eighteenth-century atlas. Many of the Yakut natives were driven to penury through conscripted labor and the requirement to supply horses to the Great Northern Expedition.

Dogsled caravan in northern regions of Kamchatka, from an eighteenth-century atlas. Many hundreds of dogsleds were conscripted to haul equipment across Kamchatka for the Great Northern Expedition.

CHAPTER 4

ST. PETERSBURG TO SIBERIA

To an observer of a parade or an army on the march, such as the cavalcade Bering led over the mountainous roads to Tobolsk in 1733, all may appear in order: the timing impeccable and the different components working harmoniously and efficiently, leaving nothing but clouds of dust as it winds over the horizon. In the view of the one responsible for making sure it operates so smoothly, this is rarely the case. When the grand and well-laid plans of the Admiralty College and the senate came up against the reality of Siberia, Bering, who was ultimately in charge, faced a series of logistical problems, struggles, and complaints. The difficulties Bering had to contend with on the second expedition were actually greater than on the first, due to the greater quantity of people and baggage, unmatched by a proportionate increase in resources for transportation.

The expedition was an unwieldy and diverse contingent, with different and competing interests all looking to Bering to see to their comfort and needs and with insufficient people to whom to delegate tasks. This logistical nightmare was compounded by an often hostile reception. When the advance contingents rode into Siberian communities, they were seldom met with smiles and open arms.

People still remembered the hardships caused by the First Kamchatka Expedition. The official demand letters for labor, food, and supplies severely strained local economies and brought hardship to local peoples. Some of the Russian Siberians were former serfs who had fled east in search of more freedom, some had been Swedish prisoners of war, and others were criminals or political exiles (including many from the highest ranks of the old nobility). But the majority were Cossacks, the real conquerors of Siberia. The Cossacks hailed from the region north of the Caspian and Black Seas, greatly increasing the population of Siberia at the expense of the native populations. These descendants of the original Cossacks were technically Russians and certainly spoke the language, but they were just as hostile to the intrusion of traditional Russians like Bering's massive entourage as they were toward the natives. They were not inclined to accept the authority of western Russians or to offer assistance just because someone produced a letter of command from a distant empress or because scientists used to life in St. Petersburg expected to be treated with deference on the frontier. A certain lawlessness pervaded the entire massive region, which few in the Russian court had ever visited. The various nomadic tribes frequently launched raids and stole livestock when they felt they could escape retribution, while the Cossacks subjugated the people and extracted tribute, usually in the form of furs. In addition, during Empress Anna's reign more than twenty thousand new deportees were sent east to Siberia for various crimes against the state, increasing the "Wild West" atmosphere.

THE LOGISTICAL PROBLEMS BECAME apparent as soon as the expedition crossed the Urals and arrived in Tobolsk in early 1734 after months of travel on roads. This was the easy part of the journey. The first, slower-moving contingent had left St. Petersburg on February 21, led by Captain Spangberg. His job was to shepherd the sled loads of unwieldy and heavy materials that would be needed for the ships. Captain Chirikov followed in April with a force of more than five hundred, including all the officers' wives and children, riding horses and hauling creaking wagons, and they soon, by coercion or conscription, joined nearly five hundred more soldiers and eventually as many as two thousand laborers as they progressed through Siberia. Lieutenant Waxell called them "deported persons who were to work on board our vessels on the rivers." Bering himself followed soon after, on April 29, with Anna and his two youngest children, aged two and one. Their two older children, aged ten and twelve, were left in the care of family friends and relatives to ensure their education—the frontier was no place for them during these critical years. They would be adults before the family would be reunited, so it was a farewell for many years, even if all went well. The final group to depart St. Petersburg was the scientific contingent, who belatedly rushed east in August with their mobile miniacademy.

While Spangberg merely passed through with his group, taking seventy-four workers and using riverboats to transport about seven thousand pounds of raw iron in fifteen hundred leather saddlebags, the others planned on overwintering. The main parties of the expedition regrouped in Tobolsk in January 1734 after a mostly uneventful journey. Although they were expected, there was no way a town of around thirteen thousand people could possibly prepare for the arrival of this many in winter. It was a season of fierce grumbling. Not only did Bering commandeer most of the best houses for his entourage when he arrived, but he also had orders to hire, or take against their will if they did not want to go, many hundreds of the local population when the expedition departed in the spring.

At the end of February, he and a small contingent set off overland on a winter trek southeast to Irkutsk, near Lake Baikal, to acquire trade goods of mostly Chinese origin, such as green tea, silk, and porcelain, to be used as gifts as the expedition fanned out across Siberia in the coming years. Bering and a few dozen people then pushed on to Yakutsk, arriving in October 1734—only a year and a half after departing St. Petersburg.

Captain Chirikov had the more difficult and unpleasant job of bringing the main body of the expedition east once the ice melted. It was not until mid-May that Chirikov had readied the approximately two thousand people of the main contingent of the expedition. They departed Tobolsk, no doubt to the relief of the locals, on riverboats following the route of the First Kamchatka Expedition. They planned to cruise down the Irtysh River to the Ob and ascend it, hauling the boats over the usual portage to the Yenisei, and then float down the Yenisei River, to the Ilim and Tunguska Rivers, and finally to the Lena. Each river system, as before, presented new challenges and obstacles and needed a new style of boat or cart and the unloading and loading of tons of equipment, hauling it over brutal portages during freezing storms or sweltering through maddening clouds of biting insects. And always, there was the feeding and management of thousands of horses and people of all ages, as they worked their way to the town of Yakutsk, with a population not much larger than the combined expedition.

It should not be surprising to note that nothing went according to the well-laid plans drawn up in St. Petersburg. The workers who were supposed to construct the boats in advance did not do so, the food supplies that were to be ready and waiting never materialized, the wagons and sledges were not constructed in a timely manner, the promised horses were not ready, and many of the workers who were pledged to assist or join the expedition were mysteriously absent. All the support that had been so graciously proclaimed, and the promised resources, proved to be a chimera. Merely keeping the ponderous expedition and its tons of unwieldy equipment moving east through Siberia without drownings or starvation was a constant dilemma. Deserters were so numerous that the turnover in manpower occasionally threatened to stall the expedition's progress, leaving tons of supplies behind. The working and living conditions must have been truly atrocious if so many risked fleeing the expedition, since in Siberia there was nowhere to flee to, with hostile peoples, little food, few settlements, and a killing winter. Escaping the discipline and hard labor of the expedition was an uncertain prospect.

Lieutenant Sven Waxell recalled that "we sought to prevent further losses by introducing a harsh discipline; we set up a gallows every twenty versts along the River Lena, which had an exceptionally good effect, for after that had been done we had only very few run aways." Then in his midthirties, the Swedish Waxell had served in both the English and the Russian Navies. He was a sensible and unpretentious man who brought along his wife and boy, named Laurentz, who had been born only in 1730. Waxell and his son would play a greater role in the dramatic events of the voyage than they ever could have imagined. The main contingent of the expedition arrived in Yakutsk in June 1735 and reunited with Captain-Commander Bering.

THE JOURNEY WAS NOT all hardship for the Berings—now that they were nobility, their rank had privileges, even in Siberia. As the leader of the massive expedition, the largest ever and most disruptive migration of people from Russia to Siberia, which was to bring the most immediate changes as well as the promise of future transformations and greater governmental presence in the region, Bering was a symbol of power and progress. He had to play his role. Anna Bering was equally devoted to promoting her family's interests as she saw them—a rise in social status and rank and the respect, at least officially, of those of lower rank. These social ambitions were one of the main reasons Bering agreed to such a challenging and arduous position. Anna was obviously devoted to her husband to be willing to follow him to the ends of the known world and leave two of her children behind. In Siberia, primitive as were the conditions, Vitus and Anna were like a lord and lady, the pinnacle of Siberian society and living symbols of imperial authority.

Although a select few high-ranking Siberian officials affected the trappings of western European privilege, such as the governors or vice governors of Yakutsk, Irkutsk, and Tobolsk and a handful of wealthy merchants in the fur trade, for the most part culture, as Anna and Vitus Bering would have considered it, was absent. So they brought it with them. Many of the thousands of people who were connected with the Great Northern Expedition over the years and hundreds of the packhorses were employed in making sure the Berings suffered as little as possible from Siberia's want of creature comforts. They slept in tents as infrequently as feasible and traveled with their own entourage of servants. On the trail, Bering lived up to his rough-and-tumble reputation, and they all had to endure clouds of flies and mosquitoes while floating down rivers on barges. But when they arrived in towns and usurped the finest house for their use, the servants brought out silver table plates for daily use and reserved the fine porcelain settings of thirty-six for more ceremonial dinners. The Berings presided over events in clothing that also set them apart: Anna's luggage contained a large collection of silk, velvet, and cotton gowns, trimmed with ermine and brocade. Bering was resplendent in starched collar, powdered wig, and satin pants. They wore linen shirts and fine polished shoes and silk stockings more appropriate to the court in St. Petersburg, and they donned stylishly crafted furs for chilly outings. Their apartments were decorated with candelabra, and lacquer storage boxes contained a selection of jewelry and other trappings of imperial sophistication and luxury—all an affirmation that they were above the local Siberian hierarchy.

One of the most ostentatious luxuries that the pack trains hauled for the Berings was a clavichord, an instrument similar to a piano.

Pity the poor beast of burden that had it strapped to its back. To Anna, however, during years of cold and dust in Siberia, it must have been a welcome distraction both to teach their children and to enliven dull evenings with the other officers' wives and Siberian dignitaries.

BERING ARRIVED IN YAKUTSK in October 1734 and found a state of affairs not to his liking. Chirikov had left behind in the town most of the bulky provisions that he was supposed to have hauled to Okhotsk because the promised boats to transport all this heavy material had not been built. All the tons of equipment remained in Yakutsk. Skornyakov-Pisarev, the former noble and now exile who had been ordered to organize the construction of the riverboats and to prepare Okhotsk for the expedition, was only then departing Yakutsk for Okhotsk to begin his task. When he and Bering met, they took an immediate dislike to one another. Skornyakov-Pisarev claimed that the men he had been expecting to help with his tasks had never materialized and blithely explained away his lack of progress, placing the responsibility onto Bering to solve. But Bering had no time or resources to solve every problem personally and had counted on Skornyakov-Pisarev: How was he to transport the expedition's equipment over the mountains without the boats? If he had to organize the construction of the boats, it would cause yet another season of delay. With thousands of people buzzing around without food or a place to stay, Bering was kept running from one problem to another, stamping out little fires of discontent and innumerable minor unexpected problems, never having time to deal with the larger executive planning of the expedition.

One of Bering's main tasks as outlined in his orders was to explore and chart all the rivers flowing into Lake Baikal and to follow the three major Siberian rivers, the Ob, the Yenisei, and the Lena, north to the Icy Sea and along the Arctic coast. The hope was to determine whether the Arctic coast would ever be a viable sea route for European merchants to gain access to Asian markets. English and Dutch merchant adventurers had made several attempts at the Northeast Passage route in previous centuries, all of which ended in failure or disaster. This task alone, tacked on to the Great Northern Expedition's orders almost as an afterthought, was an undertaking nearly as complicated as the Pacific voyage, which was supposed to be the ultimate objective of the entire expedition.

One of the first exploration parties Bering organized was led by Dmitry Ovtsin, a young lieutenant who commanded a detachment of about fifty-six men. They built their sloop, *Tobol*, throughout the latter half of 1733 and sailed north from Tobolsk along the Ob River in 1734, accompanied by four flat-bottomed riverboats and around eighty soldiers. The soldiers were to accompany the expedition overland by marching adjacent to the river in the event of hostility of northern peoples. Their goal was to follow the Ob Gulf north to the Arctic coast and then sail east along the coast to the Yenisei River. This incredible voyage was a feat Ovtsin miraculously managed to accomplish after several years of heroically working through the ice of the Ob Gulf, along the Arctic coast, and then traveling upstream, or south, along the Yenisei River in 1737.

Unfortunately for Ovtsin, during the course of this expedition he encountered and was friendly with a famous Siberian exile, Prince Ivan Alekseevich Dolgoruky. The secret police arrested Ovtsin and sent news of his encounter back to St. Petersburg. Although he was praised for the exploration and charting of his assigned section of the rivers and coast, Ovtsin was court-martialed, stripped of his rank, and ordered to join Bering as a laborer on the voyage to America. Such were the arbitrary decrees that controlled fate in Empress Anna's Russia. His demotion, in addition to being personally demoralizing, was to cause some tension on the return voyage from America, when the chain of command became unclear.

In 1735 Bering dispatched two contingents north from Yakutsk along the Lena River on similar missions. One group was to navigate and chart the Arctic coast all the way to the eastern point in Asia, to which Bering had sailed years earlier on his first expedition. The second group was to head west to the Yenisei River and perhaps meet up with Ovtsin's party. Lieutenant V. M. Pronchishchev departed on this second mission at the end of June 1735. His men became iced in. They overwintered near the Arctic coast, and many died of scurvy, including him and his wife. His successor, Kharlam Laptev, did not complete the coastal survey to the Yenisei River until 1741. The other party, commanded by Lieutenant Peter Lassenius, also suffered miserably of scurvy and privation near the mouth of the Lena River. The survivors of these expeditions continued charting the coast as per their orders and eventually provided the government with a rough chart of the coast. "It is deplorable to hear of all the dangers and misery these poor people had to endure," Waxell wrote, as many of them had "fallen to death's sickle." Waxell also offered his opinion of the feasibility of further exploration along the Arctic coast: "As for the crew, they will be short of provisions, the air will be injurious, and the cold will undermine their health. Nor is there any need to say that they will find none of the comforts to which Europeans are accustomed. In fact, it must be anticipated that most of them will succumb, yes, die like flies."

BERING WAS BASED IN Yakutsk for several years, organizing the northern boat expeditions and the exploratory expeditions east to Okhotsk. It was a chance for Anna and their children to settle into a routine for a while but not a pleasant time for Bering, beset as he was by setbacks and work unrelated to his voyage of discovery. The innumerable tasks that seemed so easy when blithely scrawled out in airy chambers in the court of St. Petersburg were far more challenging to accomplish in Siberia with no infrastructure or supplies and a recalcitrant workforce. These tasks included many seemingly obscure activities such as importing hemp from Irkutsk and constructing a rope works, establishing a tar distillery, and building an ironworks. Bering had spent nearly a year planning and organizing for the river exploration part of his expedition tasks when Chirikov arrived in Yakutsk in June 1735 at the head of the main contingent of the expedition. Only then could work progress on the construction of houses, storerooms, and the riverboats they would need to get over the coastal range to Okhotsk.

Bering's other main task was to pioneer a new and better route to Okhotsk rather than the Yudoma Cross route that had proved so disastrous years earlier. He sent two major expeditions out to search for a new route, but both ended without success. The wall of steep mountain ranges ran in an unbroken line along Siberia's eastern coast. There was no viable alternative to the old route, and it would take another two years and several trips to get all the supplies over the mountains. The heavier loads went by river, while the lighter loads went by the dreadful overland packhorse route. Waxell was stunned once he had made the traverse, writing that "the country between Yudoma Cross and Okhotsk is a complete wilderness." Another member of the expedition, the young naturalist Stephen Petrovich Krasheninnikov, noted that the terrain was too steep for carts or wagons and was "as miserable and difficult as one could possibly imagine. . . . The banks of the rivers are filled with huge rocks and round stones; it is amazing that the horses were able to walk on them at all," and many went lame or died. "The higher the mountains are, the muddier they become. On the summits are huge marshes, and places filled with quicksand. If a packhorse becomes mired there is no way to pull it out."

In an attempt to improve the route, Bering ordered the construction of warming houses every two miles along the entire trail and sent men out to construct better roads over the swampy sections.

The warming houses were to be staffed and kept heated all winter so that when the cavalcades arrived, the men and horses could seek shelter. To get the supplies to Okhotsk, there would be four to five hundred men continually on the march back and forth. This time Bering did not just want to get to Okhotsk with his expedition; he wanted to stamp the region with Russia's visible presence, to make all future expeditions that much easier. His goal was to establish an official route worthy of being marked on a map, something that people could count on, a known entity, even if it was harsh and rugged. But even with Bering's improvements, the Yudoma Cross route remained dangerous and slow. On one occasion, Anna Bering and her children were nearly lost when their horse ran off and no one knew where they had gone.

IN THE SUMMER OF 1735, Okhotsk was scarcely ready to accept thousands of newcomers. It was a village of Russians and several hundred Tungu and Lamut natives living in skin houses. When Spangberg and his advance contingent arrived, he expected to be welcomed by a host of new dwellings and storehouses ready to receive his men and equipment, with new provisions being brought in from the surrounding countryside and people moved to the vicinity to begin cattle ranching and sheep raising. He anticipated a wharf with ships under construction. But nothing had been done. Skornyakov-Pisarev, the exile who had been ordered to this task, had accomplished little. Although he was commissioned to travel to Okhotsk in 1731, he did not arrive there until 1734. Apparently, he had sent a small number of men to Okhotsk, but they died or deserted en route. Skornyakov-Pisarev had done nothing that he was ordered to do—perhaps the orders being so extravagantly impossible for him to accomplish that he felt they could be ignored. There were no new houses, no roads, no farms, no cattle ranches, and no schools or significant trade with Kamchatka. Okhotsk remained a dusty frontier town surrounded by grasses and pebbles, and the inhabitants were shocked to see so many weary people arriving and expecting to be looked after.

Waxell was not impressed with the town. "It is an unhealthy place," he wrote, "that offers no means of obtaining foodstuffs of any kind, except just in the spring, when large quantities of fish come into the river from the sea." His negative assessment deepened the more time he spent there. "The place itself is quite low-lying and is often under water altogether when there is an exceptionally strong high tide. . . . The whole of this area is composed of nothing but small pebbles, which the sea has heaped up and which in the course of time have become overgrown with grass." It was hardly an inspiring place to build a town. But at least the local salmon "has a particularly pleasant taste" and was especially good with wild garlic.

Because Skornyakov-Pisarev had made no preparations, Spangberg first had to build storehouses to shelter the provisions and equipment he had brought and then build barracks for all the men so they didn't freeze to death in the coming winter. Only after these prosaic survival tasks were complete could he begin work on the dock and shipyards, which were his main priority. Without a shipyard, he could not build the two ships that he needed for his planned voyage to Japan. But even here, Waxell cast a critical eye on Okhotsk. "There is, besides, danger in the spring that the ice may wreak destruction. To put it briefly, this is an emergency harbour and not one that you can use with any confidence." Nevertheless, Bering kept the supplies and equipment moving slowly over the treacherous passes to give Spangberg and his carpenters and shipbuilders the supplies they needed.

The unreadiness, and perhaps unsuitability, of Okhotsk to serve its intended purpose as a deepwater port was not the only major challenge Bering faced. Despite the years of planning and the staggering resources deployed, another one of the key problems of the first expedition had not been solved—compelling eastern Siberians to respect the authority of St. Petersburg. Imperial authorities were used to seeing their edicts and commands promptly obeyed. Merely writing out an order was as good as seeing it fulfilled. But the lesson that these authorities were only slowly learning, and that Bering had warned of, was that while technically part of the Russian Empire and under the authority of the emperor or empress, the disparate, illiterate, and hardscrabble residents of these distant lands did not jump to attention and produce what was ordered of them. It was another world. If he wanted things done, Bering would have to impose his commands by force.

The biggest problem in Okhotsk, however, was with Skornyakov-Pisarev. He was rude and disrespectful, and he set up his own competing fort a distance away. He misused his imperial authority to hire away workers for his own projects and generally impeded Bering's and Spangberg's activities. A haughty and hierarchal man, he took an immediate dislike to the no-nonsense Spangberg and clashed with Bering. He considered them to be of inferior social standing, not true Russians but "foreigners." Although seventy years old, Skornyakov-Pisarev, who was "made vicious by a long and unjust banishment, . . . became Bering's evil spirit. . . . He was violent, restless and fiery as a youngster in both speech and action, dissolute, bribable and slanderous, a lying and malicious gossip." Bering wrote that he could have kept three secretaries busy just responding to the criticisms leveled at him from Skornyakov-Pisarev alone.

CHAPTER 5

QUARRELING FACTIONS

T HE BRILLIANT OBSERVATIONS AND theories of enigmatic naturalist Georg Wilhelm Steller were one of the great legacies
of the Great Northern Expedition. But he was a difficult and lonely
man whose complex and contradictory personality ensured that he
was neither loved nor respected by most of those with whom he
spent his final years. On the expedition, his arrogant assertions, although frequently correct, were delivered in such a shrill tone and
superior and abrasive manner that he was routinely ignored. His
Russian shipmates regarded him as an overbearing and offensive
foreigner who was best left alone. While Steller was insensitive to
the feelings of others, he was hypersensitive to any slight, real or
perceived. He could not tolerate contradictions of his opinion and
lacked tact and humility. Despite having no nautical training, he
boldly asserted his opinion on naval matters, was quick to point out
when a mistake had been made, and always implied that everything
would have been done properly if only he were in charge.

That Steller was right in his assessment of situations, at least as
often as he was wrong, was of little consolation in Siberia and on
the American voyage. His rigid insistence eventually provoked the

officers to do the opposite of what he suggested, so that none need admit they heeded his advice. When Steller was present, decisions tended to be made not in a sober and judicious manner but under a cloud of acrimony and knee-jerk reactions. Steller grew to hate his Russian cohorts, and they hated him in return.

When it came to the study of the natural world, however, Steller was a near fanatic, furiously laboring to record all that his nimble and brilliant mind took in. He was ceaseless in his labors, placing himself in great danger and willingly suffering deprivation, cold, and hunger in his quest to collect and study the newly discovered species. His studies of the flora and fauna of the Northeast Pacific coast of Siberia and the Northwest Pacific coast of North America were the most reliable and insightful for nearly a century afterward. Steller made these records under the harshest conditions. In what was to be the worst case in the winter of 1742, he scrawled his observations in Latin while he shivered in a crude and drafty sailcloth hut on an uninhabited island, while around him mariners were dying from scurvy and blue foxes burrowed into the shallow graves to feast upon their flesh.

BORN ON MARCH 10, 1709, Steller was the second son in a family of eight in the German town of Windsheim, raised in a secure middle-class home. His father was the town cantor and also the organist. Being a cantor, the one who led the singing in church, brought little wealth but considerable social prestige, and the distinction was marked by the privilege of carrying a sword about town. Both Bach and Handel were cantors. In school Steller was consistently at the head of his class and won a scholarship to the university at Wittenberg in 1729 to study music and theology. As a youth he demonstrated, according to his brother, "a great inclination towards the investigation of natural things," and his tenure at the staunchly

Lutheran institution was cut short by his desire to understand the world rather than preach doctrine. Eventually, Steller transferred to the University of Halle to study anatomy and medicine, and within two years he was giving highly attended lectures on botany. But the jealousy of the salaried professors and his own temper drove him to leave in 1734 for Berlin and the possibility of an official government appointment.

The prospects for a freelance botanist in Berlin in 1734 were not promising, and the short, blue-eyed, and ambitious young man cast his eyes to St. Petersburg and Russia. Among the progressive reforms initiated by Peter the Great in the previous decades and continued by his widow, Empress Catherine, and his niece Empress Anna was the ongoing support of the Academy of Sciences in St. Petersburg, chiefly staffed by foreign intellectuals.

When Danish mariner Vitus Bering proposed a second voyage of exploration in the Pacific for the Russian government, news of this scientific and exploratory journey on a scale unheard of in Europe traveled within the scientific community. To a twenty-five-year-old man, reports of the ambitious Great Northern Expedition—the great distances to be traveled, the vast extent of land to be explored, and the possibility of somehow reaching America across the Pacific—were a siren call to action. He admitted later to having "an insatiable desire to visit foreign lands." Steller set off for Danzig, Poland, which had been besieged by the Russian Army earlier that spring. He presented himself as a surgeon to the authorities and was eventually put in charge of a transport returning wounded Russian soldiers to St. Petersburg. He then earned a position as physician to the archbishop of Novgorod.

Through contacts and ceaseless efforts, Steller managed, at age twenty-eight, to obtain work at the Academy of Sciences. There the inner clique of Germans and other foreigners was disdainful toward the Russians. It was an attitude that obviously influenced the impressionable young adjunct. That environment seemed to have brought out the worst in his arrogance and would be the cause of many of his troubles on the American voyage. His wished-for commission as a botanist to join the Great Northern Expedition came in 1737. During his brief sojourn in St. Petersburg, he met and married Brigitte Messerschmidt, the attractive widow of one of his former colleagues. She promised to follow him to Siberia as soon as they were wed. When the time for departure drew near, however, she began to reconsider the practicality of her decision, and by the time she had reached Moscow after an arduous winter journey, her mind was made up. She had a daughter from her earlier marriage, and the winter travel showed her that Siberia was not the place to raise her child. She would remain in Moscow while Steller continued east.

Disillusioned and bitter, Steller set off to seek his fortune in Siberia alone, with orders to meet up with Gmelin and Müller and perhaps to join Spangberg's voyage to Japan. The romantic setback seems to have further soured Steller's demeanor. He became short tempered and irascible—more prone to dogmatic disagreement and rude behavior, although he did declare to Gmelin in a letter that "I have entirely forgotten her and fallen in love with Nature." The journey across Siberia consumed two full years, yet he made few friends, devoting himself thoroughly during this time to his studies of the flora and fauna of the land. His style of travel reveals a personality very different from that of the other scientists. Steller was suited for the primitive conditions. Gmelin wrote with shock that Steller "had reduced [his entourage] to the least possible compass. His drinking cup for beer was the same as his cup for mead and whiskey. Wine he dispensed with entirely. He had only one dish out of which he ate and in which was served all his food. For this he needed no chef. He cooked everything himself. . . . It was no hardship for him to go hungry and thirsty a whole day if he was able to accomplish something advantageous to science." Gmelin and Steller clashed over Steller's responsibilities, with Gmelin attempting to order Steller about as if he were an assistant and Steller resisting and sending many formal complaints and commissions back to St. Petersburg. Gmelin assumed that he was senior to Steller in the hierarchy, while Steller believed he was to act independently, particularly since they were the same age and had the same education and credentials. Other than his conflict with Gmelin, Steller's one enduring impression of Siberia was an unsettling fury at the general and persistent abuses of the native population by the *yasak* (tax) collectors, who were notoriously corrupt and cruel in their demands for furs.

The scientific goals of the Great Northern Expedition included gathering general information about Siberia: How cold was it in winter, how many hours of sunlight were there in each season, was it dry or humid, how many lakes and rivers could be used for navigation, and what valuable minerals were there? They were also to record the customs of the various non-Russian peoples as well as all the commonly used place-names and a general local history of each town or region. Artists were to sketch buildings, landscapes, and peoples. Observing and compiling information on the flora and fauna of the land were also major objectives, and this aligned with the spirit of the era. The cataloging of all nature was one of the preeminent scientific goals of the era, and most common plants and animals known today were collected, classified, and named in a frenzy of scientifically motivated exploration. Until the 1859 publication of Darwin's *The Origin of Species*, it was believed that there was a finite number of species on the planet and through diligent effort all of nature might be collected and studied. Compiling an enormous chart of all living things was seen as the starting point to understanding the bewildering variety of the natural world. As maritime trade flourished and the ships of seafaring nations such as Britain, the Netherlands, France, and Spain girdled the globe, mariners returned from their journeys with multitudes of new specimens of animals, plants, and natural curiosities that were not listed in any of the descriptions found in ancient texts. The evidence of so many new and unfamiliar life forms rendered obsolete the old bestiaries and herbals, which had previously described the common animals and plants. Most of these texts combined pictures and descriptions of the known animals of a region with fantastic creatures such as mermaids, unicorns, and sea monsters, which were said to live conveniently in the blank spaces on maps.

Close to the time of the Great Northern Expedition, Swedish naturalist Carolus Linnaeus (1707–1778) was developing his renowned classification system. First outlined in 1735 in *Systema Naturae*, it required two Latin names for each species, what is known as binomial nomenclature—the distinctions of genus and species as the identifiers of any given specimen. His decision to classify them based on their sexual organs and method of reproduction, however practical, was an approach that provoked indignation among certain prudish members of the intelligentsia. English botanist the Reverend Samuel Goodenough remarked that "a literal translation of the first principles of Linnaean botany is enough to shock female modesty." In spite of these reservations, Linnaeus's system was quickly adopted as the standard for communication among botanists—although it was not sufficiently established by the time of Steller's journey through Siberia and Pacific America for him to have consistently used it in his own descriptions. Each of the three "Kingdoms of Nature"—animal, mineral, and vegetable— was subdivided into classes, orders, genera, and finally species. The kingdom of animals, for example, included mammals, birds, amphibians, fish, insects, and worms. Linnaeus imagined every living thing a part of a great hierarchy from the lowest creatures to the highest, with humans at the apex. Siberia and Kamchatka had never been visited by trained naturalists before, and there were many plants and animals unknown in Europe, or variations of familiar ones, such that it could take years to locate, identify, and describe them all. It was an enormous undertaking that required logical organizing and a deft and curious mind, traits that Steller possessed in abundance.

When Bering met Steller in Okhotsk in August 1740, he was immediately impressed with the young naturalist and began incorporating him into future plans.

STELLER'S PERSONALITY IGNITED THE simmering factions within the scientific contingent. It had also been a thorn in Bering's side since the earliest days of the expedition. When Müller, Gmelin, and Croyère first floated into Yakutsk with their band of assistants and laborers aboard a dozen riverboats in September 1736, they found the town already bursting with people, swelled by Bering and Spangberg's men readying for the transport of goods over the mountains to Okhotsk and the preparations for the Japanese voyages. Between all the newcomers of the expedition, perhaps eight hundred additional people were in the town of four thousand. There were only 250 houses. Although the expedition usurped the houses of locals for their own use, not everyone was satisfied. Müller and Gmelin had a high opinion of their status and coveted the commodious abodes of the wealthy fur traders, not the humble but serviceable dwellings Bering had secured for them. Of course, they complained at this slight to their honor and prestige. Bering brushed them off brusquely, but they continued to complain to various officials. Siberia had proved to be an eye-opening experience for them—the harsh conditions, lack of any amenities, truculent and rude officials who did not understand or appreciate their scientific objectives and refused them aid, and now in Yakutsk inadequate housing. They were distracted by mosquitoes and other insects, vermin infested the food, and there were blasting heat and dust in the summer and dark, wind-lashed, freezing winters. But to their credit, the scientists were not kept from their work. Gmelin collected plants for his opus *Flora siberica*, and Müller traveled, interviewed, and consulted local archives for his history. He spoke to many Russians who had undertaken fascinating and dangerous journeys and discovered numerous original documents in isolated archives in Tobolsk, Yakutsk, and Irkutsk.

On top of their dislike of Siberians in general, who did not respect their status or offer them proper deference, the academicians were plagued by the same problem Waxell wrote about: desertion. Gmelin wrote that the workers, or, as Waxell more accurately described them, "exiles" compelled to provide their services, could never be given any responsibility. "No kindness, no lenience, no friendly address is of any avail," Gmelin wrote. "He must be treated with the utmost severity if he is to behave. The worst part, as far as we were concerned, is that we have had to learn all these things by experience, since we had nobody to advise us." Gmelin was also appalled by the Siberians' drinking habits, on one occasion noting that Easter celebrations had to be done early in the morning, as a sort of prelude to the bacchanalia that followed: "This ungodly drinking lasted four or five days without interruption, and there was no way of stopping the madness." Some of this discontent was directed at Bering, the commander, whom they felt should have been looking after their interests. Gmelin and Müller sent damning letters back to St. Petersburg, criticizing their leader's abilities and decisions, claiming that everything was progressing too slowly and that Bering was lenient where he should be harsh and harsh where he should be lenient, and many other criticisms implying that the problems of the expedition were not due entirely to Siberian conditions but exacerbated by Bering.

Gmelin and Müller would not have gone far in Siberia without Bering's authority and presence to back them up. But they failed to see it this way, believing that he was the cause of at least some of their setbacks. The academicians and the naval hierarchy of the main expedition did not have much common ground, and they did not believe they shared the same objectives. It was an unwieldly authority structure in which Bering was responsible for them and their needs but technically had no authority over them. They kept busy with their work, using the imperial presence of Bering's contingent to bolster their own respect and fulfill their own demands from the local populace, while irritated with being under Bering's overall authority. Bering refused to guarantee the speed or safety of their provisions in transport from Yakutsk to Okhotsk, nor would he promise them well-appointed accommodation in the rugged Pacific town that basically had no infrastructure except that which Spangberg was hastily building. Nor would Bering satisfy their demands for commodious berths aboard the ships that would be sailing to Kamchatka from Okhotsk.

Faced with these logistical challenges and Bering's inability, or unwillingness, to ensure their comforts, Gmelin and Müller decided to postpone or abandon their own journey east from Yakutsk. Instead, they sent a young Russian assistant, Stephen Krasheninnikov, to accompany Croyère and the recently arrived naturalist Steller, who also had been collecting plants in Siberia. Steller had met Gmelin in Yeniseisk in January 1739, a year after he had departed St. Petersburg, and Gmelin suggested that Steller take his place as the lead scientist to explore Kamchatka. Steller eagerly agreed, as it would be his chance to be singled out as a pioneer, working on something new and noteworthy. And it would get him out from under Gmelin's nominal authority.

THE QUARRELING FACTIONS SENT charges and countercharges by courier back to St. Petersburg. Each accused the other of improper behavior and neglect of duty or drunkenness and other illegal acts. In addition to the quarreling among scientists, Spangberg and Chirikov had no love of each other. Spangberg was not a native Russian but Swedish, and he found Chirikov to be preoccupied with social hierarchy and too fussy about equipment. Spangberg, although a competent and trustworthy officer, often did what he pleased and used intimidation and the threat of his huge dogs to get things done. Chirikov chafed under Bering's command like an eagle tethered to a post and clamored for more action and less plodding. He considered Spangberg his "archenemy," so different were their dispositions. He peppered Bering with proposals for new miniexpeditions and for opportunities to make new discoveries, and he was rebuffed repeatedly by the overworked commander, whose inclination was not to seek out exciting new possibilities but to adhere to his imperial instructions. Chirikov claimed that he was "reduced to virtual uselessness since my proposals to him [Bering] are not accepted. . . . He bears only malice toward me for them." Chirikov and Spangberg, however, did band together to send back to St. Petersburg disparaging reports of Bering's leadership.

Skornyakov-Pisarev also continued to obstruct and dither and sent derogatory reports on Bering's actions and progress: that he was neglecting his duties to go on sleigh rides with Anna and his children, that he secretly distilled liquor and exchanged it with the native people for furs, that they kidnapped local peoples and compelled them to domestic service. One of the preeminent historians of the Russian expansion to the Pacific, F. A. Golder, stated, "Just what proportion of truth and falsehood these charges contain, it is not easy to determine." Bering naturally defended himself, against his own men and against the Siberian officials' obstructionist or self-interested actions. But his main defense was to become ever more conservative in the interpretation of his orders. He knew that the land and people of Siberia could not support the grand ambitions of the Great Northern Expedition in such a short time period, and so he plodded along, working as best as he could with hostile or indifferent local authorities. By refusing any deviation from the letter of his orders, he sought to avoid arbitrary punishment, such as had been meted out to Ovtsin for the crime of speaking to the wrong exile.

Bering had been beaten down by years of bureaucratic dithering and the stress of brokering compromises among the hundreds of haughty, quarreling delegates, officers, and scientists of the mission. He had been promised everything by the Russian government before he left, yet reality intruded on the fanciful dream once he was in Siberia. Now after years of stressful work in disagreeable conditions, he was being criticized for the delays. His two staunchest defenders in the Russian government, Thomas Saunders and Ivan Kirilov, original champions of the project, had died. The expedition was behind schedule, and the costs were increasing rapidly. By 1737 the expedition had billed three hundred thousand rubles, ten times the amount originally predicted by Bering in his proposal. The Russian government had to blame someone, and Bering was the leader. "Because of failure to send necessary information and a delay in accomplishing the work assigned," his pay was cut in half starting in 1738, and he was threatened with a reduction in rank, hardly a morale boost, considering the endless work and hardships he had endured. Bering did not get himself out of Yakutsk to Okhotsk until the summer of 1737. The Russian Senate discussed canceling the expedition or replacing Bering with Chirikov, while another report suggested that Spangberg should be placed in command. The tension between Chirikov and Spangberg grew stronger as time passed, since each feared being subordinate to the other.

Bering's commander at the Admiralty College, Count Golovin, who managed to persuade the senate to continue financing the expedition despite the lack of progress, or at least the seeming lack of progress, sent a note to Chirikov, authorizing him to countermand Bering's orders if he felt they were unjustified. Bering's greatest weakness, if indeed it can be seen that way, was that he was too thorough—rather than rush off to do the crowning job of the voyage, he wanted to establish the infrastructure of the entire expedition so that it could be repeated without the same logistical challenges in the future. The Russian government, on the other hand, would have liked to see exciting claims of the success of the voyages to inspire continued support, even if it came at the expense of a more solid foundation. Bering's lack of political sense was his greatest failing, his devotion to the boring foundational aspects of his commission rather than to the exciting details. So far he had provided no rousing stories and dramatic discoveries around which to rally support. As the complaints against him grew, he felt threat-ened and dared not deviate from the letter of his orders, so that none could hold him accountable for any failures. This position, while sensible in Empress Anna's Russia, was a position that chafed the younger officers like Spangberg and Chirikov, who strained for adventure and risk and great deeds.

There is no doubt that the Siberian dignitaries had little incentive to aid Bering other than fear of reprisals, and St. Petersburg was far away. What was demanded of them by Bering and the expedition was nearly impossible to provide if they had any hope of maintain-ing order. There were too many people for the resources available, and they required too much assistance—food, iron, leather, horses, and laborers from a society that was already marginal and sparsely populated. The peasants who were conscripted into service fell into "extreme ruin," unable to tend their subsistence farms, harvest crops, or see their families.

One political exile in Siberia, Heinrich Von Fuch, reported some of the direct consequences of the expedition's demands on the local populace: "Every year Russian peasants are required to transport provisions over a distance of 2,000–3,000 versts to the town of Iakutsk for this expedition. . . . Consequently, many of the peasants are away from their homes for as long as three years at a time. When they return they have to live on charity or by hir-ing themselves out." The nomadic Yakuts were not spared, either: they are "required to send several hundred fully equipped horses to Iakutsk [Yatutsk] in the spring, plus one man to care for every five horses. These horses are used to transport provisions and supplies overland to Okhotsk. Because the land between Iakutsk and Okhotsk is marshy and barren steppe, very few of these horses come back. The officials who are sent out to requisition these horses burden the Iakuts [Yatutsk] in every possible way to enrich themselves." Von Fuch reported that when the exorbitant demands for tribute were not met, or if a relative died or ran away, the officials could confiscate a man's livestock in compensation, and if the livestock proved insufficient, they would then seize his wife and children into servitude, at which point suicide was common. "If the newly commenced Kamchatka Expedition continues to burden the local people, it will obviously become necessary to take measure to prevent them from completely ruining the local population."

Bering's report to Golovin is also revealing of the general hardships during these years: "There are no clothes or shoes for the servitors of my command . . . because no salaries have been sent from Irkutsk by the provincial administration. . . . While transporting provisions, they became very emaciated, and in wintertime some hands and feet were frozen by the severe cold, and because of such difficulty and the lack of other victuals many can barely walk, and throughout the month of June, 22 men were very sick, and all became emaciated." The constant food shortages and lack of proper supplies hindered the work and withered morale. It was not until the late summer of 1740 that the majority of the expedition and all the supplies and equipment were transported over the mountains and stored in Okhotsk. This had been the total time estimated for the entire expedition. Nearly all the delays were at least in part caused by the rugged geography between Yakutsk and Okhotsk. Bering himself advised in his report that a faster, cheaper, and safer route was needed, despite the years of effort he devoted to securing and formalizing the current route. "It is very necessary to find a way of transporting provisions and all other supplies to Okhotsk without such difficulty as before." Despite the ridiculously laborious and dangerous route, the trail pioneered by Bering between Yakutsk and Okhotsk remained the primary route to the Pacific until the Amur River was annexed from China in the 1850s.

While these tons of equipment and supplies were slowly being transported from Yakutsk to Okhotsk, a task that took more than two years, Bering had sent Spangberg on to Okhotsk to supervise the construction of the ships that Spangberg would sail to Japan and the Kuril Islands and other ships that would eventually cross the Pacific. Crews were sent up the Okhota River to chop the timber, more than three hundred trees for each ship, and, as usual, ongoing food shortages and unreliable laborers prolonged the task. When the three ships with 151 men aboard finally launched a year later than planned, on June 29, 1738, they took with them all the food supplies stored in Okhotsk. The flotilla consisted of the old reconstructed *Gabriel* from the first expedition and two new vessels, the *Archangel Michel* and the *Nadezhda*. They cruised first through pack ice across the Sea of Okhotsk to Bolsheretsk on the western coast of Kamchatka, a distance of more than 680 miles, and then turned south into uncharted foggy waters around the Kuril Islands, north of Japan. They were soon separated in storms. Each of the ships independently spied and charted about thirty islands, and they all returned safely to Bolsheretsk in September without having landed anywhere. The following summer, Spangberg made a second expedition. With an earlier departure and starting from Bolsheretsk, he planned to head farther south before the fall storms. As far as the Russian government was concerned, his job was to establish the location and relationship between Kamchatka and Japan with the intention of promoting trade. Trade between the two nations would help solidify Russian claims to the eastern portion of their empire. Along with increased population, the eastern region could become less dependent upon the West and stop being such a drain on the national treasury.

The second voyage departed in May 1739 and produced far more valuable and interesting results. The flotilla was soon engulfed in "thick" weather, and one of the ships became lost and returned while two continued on south, one commanded by Spangberg, the other by Lieutenant William Walton. They reached the island of Honshu in northern Japan in late June. Here they spied many small ships in the shallow bays. Coastal villages were surrounded by people working in fields of grain of a variety they did not recognize, while large forested hills dominated inland. On several occasions, boats sailed out to meet them, and men came aboard their ships to trade fresh fish, water, large tobacco leaves, rice, fruit, salted pickles, and other foods for Russian cloth and clothing. They were small men who bowed when entering the ship's cabin and were "excessively polite." Spangberg did not allow his men to go ashore, nor did he allow many Japanese to board his ship, "since Japan's history abounds in accounts of attacks on Christians." He observed that "in each Japanese craft was a number of stones, each of about two to three pounds weight. Perhaps the stones served as ballast, but being of that size, they could also have been used as projectiles, if things should have gone wrong." The Japanese people he described as

> mostly small in height, and it is seldom that anybody really is met with. Their complexion is brownish, their eyes black. They have strong black head-hair, of which the half is cut off, the rest being combed back quite flat. Their hair is smeared with glue or grease, and then wrapped up in white paper. . . . The Japanese have small flat noses, yet not as flat as those of the Kalmuks; it is most exceptional to meet anyone with a pointed nose. Their dress is white and fastened with a band round the body. The sleeves are wide, like those on a European dressing gown. None were seen with trousers and all went barefoot.

They understood sea charts and made it clear to Spangberg that their land was called Nippon and not Japan.

Once Spangberg was sure that he had reached Japan, he hastened north with this new information, stopping for water on one of the larger Kuril Islands. Here he encountered eight men who called themselves Ainu, whom he reported were quite hairy all over their bodies but friendly. The Ainu fell on their knees and bowed to the deck when "entertained" with gin. "They have black hair, and the elderly are altogether grey-haired. Some of them had silver rings in their ears." Spangberg's account of visiting Japan is similar to countless descriptions from other travelers, following the age-old lurid interest in foreign peoples and strange customs since the time of written records and undoubtedly before. He arrived back in Okhotsk on September 9, 1739, and gave a detailed report of his voyages to Bering, who was then finalizing the construction of the two ships for the American expedition, which he wanted completed by the next spring. Spangberg wanted to return to the Kurils to subjugate them into the Russian Empire, but Bering refused to authorize the action, instead giving him permission to return to St. Petersburg and present his case.

When Skornyakov-Pisarev saw Spangberg's charts of the Japanese voyage, he proclaimed that they were poorly done and erroneous because they failed to show the large series of islands then believed to be located in those waters. He dashed off an official communication to St. Petersburg, denouncing Spangberg for incompetence. Spangberg decided that he would have to defend his findings in person before proposing another voyage. After traveling west for many weeks through Siberia, he met an eastbound courier from St. Petersburg, ordering to him to return to Okhotsk and make a third voyage to Japan, this time to search for the fabled islands. On his way back to Okhotsk, Spangberg met with Steller, who was also heading east, and they returned together to Okhotsk in August 1740. While Spangberg's voyage was delayed, Bering was happy to have Steller come to Kamchatka and perhaps to America. Steller was then thirty-one years old, outspoken and brash, full of enthusiasm for new adventures, with no dependents to distract him. Bering was now fifty-nine, determined and plodding, yet bent under the weight of seven years of responsibility for the expedition, worried about his wife and children and his future career.

After all these years, Bering had still not yet crossed the Sea of Okhotsk to Kamchatka, let alone America, and the officials in St. Petersburg were wringing their hands. The Admiralty College realized that all their directives were not speeding up the process. They sent officers to demand compliance from the Siberian officials and to threaten them with torture if their attitude did not change. In 1739 two officers, named Tolbuchin and Larinof, arrived with the commission to investigate the claims against Bering and his many counterclaims. The imperial cabinet was pressuring them "to look into the Kamchatka Expedition to see if it can be brought to a head, so that from now on the treasury should not be emptied in vain." Skornyakov-Pisarev was finally replaced by a more competent and less contrary and obstructionist official, a political exile named Anton Manuilovitch Devier. The mere threat implied by the arrival of these special officers sped up the work, compounded by the fact that the penalty for not sufficiently aiding the expedition could now be torture: men worked harder, boats were launched, and supplies and horses materialized, so that by 1740 nearly everything needed for the American voyage had been brought from Yakutsk to Okhotsk over new rudimentary roads. Okhotsk boasted many new buildings, industries, and farms. But one unintended consequence of the new imperial pressure was that the officers, and Bering in particular, who was in the spotlight, were even more afraid to deviate from their written orders, even when circumstances pointed to the need for a new plan. Thus, all proceeded as had been envisioned and laid out in St. Petersburg, by officials who had never been to Siberia or America.

CHAPTER 6

PHANTOM ISLANDS

T HE TWO NEW SHIPS for the American expedition, the *St. Peter* and the *St. Paul*, were slowly taking shape at the Okhotsk dockyards—like the ribs of a giant whale, with men scampering over the frame, covering it with planks of Siberian timber and fitting it with metalworks, much of it hauled all the way from Russia. By June 1740, they were ready to float. Once in the water, the work could begin on the ballast and rigging, and supplies and food could be loaded. They were identical twin ships, ninety feet long by twenty-three feet wide by nine and a half feet high to the deck, each with two masts and displacing 211 tons. Built on a Dutch design for moderately sized light cargo and passenger duty in the Baltic and North Seas, the design was adjusted to accommodate fourteen small cannons, two- and three-pounders, and three falconets. The captain's cabins were large and spacious for the ship size, capable of comfortably hosting a dozen officers, while each ship had sleeping quarters for seventy-seven men. Each ship would be loaded with about 106 tons of provisions, one hundred barrels of freshwater, firewood, and ammunition. There were spare anchors, pumps, a capstan for hauling heavy rope, and a windlass for raising the anchors. The decks had three hatches and a larger cargo opening, and they each were outfitted with two smaller shore boats, a ten-oared longboat around twenty feet long and a six-oared yawl, each with a small mast and simple rigging and sail. The interminable delays were finally coming to an end.

SINCE HE FIRST ARRIVED in Okhotsk in 1737, Bering had been organizing the construction of shipyards and numerous ships, first for Spangberg's voyages to Japan and then the two ships for his own grand voyage across the Pacific. All the construction of ships for the various voyages was certainly time consuming, but the main difficulty had been the need to get the supplies over the final mountain range from Yakutsk. Waxell wrote, "We were forced to send most of [twenty carpenters] to the storehouses on the Urak and to Iudoma Cross to assist in transporting our supplies from those two places." Even skilled tradesmen had been conscripted into general labor duties. For two years, the outfitting and provisioning for Spangberg's Japan voyages had sucked resources from the American expedition, but by the fall of 1739 the final work on the *St. Peter* and the *St. Paul* had sped up considerably. The canvas for the sails had arrived only that spring after a year on the trail from St. Petersburg. And it was only in early 1740 that Bering had a full complement of men working on the ships, a workforce that included about eighty carpenters, in addition to dozens of blacksmiths, blockmakers, and sailmakers.

On August 19, 1740, the final loading was nearly complete, and Bering said good-bye to Anna and their two youngest children, aged nine and ten. The servants who had packed all of their baggage and belongings departed on the long road to St. Petersburg, along with many hundreds of the workers, shipwrights, carpenters, and soldiers who would not be sailing to Kamchatka or America. The families of the other officers also departed. Although it had grown over the years into a small town, Okhotsk was not a desirable place to wait for the return of the *St. Peter* and the *St. Paul*. The voyage could take two years, and the families had decided it would be safer to reestablish their lives in western Russia. It must have been a difficult parting for Bering, since he and Anna were a devoted couple; she did follow him to the ends of the earth, leaving their two oldest children behind with family friends and relatives. Personal correspondence from them from before they parted in 1740 reveals a couple desperately trying to keep their extended family unified and the challenges they faced, particularly Anna, in doing so from such a great distance, where letters could take six months to be delivered. Anna refers to her husband as "my Bering," and the letters are concerned with the career choices of their absent children and the health of Anna's parents. They are scandalized at nineteen-year-old Jonas's decision to join the infantry, worried that he would meet the wrong type of people, and hoping that he hadn't "staggered into pubs." Despite Bering's career in the navy, Anna fretted that their son's "arm or leg will be shot to pieces in the first flush of youth." The parents were so far away and unable to do much more for their two older boys than write advice and send it off by courier. Bering wrote a formal letter to the admiralty, requesting retirement from active duty upon his return. "I have been in the service for 37 years and have not reached the point where I can have a home in one place for myself and my family. I live like a nomad."

Barely a week after the dozens of workers and the officers' families departed and the ships were readying to sail, an unexpected visitor rode his horse into Okhotsk, exhausted and road weary. The rider was a courier from the Imperial Household Troops in St. Petersburg, and he had letters for Bering. The empress demanded a detailed report of the expedition's progress to date, specifying how closely he had followed his instructions, and the document was to be signed by all the officers. It was a record that could take many days, perhaps even weeks, to prepare, if they wanted to be accurate in accounting for their years of activity in a manner that would preserve their careers and ward off punishment. But they could not delay if they wanted to sail to Kamchatka before the fall storms and ice made the voyage dangerous. Missing the sailing window in 1740 would add yet another year to the expedition. Bering convened the officers, and they all agreed that further delay was impossible. Bering wrote up a document for the courier, stating that Spangberg, who was remaining in Okhotsk until ships were available for his third voyage to Japan, would write everything he could about those voyages and that Bering would prepare the larger document over the winter in Kamchatka and then send it. Bering would also respond to a query about the status of another as yet unfulfilled job that he had been ordered to complete, the creation of Siberian post offices. Naturally, this was a near-impossible task. How could he possibly construct these post offices and then staff them, particularly on the route between Yakutsk and Okhotsk and then throughout Kamchatka? The mail service between Kamchatka and Okhotsk was supposed to run every second month, yet the sailing season across the Sea of Okhotsk was safely open only between May and September. Nevertheless, the lack of post offices could be construed as an example of Bering's failure to follow his orders satisfactorily.

On August 30, the *St. Peter* and the *St. Paul* hauled anchor and sallied forth east, leaving these problems behind—and embracing new ones. Their first destination was Bolsheretsk, several miles inland along the Bolshaya River, amid low-lying sand dunes and lagoons. The winds were contrary and the captains impatient, so it was with sinking horror that before the ships cleared the Okhota River, they looked back to see one of the supply ships, the *Nadezhda*, commanded by Lieutenant Sofron Khitrov, aground on a concealed sandbar. Eight days of delay followed, as the ship was unloaded and refloated, repaired, and then reloaded. Incredibly, the *Nadezhda* had been carrying most of the sea biscuit destined to feed the men on the American voyage the following spring. It was now ruined by saltwater. Bering's original plan was to sail east from Kamchatka across the Pacific in the spring of 1741, explore Pacific America, find a safe harbor to overwinter, and return to Kamchatka in the summer of 1742. The unanswered question now on everyone's mind was how this would be done without proper food.

Steller and Croyère followed four days later in a smaller boat chiefly devoted to the scientists, their baggage, and servants. The whole flotilla reached the Bolshaya River by September 20. Here the academicians disembarked, while the rest of the ships continued south to round the tip of Kamchatka and sail north to Avacha Bay. Owing to the delays, Bering judged the fall storms too rough for one of the supply ships, and only the *St. Peter*, the *St. Paul*, and the *Nadezhda* headed to sea. It was a new moon, and the currents and tides around Cape Lopatka, the southern tip of Kamchatka, were a turbulent swirl of thrashing white water. The distance between the cape and the first of the Kuril Islands is only four miles, and the center of the channel is plugged by an enormous outcropping of rocky reef, with waves sweeping and crashing over it. On this day, a powerful easterly wind surged them forward, while the pendulous westerly tidal waves pushed them back.

The *St. Paul* and the *Nadezhda* watched as Bering led the *St. Peter* forward into the maelstrom, unaware of the competing power of the wind and tides. Lieutenant Waxell later wrote, "Never in my whole life have I ever been exposed to such great danger as then." For more than an hour, they made no progress, pushed and pulled between the wind and the waves. The bow of the ship plunged into deep troughs as the sea broke over the deck on both sides. "The ship's boat, which we were towing behind us on 40 fathoms of rope, was thrown by the waves against our stern," cracking timbers and scattering men before being sucked back. The wind screeched and pulled at the sails, nearly cracking the main-topmast under the strain as they struggled to keep the ship headed into the waves. "Had we come athwart it among those waves there would have been no saving us." Only when the contrary tide began to abate did the *St. Peter* slowly begin to move forward and round the cape. Chirikov waited about an hour and then ran the *St. Paul* through without difficulty, exiting the Sea of Okhotsk and entering the Pacific Ocean.

The two ships then waited and watched, but the *Nadezhda*, still commanded by Khitrov, was nowhere to be seen. The supply ship had not followed. They later learned that Khitrov, seeing the terrifying predicament of the *St. Peter*, ordered his ship to return to Bolsheretsk instead of challenging the channel. To Bering, it was a second example of Khitrov's poor seamanship and contributed to ill will between the commander and the junior officer. The ordeal served as a reminder that from now on, they would be voyaging into fickle and unknown seas.

When the *St. Peter* and *St. Paul* arrived at the new harbor they called Petropavlovsk (Peter and Paul Harbor, after their ships) in Avacha Bay, they saw that a place for a settlement had been roughly cleared from the forest and some barracks and storehouses erected, the work of Ivan Yelagin and men sent the previous year. It was an ideal shelter, but at this time the *St. Peter* and the *St. Paul* were the first two seagoing ships to sail into the beautiful sandy-bottomed harbor. They noted that it could easily hold a score of ships without even the use of anchor, so sheltered was it from wind and swell. Avacha Bay is eleven miles in diameter and is surrounded by impressive snowcapped conical volcanoes. These were active volcanoes. One of them had erupted in 1737, smothering the land in ash and sending mighty tidal waves against the shores.

While they were settling in for the winter in Petropavlovsk, world events were unfolding that would change Russia's political landscape. Empress Anna, who shared her great-uncle Peter's fondness for western European culture, died in 1740. During the struggle for the throne, Peter's daughter Elizabeth emerged triumphant, assumed power after a coup in November 1741, and was crowned on April 25, 1742. Elizabeth and the court she presided over were much more suspicious of foreigners and ideas from outside. Germans began to be removed from positions of authority and respect, and any criticism of the government, however innocuous or routine, was now being frowned upon; publications that did not please the ruling cadre were suppressed. The Academy of Sciences began to have its freedom curtailed and its funding squeezed. No news of these ominous developments, however, reached Kamchatka before the ships departed.

STELLER AND CROYÈRE FOUND Bolsheretsk in a miserable state. The commander, Yakutskian Kolesov, was a drunkard; commerce was sluggish and hampered by corruption; the soldiers were dissolute and ill-trained and the surrounding population demoralized and rebellious. The officials squeezed the natives for taxes paid in furs, enriching themselves with the difference between what they collected and what they remitted to senior officials in Siberia. The town itself was situated upstream along a gloomy, heavily forested shore of the river. The ostrog on the shore and a chapel were surrounded by palisades, but the civilian dwellings, about thirty in total, were situated on a series of small islands in the river. The most prominent buildings were a whiskey distillery and a drinking establishment. Steller and Croyère found lodgings outside the ostrog and set to work organizing themselves for a long winter of mist and heavy snow. Steller met with the younger natural historian Krasheninnikov, who had thoroughly explored large parts of the peninsula. They worked together, collecting and studying the plants and animals and recording the weather.

Steller also began thinking about one of the most perplexing medical mysteries of the time, scurvy. Why did Bering's various Icy

Sea expedition members suffer so badly from this horrible blight—including blackened bleeding gums, morose disposition, and the opening of old wounds—while the natives never seemed to suffer from it? He concluded that it must somehow be associated with diet—an astute observation decades ahead of its time and with vital implications. Steller also interviewed many Cossacks and Kamchadal natives about their opinions about the possibility of land to the east, plying them with brandy when necessary to loosen their tongues. He became convinced that sporadic trade existed between Kamchatka and other lands in regions to the northeast. But when Steller later told Bering of these rumors, Bering said, "People talk a lot" and "Who believes Cossacks?" Bering had too much to deal with as it was and spared no thought to the health of expedition members or hearsay and rumors of native activities; it was just another in a long list of things out of his control. Bering was weary of even trying to enumerate the staggering problems that Siberia faced in developing a civil society. Investigating possible trade networks farther north would be just another thing preventing him from obeying orders.

The most pressing emergency, however, was Khitrov's retreat with the supplies. It caused great strain, delay, and further hardship over the winter and nearly wrecked the whole expedition. They now had to unload the *Nadezhda* at Bolsheretsk and repack the goods for transport 140 miles across Kamchatka to Avacha Bay, right through the mountainous heart of the peninsula where there were no roads or rivers to follow. Since there were no horses and no trail, natives were conscripted from hundreds of miles around. They were required to bring their sleds and their dogs, more than four thousand of them, to begin the months-long task of ferrying tons of supplies through the snow to Avacha Bay. Waxell was appalled at the treatment of the natives:

> Some of these Kamchadals had no previous experience of the work
> of driving with dogs; they had never heard of such a means of

transport. Nor had most of them ever been farther than five miles away from where they were born, and now here they were having to go off with us, as they understood it, to the end of the world, and that, into the bargain, with their dogs, which they loved above all things. In the main they did not care about money, having no means of using it; in fact most of them had no idea what money was.

The hardship, strain, and ill treatment of the conscripted Kamchadals was so great that there was a revolt, and many refused to work. One disaffected and abused band burned seven Russians in their hut and fled into the mountains. Retribution was swift and severe. A troop of fifty soldiers tracked them down through the snow and surprised them in their winter huts, which were located on a collection of remote rocks at the mouth of the Okola-vaem River, at the base of a mountain. The soldiers tossed grenades into the houses through the smoke holes in the roof. Not knowing what a grenade was, they moved to investigate, and it exploded, killing and injuring many, including women and children. The survivors were captured and taken to Avacha Bay and "given a good dose of the knout to find out the guilty ones." The punishments meted out were, according to Steller and Waxell, cruel and inhumane. In addition to the time spent ferrying supplies across the peninsula by dogsled, hunting and punishing the Kamchadals also consumed many precious weeks, already in short supply.

These further challenges were yet another strain on the weary and aging commander. Bering despaired of ever setting sail. The seemingly endless misfortunes all added to the interminable stress that he had been under for years. Now he no longer had the presence of his wife. Each misfortune incrementally added to the likelihood of another misfortune, compounding as the expedition progressed.

DURING THE WINTER OF 1740–1741, Bering was creating the final list of crew for the voyage. He relieved Khitrov of his command of the *Nadezhda* and ordered the younger man to join the *St. Peter* as a second officer, where he would be under Bering's watchful eye. Bering also decided that he wanted Steller to join the expedition to America, despite the mutual hostility between Steller and Khitrov, who would have to sail on the same small ship for many months. Bering's physician had recently requested to be sent back to St. Petersburg due to illness, and Bering had no other replacement. But Steller had medical training, and his Lutheran background as a theologian would be comforting, since Bering and several of the officers were of that faith. The commander sent Steller a note with one of the returning sled teams, asking Steller to cross Kamchatka and join him to discuss "certain matters." Steller received the message in Bolsheretsk on February 17 and had an inkling of what it might mean. Terribly excited by the prospect, he wound up his work and with a lone companion crossed the peninsula by dogsled in ten days, arriving in early March. "As soon as I arrived," he wrote, "[Bering] represented to me with many arguments the important and useful service I could render and how my undertaking would be appreciated in high places, if I should consent to go along with him."

They soon worked out the details. Bering promised to ensure that Steller would not be going against his prior orders from St. Petersburg. Bering "swept aside all my objections by taking upon himself the responsibility for all the consequences." According to Steller, Bering also promised to give him all the opportunity to pursue his studies in natural history and to allow him the services of men so that he "might accomplish something worthwhile" when he was in America. Steller would share Bering's cabin and serve as the commander's personal physician. Steller was concerned that he would have nothing to show once he returned from "a miserable and dangerous sea voyage." But the voyage was not merely a voyage of discovery, one of science; it had very practical and territorial ambitions. Bering believed that Steller had the skill and knowledge to locate and identify metals and minerals.

Petropavlovsk quickly evolved into a small but clean and pleasant town in a magnificent natural setting. The remainder of the winter, however, was not a pleasant one for the explorers, overburdened as they were with work and the harsh aftermath of the native rebellion. Steller was mortified at the ignorance, cruelty, corruption, dissolution, and brutality of the Cossacks and, as was his nature, complained loudly, condemning the practices. He had become involved in the establishment of a school at Bolsheretsk, but he unfortunately had a manner that engendered dislike if not hatred in the people around him. As he sought to reform what he considered un-Christian and immoral behavior and abuses, Steller was earnest but abrasive and too obvious in his scorn of the Cossacks' lifestyle. He wrote a report and petition and sent it back to St. Petersburg, urging that the Kamchadals be treated with respect and restraint and pointing out that they had rights. He also offered his unsolicited advice on how to better administer the distant land. Steller voiced strong advocacy for social justice that fell on deaf ears, or at least overworked and weary ones.

Bering and the officers were now years behind and anxious about the impending voyage and their careers. Scolding them for not being patient and nice in a brusque manner was just another irritant. Bering had an increasingly narrow focus on getting the job done and seeing his family again, a preoccupation no doubt shared by the other officers. Steller, on the other hand, was relatively fresh and unburdened by the history of the expedition. He was not laboring under the same smothering weight of precedent and expectation—he was still excited and curious. To him it was an adventure, not an obligation or hurdle to be surmounted as quickly as possible so that he could get on with his life. "No proposal of mine," Steller wrote during the winter before they departed, "not even the most insignificant, was considered worthy of being accepted, because those in command were too much imbued with their own wisdom, until the disastrous end and a just dispensation exposed their unfortunately too naked vanity." Steller was already in conflict with Bering, just as Bering was in conflict with Chirikov, who chafed to get going after years of being held back by what he perceived as Bering's timidity. Not many were favorably disposed toward Captain-Commander Bering by this time, but he no longer seemed to care.

By May 1741, the ships were finally getting ready to sail. May was the prime month for embarking on a voyage across the Pacific, but they were delayed until June in bringing supplies across from Bolsheretsk. Once the supplies were tallied, it was apparent that they had supplies for only a single season and not enough to overwinter, as had been the plan all along. Into the unknown they would sail, across the vast Pacific Ocean, with the necessity of returning in the same year, in the fall, before the known and aggressive winter storms of the Kamchatka coast set in. They had already been so long in Siberia that even contemplating a further year was maddening. Their families had all returned home, and the thrill of the East had long worn off for most.

The final major decision that remained was to decide upon the exact route they should take to reach the new land across the ocean. On May 4, Bering called a sea council of officers and read aloud the orders from St. Petersburg so they could discuss the various options and determine how closely these options aligned with their orders. As was the custom of the Russian Imperial Navy, a vote was called of all the senior officers before major decisions were enacted. Bering was not a dictator but more of a first among equals. Steller was not invited to the meeting. Had he been present, he might have influenced the council to choose a different course than the one ultimately taken, since he had heard the Cossacks' rumors of land closer to Asia farther north. All winter the officers had been discussing the possibilities, weighing the reasons, and assessing the available geographical evidence, scant as it was. Bering's official orders from Empress Anna called on him to hold a meeting and to "take counsel concerning various routes to America with the professors sent by the Academy of Sciences," and at this point in the expedition he would not deviate from these official instructions—fear of punishment was common for disobedience of orders, and he was weary of any arguments for change. Croyère, representing the academy in these meetings since Steller was not invited, brought his maps to the council and strenuously argued in favor of searching first for those lands and islands that theoretically lay between Asia and America. These were prominently displayed on the charts made by his brother, French geographer Joseph-Nicolas Delisle, who was also employed at the Academy of Sciences in St. Petersburg. Delisle had created a chart of the North Pacific to help Bering navigate to America.

Delisle was respected in St. Petersburg, and his charts showed the large islands to be as yet unclaimed by any European power. Bering dared not disobey his orders after all the delays and perceived failures—what if these islands existed and he was the one responsible for not claiming them for Russia? Unfortunately, Delisle had populated his chart with several imaginary islands rumored to lie along the route of the expedition, most notably Yezo and Gama Land, the very nonexistent islands that Bering had sought unsuccessfully to find at the end of his first voyage a decade earlier. Since these lands were rumored to be potentially wealthy, finding them had been added to Bering's official instructions.

Spangberg had all but disproved the existence of Yezo, or at least showed that it was one of the Kuril Islands exaggerated beyond reality, but had not been believed. Waxell, Bering's second in command on the *St. Peter*, concurred, saying that "Spangberg's map is based on actual experience and pays no attention to the statements or guesses of others. . . . Spangberg will not associate himself with the view that these islands are the land Yezo. . . . As far as I am concerned, I am now firmly convinced that if there is a land of Yezo in these regions, it can only be these islands. Had there been any other Yezo, it certainly would have been discovered." Croyère was strenuous in his arguments, claiming that Bering and Spangberg had not seen the islands because they were farther east than everyone supposed. He was persuasive and had the backing of the academy in St. Petersburg, and Bering had orders to consult him.

Despite Spangberg's expeditions and the opposition of Chirikov and Waxell, who believed the lands to be phantoms, Bering decided that the first order for the *St. Peter* and the *St. Paul* was to head south to search for these mythical lands, so that he could not be faulted for not adhering to his orders. The other officers at the meeting reluctantly affixed their signatures to the document, agreeing on the course of sailing, southeast and east rather than northeast. Chirikov later reported that they felt compelled to agree to the southern course because of the charts showing that Gama Land "was part of America because, on the general charts, land is indicated all the way from California to Juan de Gamma [*sic*] Land, and this indication is also on the map of Professor Delisle de la Croyere [*sic*]."

The decision led to a huge and time-consuming circuit of the vast uncharted expanse of the Pacific Ocean. This proved to be a disastrous course, especially when they were already a month late in departing and lacking in provisions. Writing a decade later, Waxell fumed that Delisle and his associates at the Academy of Sciences "who drew up these plans obtained all their knowledge from visions or that being very credulous they were dupes of others. . . . [M]y blood still boils whenever I think of the scandalous deception of which we were the victims."

THE SEA COUNCIL ALSO officially confirmed the decision that had not been made known to the crews, that both ships would return to Petropavlovsk by the end of September. With the loss of the supplies the previous fall, they had no means to winter over in Alaska. Now, given that they were already late and first to set sail southeast in search of mythical islands, this was a nearly impossible task for a single sailing season.

The remainder of May was consumed with last-minute details—making ropes, caulking the hull, testing the rigging, making pitch and sealing cracks, scrubbing and scraping, woodcrafting, hauling and stowing supplies, and repairing damaged items. They were testing and fitting out both vessels to make sure they were in perfect condition and making the final crew assignments. Steller, seemingly oblivious to the frantic final preparations for the voyage and unaware of the sheer logistical complexity of the enterprise, was busy collecting and describing an unusual new species of fish he found in Avacha Bay. In addition to fourteen cannons and balls and gunpowder for dozens of small arms, they had loaded into the ships approximately six months of provisions per sailor: 4 tons of groats, 3 tons of salted beef in barrels, 3 tons of butter in barrels, more than 1 ton of salt pork in barrels, 650 pounds of salt, 102 barrels of water (about a two-month supply), 3.5 tons of crackers, as well as 17 barrels of gunpowder, firewood, iron, spare sails, rope, tar, and more.

On May 22, the crew rowed out to the ships with their bags of personal items and occupied their quarters. There were seventy-six men and one boy, Waxell's fourteen-year-old son, Laurentz, aboard the *St. Peter* and seventy-six men aboard the *St. Paul*. They would be living in crowded quarters. The *St. Peter* was commanded by Bering, with his second in command being Lieutenant Sven Waxell, followed by Lieutenant Andreyan Hesselberg, Shipmaster Sofron Khitrov, and Second Mate Kharlam Yushin. Georg Steller was surgeon and naturalist. Aleksei Chirikov commanded the *St. Paul*, with two lieutenants, Chikhachev and Plautin, as well as astronomer and geographer Louis Delisle de la Croyère. Alongside the direct command structure were nineteen marines and their officers and other professional tradesmen, including the purser, an assistant surgeon, coopers, caulkers, a sailmaker, a blacksmith, four carpenters, and the general sailors. There was one artist, Friedrich Plenisner, who was one of Steller's only companions, and three "interpreters," Kamchatka natives compelled or persuaded to come on the voyage to help speak to any people they might encounter in the foreign lands across the ocean.

On Sunday, May 24, Bering hoisted his flag aboard the *St. Peter* and made a final inspection of both ships, which were to sail together, to offer aid in case of disaster. At the moment of great excitement, the wind died and the ships were becalmed, sails limp and powerless until May 29. When the winds picked up, the ships were towed into the outer harbor. Unfortunately, the winds blew erratically and from the wrong angle for several days: "During the whole twenty-four hours the winds veered back and forth between S and E." The ships floundered and were towed about Avacha Bay until Thursday, June 4, when a mild northwester arose, plumped the sails, and powered the ships slowly through the narrows and out of the harbor. They hoisted sails and eased out of Avacha Bay in fine weather, setting off toward the uninterrupted horizon—course southeast, toward Gama Land.

On the morning of June 9, after five days of sailing in fine weather to the southeast, the two ships had reached 49 degrees latitude and began taking soundings of water depth, as they were in the vicinity shown on the charts of the elusive Gama Land. They were on alert for anything unusual. "Straight ahead of us," wrote Waxell,

and at some considerable distance, we caught sight of something black on the water. It was thickly covered in an incredible mass of sea birds of all kinds. We could not conceive what it was and took a sounding, but without reaching bottom; then we altered course slightly, yet not so much as to put the black that we could see at too great a distance from us. In the end we realized that it must be a dead whale, and so sailed right close towards it. To begin with, we had been quite dismayed, thinking that it was a shoal of rocks of which we ought to be beware, for you can never feel safe when you have to navigate in waters which are completely blank.

For the next three days, they continued to slowly track the ocean to 46 degrees latitude, finding no depth at ninety fathoms and seeing no land. On June 12, Chirikov wrote in his journal, "It became quite evident that it did not exist, since we had sailed over the region where it was supposed to be." Steller, in the first of the recorded quarrels he was to have with the naval officers, disagreed with this assessment. He claimed to see in the wake of the ship "for the first time rather distinct signs of land to the south or southeast of us. The sea being quite calm we observed various kinds of seaweed suddenly drifting about our ship in large quantities, especially the sea oak, which do not as a rule occur very far from the coast, inasmuch as the tide carries them back towards the land." He also claimed to have seen gulls, terns, and harlequin ducks—which he imagined were sure signs that land was near. He boldly made his opinions known to the naval officers, but having no rank in the naval hierarchy, he had little voice in the decisions on the ship. They were men of the navy, and most of them were Russians, or, in Waxell's case, a soft-spoken Swede. Steller was German and from a very different educational and cultural background. He was used to open, though structured, argument with peers as practice for rhetoric, while the officers were accustomed to making opinions known when asked and otherwise obeying orders from superiors.

Steller and the officers were doomed to misunderstanding and conflict and an animosity that swelled as time passed. Steller was increasingly ostracized and mocked by the seamen and retreated to his journal, where he poured his anger and resentment onto the pages. "Just at the time when it was most necessary to apply reason in order to attain the wished-for object," he fumed, "the erratic behaviour of the naval officers began. They commenced to ridicule or ignore every opinion offered by anybody not a seaman [Steller was one of the only men of this description aboard the *St. Peter*] as if with the rules of navigation, they had also acquired all other science and logic." To Steller, the fate of the voyage depended on his scientific observations and opinions, and they were being idiots not to listen to him. This waste of his expertise occurred "at the time when a single day—so many of which were afterwards spent in vain—might have been decisive for the whole enterprise." Of course, the ships were nowhere near land of any sort, but Steller felt wronged to have been dismissed—he was used to having his opinions taken seriously. To the mariners, he was an abrasive and puffed-up meddler who felt comfortable giving orders to naval men who had spent their lives at sea and surely knew the signs of land.

Steller did not easily give up when he felt he was right, which was most of the time, and he continued to make his opinions known. The mariners provoked him and teased him to relieve the monotony of shipboard life. Steller became the entertainment, and sometimes he did not know it. At times mariners would pick an argument with him just to get a response. One claimed that there was no such thing as ocean currents. Another pointed to a world map and boldly proclaimed that they were in the Atlantic Ocean, off eastern Canada. A mariner told him confidently that the Maldive Islands were actually located in the Mediterranean Sea rather than the Indian Ocean. So earnest and superior was Steller, and so much did he underestimate the knowledge of Russians and mariners in general, that he believed the men were serious, and he vociferously argued with them. Perhaps his irascibility was the result of excessive drinking: among other subtle references, the log for the *St. Peter* from May 1741, soon after the voyage began, notes that "Ensign Lagunov took out from one of the casks on board a bucket of vodka and gave it to Adjunct Steller."

On June 13, the two ships pulled close together, and Waxell called over the rush of wind and waves through the "speaking trumpet" to Chirikov on the *St. Paul*. As agreed, Bering now commanded the two ships to abandon the search for Gama Land and to head northeast to America, having fulfilled their orders to search for the mythical Pacific islands. The two ships, each the only lifeline to the other in a vast uncharted wilderness of ocean, sailed off together to the east. But in the early morning of June 20, dirty weather blew in. In the fog, darkness, and "stormy winds" common in the region, the two ships lost sight of each other.

They had previously agreed upon a plan for just such an event, so the two ships circled around the vicinity, searching for any sign of the other for three precious days. To no avail: impeded by contrary winds and rough weather, they could not catch sight of the other, despite sailing close by. After the allotted time, which had also been agreed upon beforehand, Bering and Chirikov sailed their ships on separately. Bering ordered the *St. Peter* to head south for four more days through dark, foggy weather, to 45 degrees north latitude, to test Steller's theory that land was near. But after this additional wasted time, Bering ordered a northeast course in frustration. At least no one could say he had not fulfilled his instructions to take counsel from the members of the academy, and no one would again be inclined to give credence to Steller's opinions, however strenuously he argued them.

PART THREE

AMERICA

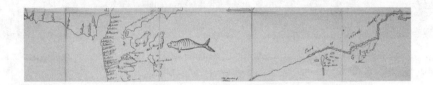

Tlingit boats are seen in this engraving of the Alaskan coast from the 1790s, from a sketch by John Sykes, in George Vancouver's *Voyage of Discovery*.

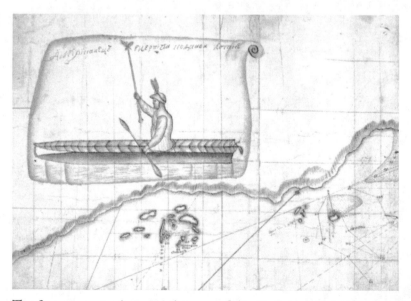

The first encounter between the men of the *St. Peter* and the Aleuts of Shumagin Island is shown in this sketch by Sven Waxell.

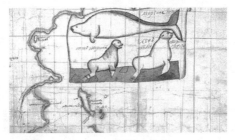

Sketch of Bering Island and the strange beasts the shipwrecked mariners encountered; the Steller's sea cow and the Steller's sea lion, by Sofron Khitrov, similar to a drawing by Sven Waxell.

Otaria ursina, the Ursine seal, or Steller's sea bear, from an early edition of Georg Steller's famous natural history treatise, *Beasts of the Sea*.

This illustration from a 1753 German edition of Georg Steller's *Beasts of the Sea* shows Steller, Friedrich Plenisner, and Thomas Lepekhin engaged in their famous dissection of a Steller's sea cow, a now extinct species of manatee.

CHAPTER 7

BOLSHAYA ZEMLYA, THE GREAT LAND

T HE WEATHER WAS FINE, and men crowded the railings of the *St. Peter* when they were not working, discussing their predicament—the incredible distance they had sailed without seeing even a hint of land in any direction. By the end of June, the water barrels were half empty and the rations had been cut back just in case land was still more distant. The cook prepared the mush of the evening meal with a slightly altered recipe, so that it was thick rather than watery. For weeks the ship had surged east through fair wind and weather. "We saw nothing but sky and sea and heard only the officers exclamations and expressions of amazement over how we could have erred so fundamentally as to believe Kamchatka to be separated by a narrow channel from America." Bering spent much of his time laid up in his cabin with an unknown energy-sapping illness, and the officers began running the ship without consulting him or informing him of their decisions. Second Officer Waxell and the sea council were effectively in charge, and Bering rarely made an appearance in the pages of his account of the journey. "Even thus early a beginning had been made to carry out another scheme,"

Steller recalled, "namely not to let the Captain Commander, who constantly stayed in the cabin, know more than was considered advisable." The *St. Peter* kept heading northeast, and for almost a month it was a dreary and uncertain voyage, with no imminent threats but the gnawing anxiety of the unknown. They saw nothing noteworthy and heard nothing but the swish of the ship sliding through waves and the ruffle of the wind in the sails.

As constant as the daily routine were the internal conflicts. With seventy-seven people crowded onto the ninety-by-twenty-three-foot wooden vessel, there couldn't have been much privacy. Steller was always at the center of the quarreling, and he continued to castigate the officers as fools for not taking his advice as to what direction to sail the ship. Despite the routine disagreements and his evident disgust at being taken so lightly and having his opinions ignored or ridiculed, Steller did not view himself as a source of interpersonal problems aboard ship. Meanwhile, the Russian sailors continued to insult and mock him for his fastidiousness and his foreign and arrogant manners. Steller wrote:

> The brazen and very vulgar snubs by the officers, who coarsely and sneeringly rejected all well-founded and timely admonishings and propositions, thinking that they were still dealing with the Cossacks and poor exiles freighting provisions from Yakutsk to Okhotsk, who had simply to obey and keep still without talking back, had been the cause of closing the mouth of myself as well as of others long ago. No matter what we observed and might discuss for the benefit of the general good as well as the public interest, the answer was always ready: "You do not understand it; you are not a seaman; you have not been in God's council chamber!"

The officers, he fumed in his journal after some slight to his honor or after someone had failed to show him the respect he believed he deserved, were used to dealing with the ignorant mob in Siberia rather than an educated gentleman like himself. They "completely forgot themselves and, through habit, fell into the delusion of being infallible or feeling insulted when anyone mentioned anything of which they were ignorant."

In the first instance, in early June, it was land to the south that Steller was sure they had missed. Now in early July, it was land to the north that he was convinced lay just a little farther across the ocean. When he spied clumps of mottled seaweed lurking just beneath the ocean's surface, he assured the officers that land was near, most likely to the north, and was angered when they laughed at him and continued on their northeast course. Steller marshaled his evidence, all based on book knowledge of plants and animals rather than direct experience. There was the large clump of "reed grass" common in Kamchatka, an infallible indication of land since it would have been scattered if the ship was far out at sea. There was the strong current that he held out as being evidence of a nearby coast. There were frequent "flocks of gulls, which particularly in June, always keep close to the coast where the fishes approach the land and ascend the streams from the sea in the greatest number and thus afford them the most abundant food supply." Steller observed that the birds were usually flying north or northwest. There were "red and white stinging jellyfish," which Steller was confident were never to be seen more than fifteen or twenty miles from shore. And there were the sea otters, or sea beavers as he called them, which he occasionally spied in the clumps of seaweeds, although no one else could ever see them. Knowing what we do now about the ship's location in relation to Alaska, the otters almost certainly could not have been this far out at sea.

Even though Steller assured readers of his journal that "these irrefutable indications of a near land" were delivered to the Russian officers and to the ailing Danish commander, with "reason, great respect, and patience," and he had advised them to "lay the course toward the north in order to reach land sooner," they sighed and ignored him. Bering himself, probably regretting his initial impulse to invite Steller on the voyage in the first place, told Steller he considered it "ridiculous" and "beneath their dignity" and "annoying" to have to listen to him and that "in many parts of the ocean the whole sea was overgrown with weeds." Steller was flabbergasted that his well-reasoned conclusion, that it was "inevitable" that land was near, could be challenged and dismissed by the commander so off-handedly. "What could I say to that?" he wrote. Steller was wrong on this occasion, as on many others, and although he outlined his reasoning in great detail in his journal, and some of it makes logical sense, turning directly north at this point rather than continuing northeast would have led them astray on a much longer voyage to America or to the islands in the Aleutian chain.

Despite his dubious advice, Steller did have moments of insight. In his caustic but oddly wise style, he wrote of his growing foreboding:

> For the first time I had here the sad occasion to see how it happens that often the greatest and most useful undertakings may in the end, in spite of all care given and great expenses involved and although granted all possible resources, accomplish very much less, as far as the public good is concerned, than was planned originally; while on the other hand the smallest beginnings, through mutual and earnest cooperation in word and deed, of minds devoid of all egotistic aims and gain, may grow into mighty achievements which pay interest on the outlay a thousand fold.

By mid-July they had been at sea for nearly six weeks. Although the ship surged ahead with a good wind in its sails, the sun was pleasant, and all seemed well, they were running low on water and food, and there was a general anxiety at having been so long without seeing land. Just how far could land be? What if the ocean went on and on until they ran out of water and food, or came down with scurvy, and perished miserably, as had other famous mariners of the Pacific they had undoubtedly read about, such as Ferdinand Magellan? They knew enough of world geography to know that the ocean did not go on endlessly, but their minds began to imagine the fearful things that might befall them so far from home on uncharted shores of a foreign continent. The sea council met in the great cabin and agreed that if they did not spy land by July 20, they would turn the ship around, abandon the entire voyage, and hasten back to Avacha Bay.

July 15 was a clear and sunny day with a fine wind propelling the ship onward. In the evening, as clouds appeared to the east, Steller was strolling the deck, straining his eyes into the deepening haze. He squinted at a barely discernible outline through the swirling mist, yelled "land," and rushed to the railing. The excitement spread throughout the ship, others rushed to the railing, and men scampered up the rigging for a better view. But because of his past behavior, he could not convince others of his sighting. "Because I was the first to announce it," he sulked, "and because forsooth it was not so distinct that a picture could be made of it, the announcement was regarded as one of my peculiarities." Though it was drizzling, land was officially sighted in the East the following day, July 16. It was the third time he claimed land was nearby but the only time any actually materialized. Waxell recorded that they took observations and calculated that the *St. Peter* was at latitude 58 degrees, 38 minutes north, 50 degrees east of Avacha Bay. Though they were within sight of Alaska, it would be another three or four days before they reached it.

Steller privately gloated that he had been right all along. Had they only listened to him, instead of seeing land "six weeks after leaving Avacha, we might have made it in three or four days."

ACCORDING TO THE SHIP'S log, the first clear view of America was of a range of mighty snow-dusted spires draped in fog, "among them a high volcano." About a hundred nautical miles from the ship, the "volcano" towered over a vast range of smaller mountains snug against the coast as far as the eye could see. Endless green forests peeked through the mist. It was St. Elias Day, and they named the peak accordingly.* The mountains, Steller observed, "were so lofty that we could see them quite plainly at sea at a distance of sixteen Dutch miles. . . . I cannot recall having seen higher mountains anywhere in Siberia and Kamchatka." Waxell confirmed the sighting in his practical manner: "The land consisted of huge, high, snow-covered mountains."

All the officers and mariners cheered and congratulated each other on their greatness in discovering the new land. They slapped backs, imagined the glory and fame, and discussed the expectations of future reward that awaited them in St. Petersburg. But Bering, roused temporarily from his cabin for the event, showed no elation when he strolled on deck, beheld the scene, and heard faintly the roar of distant breakers crashing against the shore. He shrugged his shoulders, returned inside, and later noted glumly, prophetically, that "we think now we have accomplished everything, and many go about greatly inflated, but they do not consider where we have reached land, how far we are from home, and what may yet happen; who knows but that perhaps trade winds may arise, which

---

* Situated on the Alaska-Yukon border, Mount St. Elias is one of the highest mountains in both the United States and Canada at 18,008 feet (5,489 meters). Today the massive mountain is part of Kluane National Park in Canada and Wrangell–St. Elias National Park and Preserve in the United States. Sometimes called Shaa Tlein, or the "Big Mountain," by the Yakutat Tlingit, it is less romantically known as Boundary Peak 186. Some historians maintain that the mountain was not named by Bering and his officers but that its name was appended later in the eighteenth century and named after the far less impressive Cape St. Elias on Kayak Island.

may prevent us from returning? We do not know this country; nor are we provided with supplies for a wintering." Although it was the culmination of his career, of the Great Northern Expedition, and of the dream set into action by Peter the Great a generation earlier, Bering saw only more problems and took no joy in the moment. He had brought the men halfway around the world to discover new lands to be added to the Russian Empire, but how would he get them all back home? The fate of Chirikov and the *St. Paul* was also on his mind; there was still no evidence of them. Had their ship foundered and the men drowned? Or were they even now in desperate need of help somewhere along the coast?

America, Alaska, *Bolshaya Zemlya*, the Great Land of rumor and legend, meant different things to different people on the ship. To Steller, the outline of Mount St. Elias on the horizon meant the fulfillment of dreams, an exciting chance for him to make his name as a natural historian, as the first to visit a new land, to describe the flora and fauna, to uncover and reveal to the world the scientific treasures of a new continent. He imagined lengthy forays inland collecting great bundles of exotic specimens and locating the source of valuable minerals that would make the academy and the government in St. Petersburg lavish praise and appointments upon him. On the other hand, to Bering and some of the others, the unknown coast represented danger, something to be kept away from or approached with extreme caution—the abode of hostile people, dangerous sailing conditions, and hidden reefs or shallows. While Bering and Waxell and the other officers concerned with the innumerable nautical dangers awaiting to damage or wreck the ship urged caution, Steller rushed about, excitedly eager to row ashore and explore the new continent. What new animals, what new plants, might he discover and name?

For three days, contrary winds, drizzle, cloudy gusts, and fog kept the sailing ship from approaching the shore. They tacked back and forth, trying to get closer. Soundings could still not find the seafloor. Steller was in a high pitch of excitement, anticipating his chance to explore the new land, telling officers his opinion on where a safe anchorage for the ship could be found, based on his observation of currents in the water. When he was rudely rebuffed (had he been there before, then, and was sure of it?), he sniffed that "in uncertain things it is better to act on even the slightest indication than for no reason at all and only trusting to good luck." Steller was so sure of himself that he didn't try to deal respectfully with differing opinions, especially from naval officers accustomed to a chain of command. In this instance, as in many others, he was wrong in his assessment. The currents were not the evidence of a peaceful river outlet but rather a swift sea current running between the nearby Cape Suckling and an island just offshore from the mainland that they intended to anchor near. Bering was cautious, ordering the ship away from the shore of the island at night in case a storm blew in.

Only the next morning did the ship again approach the island after a night of tacking back and forth. After a day inspecting the western coast and observing some dangerous reefs, Bering again ordered the ship away from the island, and they spent another night tacking back and forth. The next morning, July 20, the officers selected a somewhat exposed anchorage on the lee side of what is now called Kayak Island, just off the mainland. They beheld "beautiful forests close down to the sea, as well as the great level ground in from the shore at the foot of the mountains. The beach itself was flat, level, and as far as we could observe, sandy." Lieutenant Khitrov reported that the island "stands out alone in the sea like a stone column; extending from it a submerged reef of rocks may be seen in low water." The *St. Peter* dropped anchor into some grayish blue clay and began lowering boats for closer investigation. Steller stared at the new land: if only he could get off the ship and get his feet onto the sand and hike down the beach.

By now two-thirds of the water barrels were empty, so getting more freshwater was the first priority. Bering ordered Khitrov to take a crew of fifteen in the longboat and cruise to the smaller island nearby, now called Wingham Island. His job was to search for a less exposed anchorage site and a place to harvest some of the huge trees for timber. Khitrov's excursion was to be brief, with a quick return to the *St. Peter* to report. Bering was taking no chances—with the *St. Paul* lost, a single miscalculation could doom them all. But his instructions called on him to note the location of a safe harbor for future expeditions that crossed the Pacific, so as always, he obeyed his orders to the letter.

While Khitrov investigated Wingham Island, the smaller shore boat, called a yawl, would head directly west to the middle of Kayak Island and look for a creek with freshwater. No one had yet spoken to Steller, and so he looked on as the boats were lowered and readied. Finally, he strolled the deck over to Bering to inquire about which shore excursion he should join. Steller was stunned and momentarily silenced when Bering told him it was too dangerous for him to go ashore and that only the water crews would embark to fill the empty barrels. Bering considered Steller's desire to collect a bunch of plants and animals from the land to be a waste of time: Would they not still be there on the next voyage? he reasoned. Bering believed their limited time should be spent studying the geography of the coast, perhaps doing some charting, and identifying harbors to make the next voyage safer and of course to solidify Russian political claims to the land. Then they would return to Kamchatka, since the season was already advanced and he did not want to be stuck on this distant and dangerous coast with short provisions. Bering also worried about the winds. The *St. Peter* was not in a secure harbor, and if the weather suddenly changed, he would be able to quickly recall the two crews in the boats—but what would he do if Steller and his assistant were off somewhere inland and unable to get back to the ship?

Steller imagined himself returning in triumph to St. Petersburg as the bearer of wonders from a new world. After he recovered from his shock, he noted in a sarcastic tone his astonishment that they had come all this way merely "for the purpose of bringing American water to Asia." Both Khitrov and Waxell agreed that Steller should go with one or the other of them, but Bering was adamant and tried to scare Steller with "dreadful tales of murder." Steller responded hotly (reflecting his eighteenth-century bias) that he had "never been so womanish as to fear danger" and that going ashore on this historic date, the first landing of a European on the shores of Northwest America, was "my principal work, my calling, and my duty." The longboat pushed off, carrying Khitrov and his crew, and Steller watched dumbfounded as it oared its way north.

He again pleaded with Bering, and then he threatened to report Bering's actions to the admiralty, the academy, and the senate "in the terms it deserved." The *St. Peter* was small enough that the argument was undoubtedly heard by many. Bering called him a "wild man," and then Steller put "all respect aside and prayed a particular prayer" and pointed out that studying the flora and fauna was his specific purpose on the voyage. The "particular prayer" that Steller wrote about sounds like a curse of some sort, but perhaps it was actually a prayer common between the two Lutherans, for apparently it produced the desired result: rather than lose his temper and toss Steller in the brig, "the Commander was at once mollified." Bering grudgingly gave his permission for Steller to go ashore in the yawl with the water crew under Waxell's command, but he was given no assistants apart from his own personal servant, Cossack Thomas Lepekhin. As Steller and Lepekhin clambered down into the yawl amid the empty water barrels at nine in the morning, Bering ordered the two trumpeters to come to the railing and sound a blaring salute, as if Steller were a naval dignitary. It was certainly a mockery, but Steller had the good sense to be gracious in his acceptance, waving jauntily. He was now convinced that Bering relented and let him go ashore only so that Bering could claim to have sent a representative to take note of the mineral potential of the land, in accordance with the official orders for the expedition. Perhaps, Steller mused sarcastically, he "would make watery observations" with the crew while the other shore party under Khitrov was "out on a windy expedition." It was a fine day of mixed sun and clouds, with a pleasant easterly breeze.

While crews filled the large barrels with freshwater at a small creek (today the creek is called Steller's Creek), Steller realized that his time was to be "scant and precious," so he rushed across the sandy beach and ventured inland into the thick forest, Lepekhin following closely. He occasionally stooped and dug up any plant that looked unusual and soon found signs "of people and their doings." Under the shelter of a large Sitka spruce tree, he found a dugout log that looked like a trough. It contained still-smoldering coals, and Steller noted that the people, "for lack of pots and vessels, had cooked their meat by means of red-hot stones." He noted that the charred bones, "some of them with bits of meat" attached, were strewn about the campsite where the "eaters had been sitting." These were not the bones of a sea mammal, and Steller surmised that they must have been caribou, but since there was no evidence of caribou on the island, the bones must have been carried from the mainland. He also found chunks of dried fish, of a type that in Kamchatka was often used to "serve the purpose of bread at all meals," and several "very large" scallops, eight inches across. He also found a fire-starting tool and moss tinder similar in style to that used by the Kamchadals. As they crept along the forest path, the two men came upon several chopped-down trees and noted that the work was done with many dull blows from stone or bone axes, "similar to those used by the Germans of old and known today as 'thunderbolts.'" Other trees were stripped of their bark to the height of a man's reach, the bark probably for use in making houses, hats, and baskets. The style of encampment and tools Steller observed is that which modern ethnographers associate with a summer camp of the Chugach of Prince William Sound. The trees were truly impressive in size, more than one hundred feet tall, easily able to sustain a shipbuilding industry "for centuries," Steller wrote with his typical exaggeration.

The two men pushed on through the damp and misty forest, along a path with other signs of recent passage. They came upon "a spot covered in cut grass" that Steller cautiously exposed, revealing a depression with a layer of rocks over tree bark. He was nervous, despite his ardent desire to meet "human beings and habitations," because he had only a small knife to defend himself, while Lepekhin had a gun and knife. It was, he surmised, a cellar or cache about fourteen feet by twenty-one feet and fourteen feet deep, and it was loaded with tools, utensils, a sweetgrass "from which liquor is distilled," and dried grasses of the sort used to make fishnets in Kamchatka. There were several bark containers containing smoked salmon, thongs of seaweed rope, and a collection of long arrows. It was a hidden food cache, storage for the winter. Steller took small samples of each item and sent Lepekhin back to the ship to warn the shore party to be wary. He continued on alone through the "thick and dark forest" to study and investigate "the noteworthy features of the three kingdoms of nature." He struggled to the crest of a nearby spruce-covered mountain for a view and saw camp smoke in the distance on the mainland. The camp on the mainland would have likely been from a different people, the Eyak from inland along the Copper River or the Tlingit from the east in Yakutat Bay. With time, Steller could have made contact with several different cultures of people. But he had to return. He "looked once more sorrowfully at the barrier to my investigations, with real regret over the action of those who had in their hands the direction of such important matters."

Although Steller burned with desire to follow the smoke and encounter the people, his time was limited, so he ran back to the beach with an armful of plants. He sent a note with the next boatload of water barrels back to the ship, which was anchored offshore, seeking Bering's permission to use the yawl and a few men to further investigate the far side of the island, which he estimated to be about thirteen miles long and only two miles wide, and to collect some more specimens. "Dead tired," he wrote. "I made in the meantime descriptions on the beach of the rarer plants which I was afraid might wither and was delighted to be able to test out the excellent water for tea."

While Steller awaited the reply to his request, he heard the squawking and chirping of unknown birds, saw unfamiliar footprints in the earth, and spied all around him plants unknown in Asia or Europe. The birds, in particular, were "strange and unknown . . . easily distinguished from the European and Siberian species by their particularly bright coloring." He continued to marvel at the abundance of natural beauty that lay before him, eager and excited to see more of the new land. "In an hour or so," he wrote sarcastically, "I received the patriotic and courteous reply that I should betake myself on board quickly or they would leave me ashore without waiting for me." Steller, always one to push his luck to the limit, was not deterred from his objective by the threats of his shipmates. He estimated the time for filling the remaining water casks and set off once again. "Since there was now no time left for moralizing," he observed (though he moralized aplenty when he rejoined the ship), "only enough to scrape together as much as possible before our fleeing the country, and as evening was already nearing, I sent my Cossack out to shoot some rare birds that I had noticed, while I once more started out to the westward, returning at sunset with various observations and collections."

Steller had lingered longer than he should have. The yawl was waiting for him, and it was with apprehension that he hastily rowed back to the ship—and was surprised at being handed a cup of warm chocolate drink, in those days a rare and special treat. And perhaps there is no more odd drink for him to have had. Consider that the cocoa was originally produced somewhere in the Americas, likely farther south in Mexico, and then shipped across the

Atlantic, probably to Spain, and then to Amsterdam and St. Petersburg. Finally, it was carted overland to Moscow and across Siberian
Asia, loaded onto the *St. Peter*, and taken back across the Pacific to
America, where Steller drank it after being one of the first Europeans to set foot in Alaska. The chocolate had traveled even farther
than the mariners, nearly circumnavigating the world.

Within an hour of Steller's return, Khitrov and his party of fifteen in the shore boat also rowed back to the *St. Peter*. He reported
the good news that he had indeed found a good safe harbor on the
east side of Wingham Island, which was about a mile long and half
a mile wide. "In going there between N. and E., the depth of the
channel was 25, 22, 18, 10, 7, 6, 4 and 3½ fathoms where it was possible to anchor." The bottom was "sandy and in spots clayey. The island is sheltered from many winds." During their exploration of the
smaller island, the men discovered a summer hut constructed with
hewn boards. The hut contained tools and domestic implements,
including a wooden basket of unusual design, a shovel, and a small
copper stained stone. Khitrov thought that perhaps the stone was
used as a whetstone for copper tools. They had met no people, but
the signs suggested that there had been people here shortly before
the explorers' arrival. Khitrov assumed that the people here, as the
ones on Kayak Island, "on seeing us ran away or hid or that they
have their habitations on the mainland and come to the island in
summer to catch fish and other sea animals." Hardly surprising con-
clusions, considering the tiny size of the island and the difficulty of
hiding from fifteen men on such a small patch of land. But the good
news to Bering was that Khitrov not only discovered but had also
roughly charted the safe harbor, one of the specific requirements of
his orders now accomplished.

Bering ordered some of the men to return in the yawl for the final load of water barrels and to leave some gifts that, Waxell noted,
"were to be left in the cabin for the natives." The gifts included
some cloth or leather, two iron kettles, two knives, twenty large

glass beads, two iron tobacco pipes, and a large package of leaf tobacco. The idea was to leave for the local people a good impression of the bearded strangers, as a foundation for good relations on future visits. Waxell proclaimed that the smoked fish they had taken from the encampment "tasted most excellently" and was pleased with the exchange. Steller had a different, and dimmer, view once he noted the additional plundering of the camp that had occurred after he had described where it was: "If we should ever come again to these parts, the natives would certainly run away even faster or they would show themselves as hostile as they themselves had been treated, especially if it should occur to them to eat or drink the tobacco . . . for them to conclude that we had intended to poison them!" Either Steller was merely being contrary, or he was jaded in his views because of the ill treatment of the natives in Kamchatka. But if evidence from other early encounters between Europeans and remote peoples is a guide, the gift of iron items such as kettles and knives would have been viewed as extremely valuable and warmly remembered.

When he was in the vicinity of the camp, Steller had a feeling that he was being watched, a vague sense of uneasiness. His suspicion was confirmed a half century later from an unexpected source. Another Russian ship under the command of Gavril Sarychev, as part of the Joseph Billings expedition in 1790, encountered a "very good-natured and intelligent" Eyak man, who told them, through an interpreter, a tale from his childhood. When he was a boy, he remembered a ship coming to Kayak Island during the summer, when his family used to visit the island after fishing and hunting on the mainland. "When the ship sent a boat ashore, we all ran away. When the ship sailed away, we returned to our hut and found in our underground storeroom glass beads, tobacco leaves, an iron kettle and something else."

AFTER THE FINAL BARRELS of water were loaded, stories told, and the hot chocolate drink savored, things resumed their natural pattern. As he wasn't immediately chastised for being a little late returning, Steller recorded that he "made my ideas known about various things"—probably in a manner that reinforced everyone's disgust with his arrogance. When he heard they were calling the southern tip of the island Cape Elias and marking it on their chart as such, he groused that "the officers were determined to have a cape on their chart" even though he "plainly represented to them that an island cannot be called a cape." He even took the liberty, for their edification, of pointing out that the projection of a cape must come from the land, "the same meaning being conveyed by the Russian word *nos* (nose), while in the present case the island would represent nothing but a detached head or a detached nose." No one likes a pedant, and one can almost hear the sighs of exasperation and annoyance, see the turned backs, and feel the dark thoughts.

The next morning, July 21, Bering unexpectedly came on deck, "much against his usual practice," and without consulting anyone ordered the ship to weigh anchor and proceed north along the coast. Waxell approached Bering and tried to convince him to delay at least a few more hours for one final trip to fill the remaining twenty water barrels, but Bering refused and claimed that "because of the approach of August and our ignorance of the land, the winds, and the sea, we should be satisfied for this year with the discovery already made." Waxell and Khitrov were not pleased with the directive, in particular sailing without a full supply of freshwater, but they chose not to demand a sea council to discuss it further and bowed to Bering's wishes, at least in part. Rather than sailing directly home through known waters, Waxell writes that "it was our intention to follow the land as it went." Bering had good reasons for his trepidation and a gnawing fear that with provisions for only one season and no knowledge of the winds and currents, they were in fact in a dangerous and precarious situation. It had taken them seven weeks to get across the ocean, so he had to assume it would take as long or longer to recross it. Bering had been looking for patterns in wind movements as recorded in the logs, and he came to the conclusion that for most of the summer, the prevailing winds were twice as likely to be northeasterly or easterly compared to the opposite direction. If the pattern held, he thought it might mean, as it does for other monsoon-type weather systems, that with the changing season, the winds might reverse. If so, the ship would be battling against headwinds that blew two-thirds of the time from the opposite direction, southwesterly. The winds would be against them. If this was the case, they had only about three more weeks to explore the Alaskan coast while working their way northwest.

Later in the morning, as the ship eased out from the shelter of the islands, Steller mused philosophically that "the only reason we did not attempt to land on the mainland is a sluggish obstinacy and a dull fear of being attacked by a handful of unarmed and still more timid savages, from whom there was no reason to expect either friendship or hostility, and a cowardly homesickness which they probably thought might be excused. . . . [T]he time spent here in investigation bears an arithmetical ratio to the time used in fitting out: ten years the preparations for this great undertaking lasted, and ten hours were devoted to the work itself." As the land drifted by, he could only imagine what interesting things lay undiscovered; he was not content with what they had done and was disdainful of the cowardice he imagined ruled Bering's and the other Russian officers' decisions. (Bering would have been even more risk averse had he known what Chirikov was dealing with around the same time farther south and east along the same coast.)

From Kayak Island, the ship sailed west and then in a generally northwesterly direction through fog, wind, and the occasional short but rough gale. One typical entry in the ship's log reads, "Stormy, squally, rainy." Heavily forested islands, such as Hawkins, Hinchinbrook, and Montague Islands, with concealed waterways, littered the coast and bedeviled their efforts to gain a clear understanding of the geography. With more time or better weather in a more clement season, the improved visibility might have revealed the glacier-fed fjords in Prince William Sound, the Copper River delta, and numerous native villages. The seas grew more turbulent with the "continuous stormy and wet weather" the farther they sailed. But the land did not trend to the north as they had supposed, but curled to the west, requiring the ship to keep angling, to avoid the unknown dangers of the coast.

As the *St. Peter* slid northwest, Steller had time to muse on the differences between Kamchatka and Alaska. The "American continent (on this side)," he wrote, "as far as climate is concerned, is notably better than that of the extreme northeastern part of Asia." Although the mountains were "amazingly high," with peaks covered in perpetual snow, they were of a "much better nature and character" than the mountains of Kamchatka. Showing the curiosity and wide range of interests common to scientists during the eighteenth century, Steller speculated that the mountains in Kamchatka were "thoroughly broken up and long since deprived of their coherency, consequently too loose for the circulation of mineral gases and devoid of all inner heat, accordingly also without precious metals. On the other hand the American mountains are solid; not naked rocks covered with moss but everywhere with good black soil, and therefore not . . . barren, with stunted dwarf trees among the rocks, but densely covered to the highest peaks with the finest trees." Steller was convinced of the correctness of the (now preposterous) theory that the inner heat of the Alaskan mountains produced the greater size and quantity of vegetation compared to the vegetation in the corresponding latitude of Asia. Steller had no qualms about theorizing and sharing his theories even with people who had no interest in them; in the absence of any accurate knowledge of the natural world, unsophisticated and unsystematic speculation was the starting point for scientific inquiry.

While watching the lushly forested and mountainous coast slowly pass by, Steller was able to study and record his observations of the specimens that he had collected, or at least the ones that Bering had allowed him to bring aboard the ship. He was already familiar with many of the plants on Kayak Island because they were similar to those found in Kamchatka, including blueberries, crow-berries, and cloudberries. But one of his most prized discoveries was a large raspberry-like plant that grew in profusion where he had rambled. The new species of raspberry, which is now called a salmonberry, was "not yet quite ripe." He had carefully dug up a few plants because he felt that he should have been allowed permission to bring several living specimens aboard ship for the return journey, kept in planters on the deck, "on account of its great size, shape, and delicious taste." But he had to content himself with dead specimens. He recorded in yet another barb at his fellow adventurers that "it is not my fault that space for such was begrudged since as a protester I myself took up too much space already."

Steller had also noted ten different "strange and unknown" birds. Only the magpie and the raven were familiar to him. Steller's ser-vant, Lepekhin, shot one bird that he was particularly excited about. It was a species that looked similar to the blue jay, which Steller remembered seeing in a book on the birds of the Carolinas that he had perused at the academy library in St. Petersburg. He had in his mind's eye "a likeness painted in lively colors" by a naturalist whose name he couldn't remember (the book was *The Natural History of Carolina, Florida, and the Bahama Islands*, by English naturalist Mark Catesby). The remarkably colorful bird, a cousin to the east-ern blue jay but with a tuft of black on its head, was later given the name Steller's jay, *Cyanocitta stelleri*, in commemoration of its first recorded observation for science. "This bird alone," Steller wrote, "proved to me that we were really in America."

Steller also took time to defend his lack of discovery of min-erals, one of the key and important objectives as defined by the expedition's instructions. His superiors in St. Petersburg, he wrote hopefully, "will easily see that my failure to discover any minerals is not due to carelessness or laziness on my part. I confess freely that I observed nothing else than sand and gray rock. It is also well known that close to the beach Nature is neither able nor accustomed to produce anything outside of marcasites and pyrites." Everyone in the Russian service was now anxious to do exactly to the letter what their instructions demanded and to defend themselves against even the slightest deviation from those instructions. Just as Bering was checking off all the points in his orders, and pursuing anything else with a decided lack of enthusiasm, Steller was making sure he could justify his actions and reasons for going on the voyage without official permission and only Bering's word that all would be fine. They were all a little afraid of the repercussions of not being diligent or of being overly independent.

On July 25, the "Captain Commander had a consultation with his officers, and it was agreed, while the misty weather prevailed, to sail SW by compass, which would take us towards Kamchatka; but when the weather cleared and the wind turned fair to sail N and W in order to observe the American coast." Waxell and Khitrov's desire to explore more of the Alaskan coast prevailed over Bering's desire to return immediately—Bering was no longer entirely in control of the ship's course. As soon as the weather cleared, the ship would head back closer to land and again follow the coast, a slower but more interesting route.

On one occasion, the visibility from the ship was so poor that they were essentially sailing blind; they could see no land in any direction, yet a sounding found them in shallow water with choppy waves. "We tried everything possible," Waxell wrote, "to escape from there, but in whatever direction we sailed, we found only shallow water. I had no idea what was the best thing to do. I decided to sail due south. For a time the depth remained the same, but fortunately we eventually came out into deep water." When the mist cleared on the morning of July 26, they spied "high land" per-haps twenty or thirty miles distant to the north of the ship. It was probably Kodiak Island or nearby Sitkalidak Island. But the storm soon returned, and the *St. Peter* pushed through the swirling soup of "drizzle" and fog and on the twenty-ninth "hove to on account of the gale." On July 30, the turbulent weather began to clear, and by the thirty-first the wind changed and they changed course to the north to come closer again to the mainland. Fog periodically rolled across the water.

Shortly after midnight on August 2, through a clearing sky and a sliver of moon, eyes peered from the deck toward a "large wooded" island that had loomed like an eldritch apparition out of the en-compassing fog. Bering called it Archdeacon Stephen's Island, after the saint's name day, but Waxell and Khitrov called it "Tu-mannji Ostrov," or Fog Island. In 1794 Captain George Vancouver called it Chirikov Island, after the commander of the *St. Paul*, even though Chirikov never saw the island. It is about one hundred miles southwest of Kodiak Island. As the weather had become "unusu-ally pleasant and warm, sunny and absolutely calm," and a sea lion swam lazily around the ship, peering up at them, Steller begged to go ashore a final time, as he could see freshwater lakes, streams, and rolling grassy hills. He was refused because Bering thought the landing might prove treacherous on account of reefs or shoals. Steller and Bering "got into a slight altercation on the subject." Ber-ing then called a sea council in the cabin, with the main purpose of agreeing that the officers would never "upbraid" Steller or accuse him of not wanting to do his duty "most zealously, to the best of my ability, and at every opportunity." It was yet another example of Steller's fear of official reprimand from the academy or the sen-ate for not doing his duty to explore and assess the natural bounty of the new lands. Once this face-saving information was duly re-corded and everyone promised to uphold his assiduous pursuit of duty, Steller agreed "to let it go at that."

The *St. Peter* weighed anchor and continued in a northwesterly direction, while Steller contented himself with casting his fishing line from the railing of the ship and catching two new species of sculpins that were lurking in the coastal waters. They had not solved their water problem, however, and there was no way they could sail all the way west to Kamchatka without stopping somewhere. While Bering worried about contrary winds, Steller just waited for his chance to go ashore. According to their calculations, Kamchatka was still around fifteen hundred nautical miles to the west.

CHAPTER 8

CURIOUS ENCOUNTERS

In the early morning of June 20, in the mid-North Pacific Ocean south of the Alaskan Peninsula and Chirikov Island, the men of the *St. Paul* saw the *St. Peter* on the horizon to the north. The visibility was poor, and two hours later the *St. Peter* had disappeared from sight, leaving them alone. Chirikov ordered the *St. Paul* to continue on the regular course with a lowered mainsail. But the next day, they were still alone on the sea, and Chirikov "gave the order to steer as near as possible" to the spot where they had last seen the *St. Peter*, in accordance with his prearranged orders. The winds were contrary, and it was hard work keeping the *St. Paul* in the proper area. On the morning of June 23, Chirikov convened the officers in his cabin, and they agreed to continue the voyage alone, hoping to meet up with their sister ship later. The *St. Paul* pressed on through the gusty sea in a general northeasterly direction.

They soon spied what they thought to be mountains to the north but that later revealed themselves to be clouds. Another week of fair winds and clear skies passed, and it was now early July. Green-looking vegetation swirled past the hull of the ship. They thought it might be grass and took a sounding, finding no bottom at one

hundred fathoms. Chirikov reported that they "examined the vegetation and learned that it was not sea grass but a species found
in thick water resembling a sea nettle which is washed ashore in
large quantities." On July 12, they saw a "shore duck in the water."
On the thirteenth, they spied a "shore duck, a gull, and two old
floating trees." On the fourteenth, their excitement was fueled by
"a large number of shore ducks, gulls, a whale, porpoises, and three
medium-sized pieces of driftwood that had been in the water for
some time." And then land materialized to the east, "quite mountainous," with bottom at sixty fathoms, consisting of "gray sand and
in places small rocks." Birds now regularly flew past the ship. It was
July 15, the same day that Steller was squinting north from the deck
of the *St. Peter* several hundred miles north along the same coast and
claiming to see land that was not confirmed until the following day.

Great flocks of murres and cormorants flew overhead as the
St. Paul sailed closer to land. They were confident that this "was
without doubt the American coast," because according to the map
of Louis Delisle de la Croyère, they were north of "parts of America
that are well known," Spanish America. They were now near Cape
Bartolome, Baker Island, west of Ketchikan, on the Alaskan pan-
handle. Of course, Croyère's chart showed only the very roughly
charted coast that was claimed by imperial Spain, even though
Spain did not actually have any presence along that coast closer than
Acapulco, three thousand miles to the south. Although it seems
absurd, no one had ever spoken to the people who lived along the
coast, and they had no idea that a far-distant empire lay political
claim to their lands. The *St. Paul* slowly cruised north for several
more hours, searching for a good anchorage. "The coast is irregular
and mountainous: these mountains had a fine growth of timber and
in places were covered with snow." The explorers were now literally
on the opposite side of the earth from where they had started in
St. Petersburg.

The next day, at four in the afternoon, Chirikov ordered a shore boat lowered, and the quartermaster, Grigori Trubitsin, led eight men closer to shore to inspect a bay to see if the *St. Paul* could safely enter. It is now called Windy Bay, on Coronation Island. Trubitsin rowed around and reported "large fir, spruce and pine trees on the beach, many sea lions on the rocks," but there was no sign of human habitation, and the bay was unsuitable as an anchorage. The ship sailed out from the coast for safety during the night, and the next day it continued cruising north by northwest through increasing fog along a coast of "high snow-covered mountains extending to the northward." Chirikov recalled that "it was my intention to make a careful survey of a part of the American coast, but my plans were ruined by the misfortune of July 18th."

When the fog cleared, the men stared from the deck of the ship and saw that the mountains had more snow on them than a few days earlier. They sailed the *St. Paul* "as close to the shore as we dared," but, unable to find a secure place to anchor, they decided to send a longboat ashore to search a bay for a safe anchorage. Then they could make a base for closer investigation of the new land. Chirikov handed Fleet Master Avram Dementiev a copy of his instructions, which he then read several times, as well as a signed paper detailing his conduct in the strange new land. Chirikov stayed on the *St. Paul*, tacking back and forth about a nautical mile from shore while Dementiev took ten armed men in the longboat. The location is now called Takanis Bay, on Yakobi Island, generally northwest of the town of Sitka. Chirikov instructed them to fire a signal rocket once ashore to announce their safe arrival, to light a bonfire on the beach at night, and to offer gifts to any native peoples, such as kettles, beads, cloth, needles, and tobacco. He wanted them to report on the quality of the harbor, to sketch it, to investigate the "trees and grass," and to "examine the rocks and the soil to see whether they contain precious minerals." They were also to fill some of the empty water barrels. As with the *St. Peter*, there wasn't enough for the return journey, and getting a fresh supply was a priority. But most important, for an ambitious imperial expedition, Chirikov instructed them to "in all things conduct yourself as a true and good servant of Her Imperial Majesty."

The men rowed off into the mist and out of sight of the ship. The longboat was loaded with provisions for a week in case a storm kept them from returning, but their instructions were clear: to "make every effort to carry out quickly the above instructions so that you may return to the ship the same day or at least not later than the next day." But no rocket was fired. When darkness came, there was no bonfire on the beach. "Strong winds and tides" kept the larger ship from approaching the land. Days passed, and still there was no sign of the shore party, and "owing to the heavy fog we could not identify the landmarks." They all had a sinking feeling that Dementiev's men had never made it ashore, or, worse, they had been attacked and killed. At first the weather was fine, but it was then followed by several days of heavy rain, fog, and winds that carried the *St. Paul* away from the shore.

On July 23, Chirikov ordered the ship to creep closer to shore at the place where he had instructed Dementiev to go. They spied rocks jutting from the ocean and lurking just below the surface as they fearfully eased the big ship closer. Chirikov fired two cannons, the boom echoing against the forest, but there was no reply. The fog lifted a little, and from the deck they spied smoke on shore in the location where they presumed Dementiev had landed. The glow of a fire on the beach rallied their spirits, and they fired seven more cannons at intervals. During the previous days, "we had seen no fire, no buildings, no boats, nor any other signs of human beings and therefore supposed that the country was uninhabited." The size of the fire grew, but no boat appeared on the water. Chirikov lit the stern lantern as a beacon and, as the weather was calm, kept the *St. Paul* close to shore. By morning the fire on the shore had died down, and only a wisp of smoke spiraled upward, blending with the fog.

Chirikov and his officers decided that the shore boat must have been damaged and was unable to row out to the ship. They prepared a written document to this effect and affixed their signatures. They would take another risk and send ashore the remaining small boat with the carpenter, the caulker, and all the tools needed to repair a boat. Boatswain Sidor Savelev volunteered to lead the second shore party, with the plan that he would return immediately with the yawl and a few of the stranded mariners. Around noon the four men set off from the ship and rowed toward shore, about nine nautical miles away, and the *St. Paul* followed carefully behind with a keen lookout for hidden rocks. By six in the evening, the *St. Paul* had retreated in the face of a heavy sea, and from the deck the men could just see the yawl approaching the shore. They waited. No signal came, and the yawl did not return to the ship. The next day, July 25, at one in the afternoon, they spied two boats emerging from the bay and coming toward the ship. Thinking it was their two boats, Chirikov sailed the *St. Paul* closer, but it soon became apparent that these were not Russian boats: "Their bows were sharp and the men did not row as we do but paddled." The larger one with many men kept its distance, while a small fast one with four men sped closer. They could see that one person wore something bright red. Some of them stood up and motioned with their hands for the *St. Paul* to come closer, and they called out twice, "Agai, Agai," before turning around and paddling back into the bay. Chirikov gave orders for white kerchiefs to be displayed, but the boats continued ashore and soon disappeared. They could not follow them, because "many rocks were seen both under and above water on which the surf was playing." A heavy surf prevented them from anchoring, and they had to retreat. There were no more signals of fires or smoke.

By now, Chirikov wrote, "we became convinced that some misfortune had happened to our men." Dementiev and the first party had been missing for eight days, and there had been plenty of opportunity to row out to the ship had they been able to. "The action of the natives, their fear to come close to us, made us suspect that they had either killed our men or held them." When Waxell later heard of the tale of the *St. Paul*'s misfortune, he speculated just how it could have happened. "When our people came ashore," he speculated, "the Americans will have hidden themselves, and thus the men from the boat will have had no inkling of any danger. Then they will have begun to roam about, one in search of water, another looking for berries and fruits, and the others this or that. In this manner they became scattered and, when the Americans thought the right moment had come, they will have run in between them and the boat, preventing them from getting back to it. That is how it must have been." He wrote that Chirikov was too naive and should have hidden some of his men belowdeck when he saw the two boats approaching, thereby to lure the Americans closer, since he believed they had "perhaps even the intention of taking the ship." Then, he speculated, Chirikov could have captured some of them and ransomed them in exchange for the Russians.*

Chirikov kept the ship close by for two more days, slowly patrolling the coast, but now both of the *St. Paul*'s small boats were lost, along with fifteen men. In the afternoon of the second day, the two native boats appeared again in the bay, but they remained close to land and then returned down the bay and disappeared. A

---

*The people were probably Tlingit, inhabiting the southern coast of Alaska and inland in northwestern British Columbia and Yukon territory. In the Tlingit language, Lingit, "Agai" or "Agou" means "Come" or "Come here." Since relations between Europeans and the Tlingit were frequently harmonious, it is generally believed that the actions of the Tlingit, which Chirikov reported, were cautious but friendly in intent, beckoning the strangers to come and see the wreckage or perhaps to trade at a nearby village. The powerful and treacherous riptides that are common along narrow inlets of the Alaskan coast had probably swamped the two small boats and drowned the men before they ever reached shore, before they could even send a flare or fire a shot, which was to be their first order of action upon reaching land.

little smoke curled into the air from the shore, but it soon dissipated. Without smaller boats to go ashore or explore shallow water, the *St. Paul* was in serious danger. An inventory revealed that they had forty-five casks of water onboard, some only partially full because the barrels had leaked. It was "hardly enough" to return, and they now had no way of filling their empty casks. They had been in America for only a few days, but Chirikov knew they had no other choice but to sail back to Kamchatka as quickly as possible. On July 27, the entire crew was placed on short rations, and the *St. Paul* began to battle contrary winds and rain on the homeward voyage.

THE *ST. PETER* SKIRTED the eastern side of Kodiak Island, zigzagging for days against contrary winds. As the ship drifted toward the island chain now known as the Semidi Islands, Steller spent his days observing large numbers of hair seals, fur seals, sea otters, sea lions, dolphins, and storm fishes (porpoises)—all the animals that seemed to flourish along the misty shores of the islands. Through thick rolling fog they proceeded, as phantasmal and eerie promontories rose from time to time from the mist. On August 4, they spied a mighty volcano (Mount Chiginagak) to the northwest, while the ship followed the curve of the fifteen-mile-long series of nine islands, each capped with towering peaks. Then the ship changed course and headed south to get some distance from the land that could be seen to the north and west, the Alaskan Peninsula. To the mariners, it looked like they were trapped in a bay, with land visible in every direction except south. Steller desperately wanted more time to investigate the land, and Waxell and Khitrov pressed Bering into agreeing to their plan to chart more of the coast before returning. However, a half-submerged reef was occasionally revealed as a ponderous wave retreated. All on board, even Steller, knew that it would have been treacherous sailing close to land without accurate charts. Waxell suspected the barely discernible land was a series of islands, because "we sailed two or three hours at a stretch through very calm water and with a light wind, yet at the same time making a good speed. Suddenly we would come out into large ocean waves and were scarcely able to manage the ship." Bering no longer had any interest in exploring—he just wanted to get back to Kamchatka—but the confusing geography of islands and mainland around the western Gulf of Alaska was confounding the direct route home. Events were proving Bering right in his fear of the unknown land, and the mist and rain amplified this fear.

On their way back south, the ship passed west of Chirikov Island again, but this time it was far off to the east, and Steller noted that "the winds, which at this time and until August 9 were mostly east or southeast and could have advanced us several hundred miles on the straight course to Kamchatka, were now utilized fruitlessly tacking up and down." As Bering had feared, they were beset by dreaded headwinds, the seasonal westerlies. The ship's speed slowed, and then the wind drove the ship back forty-three nautical miles to the southeast. Steller brooded about the abundance of "storm fishes" that he spied in the waters around the ship. It was believed that when they were "seen unusually often in a very quiet sea, a storm followed soon after, and that the oftener they came up and the more active they were, the more furious was the subsequent gale." Steller counted many of them. Then, on August 10, through the fog and drizzle, he spied something that he had never seen before. It wasn't a sea otter, a sea lion, a whale, or a porpoise. "The head was like a dog's, with pointed, erect ears," he wrote. "From the upper and the lower lips on both sides whiskers hung down. The eyes were large; the body was long, rather thick and round, tapering gradually towards the tail. The skin seemed thickly covered in hair, of a gray color on the back, but reddish white on the belly; in the water, however, the whole animal appeared red, like a cow." The peculiar beast had no forefeet but rather fins. It leaped gracefully through the water, jumping and playing, following the ship for more than two hours, diving under the slowly moving vessel and appearing on the other side, back and forth perhaps thirty times. When a piece of seaweed drifted by, the creature playfully swam up and grabbed it in its mouth and surged toward the ship, close enough that Steller could have poked it with a pole, "making such motions and monkey tricks that nothing more laughable can be imagined." After several more tricks, causing much laughter, it darted away and was seen only from a distance. Steller called it a "sea ape," and it became a mystery to many future naturalists. Clearly, it wasn't any of the other sea mammals that Steller had seen in Kamchatka or Alaska; he was sufficiently familiar with them that he certainly would have identified it. Much ink has been spilled debating the likely identity of the famous "Steller's sea ape," but the light wasn't good, "the moon and stars were out," and because of the fog and mist, a great deal was obscured. It was probably a full-grown bachelor fur seal or a young northern fur seal. We do know why the "sea ape" fled the ship. Steller shot at it because he wanted it for his collection, but he missed.*

It was around this time that the assistant surgeon, Matthias Betge, submitted an official report that five sailors were on the sick list for scurvy and that sixteen others were "badly affected." Soon there would be more cases of men unfit for service. Bering, who had been in his cabin for two days, was probably also suffering the early stages of the affliction. Since Waxell had been running the ship for most of the voyage, setting the watch, appointing the helmsman,

---

*While sailing the Aleutian Islands with his family in 1969, Miles Smeeton wrote in his book *Misty Islands* of his own encounter with a similar creature. Based on his description, it could easily have been the same creature Steller described. Two other people on the sailboat also reported seeing the strange sea mammal frolicking near their boat. They had not read Steller's account beforehand and only afterward believed they had seen the same beast.

and assigning sailing duties, Bering's present indisposition had little direct impact on the ship's operations.

After a frustrating day tacking back and forth battling contrary headwinds, Bering called a sea council in his cabin to consider their situation. Present were Bering and the senior officers, Lieutenant Waxell, Shipmaster Sofron Khitrov, and the aging navigator, Andreyan Hesselberg, then more than seventy years of age. They first went over the minutes of their previous sea council meetings, with specific attention to the directive to return to Petropavlovsk "during the last days of September." This now seemed dangerous "because of the violent autumn storms and continuous heavy fogs." It was not safe to approach land because they had no charts or knowledge of hidden reefs and rocks, currents, and sandbanks; islands compounded the poor visibility. After the discussion, the officers called all the junior and petty officers into the cabin and presented their opinion that it was time to turn directly for home along the fifty-third parallel of latitude "or as near to it as the winds will permit." The document, titled "Decision to Hasten Return," was then signed by all present. They had been at sea sixty-nine days so far. They gave orders to prepare the ship to proceed in a more southwesterly direction. Steller noted that "as usual," he wasn't called in to offer an opinion or to sign the document. But he did quietly record his opinion: "If I now draw the logical conclusion, from a comparison between the object of the sea council and their subsequent acts, it must certainly be as follows: 'These gentlemen want to go home, and by the shortest road but in the longest way.'" On this parallel, he thought, islands would surely block the path, while a more southerly route would be a detour but have better winds.

They spent the next week, until August 17, tacking back and forth along the fifty-third parallel due to contrary winds. There were no direct winds for sailing. The ship's log tells the story: endless hauling up and down of the various sails, the jig, topsails, foresails, topgallant sail, mainsail, trysail, and topmast-staysail, preparing the ship to turn and claw its way in the desired direction against the wind, through weather that was "drizzly," "wet," "heavy," "rainy," "foggy," and "thick." During this time, yet unknown to the men on either ship, the *St. Peter* and the *St. Paul* were crossing paths several times, out of sync with each other by a mere couple of days and never in sight of each other. A "real storm" set in on the seventeenth in the afternoon, and soon it was a "gale" with "heavy swell," which petered out the next day. The ceaseless struggle against wind and waves was slowly exhausting the men.

On the eighteenth of August, Steller woke in his bunk to hear talk of land, and he rushed to the deck to see what was going on. Throughout the voyage, on numerous occasions, Steller thought he saw land and loudly pointed it out, harassing the officers for not sailing closer to inspect it, so perhaps it was no surprise that when he went on deck no one would mention the land to him. "However it may already have been agreed that no one should say anything about having seen land," he groused, since none of them would confirm the sighting, which he thought was either a prank against him or because it was seen "in such a singular place, namely in the south." He then claimed the land could be seen plainly in the morning before being hidden by fog. "That it was not far from us could also be inferred from the quantities of kelp floating from that direction." And "the fact that the westerly wind died down suddenly" was in his mind additional proof that they were sailing between America and some island to the south. The officers had a distinct lack of interest in the "land," and Steller was angry because he thought they were pretending to not see the land so they would not have to investigate and put it on their chart. It was "indefensible to leave it without an investigation," he fumed.

When Steller asked what land they thought it was, Waxell replied, "Juan da Gamma [*sic*] Land" (probably with a wink to the others, since he was a well-known disbeliever in the mythical islands that had wasted so much of their time). Steller was a supporter of

"Monsieur Delisle" and his chart, and he reminded himself that he was a member of the academy, after all, and not just an ignorant seaman. On the nineteenth, Steller again thought he saw land, "but nobody but myself and a few others would believe or see it," though the usual indications were present: the declining wind, sea weeds, sea mammals, and "a species of cod which lives on the banks at a depth of 90 fathoms at the most." They may have eaten cod for dinner that night. On August 20, when they had steered farther south, Waxell "asked mockingly" whether "I was still seeing land." But Steller, never invited to take part in important decisions, wrote with his customary sardonic tone that "they could see no farther than nature and experience permitted them." No land exists in that region, and the most any of them could have seen were clouds on the horizon. The disputes and friction were escalating as the voyage wore on.

Then came several days of good easterly wind, before the ship was attacked by yet another "violent" storm during which "heavy squalls and waves" washed over the deck. On August 27, Bering called the three senior officers into his cabin again for another sea council: only a third of the water barrels remained full, and they knew there wasn't enough to make it to Avacha Bay on Kamchatka "if the contrary winds continue to blow." By their calculations, they had to travel about 1,240 nautical miles before reaching Avacha Bay, but at the speed they were traveling it would be two and a half months before they reached it. They agreed to turn the ship north again "for safety's sake" and to "go nearer the land with a view to finding good anchorage where we might take on water enough to last until our return, so that, in case of head winds we should not suffer extremely." They all signed the document. Steller wrote in his journal that of course, if they had just filled up all the water barrels when they were safely settled off of Kayak Island a month earlier, this latest delay and quest "would not have been necessary."

The ship cruised north with fair winds and clear skies, and they soon saw signs of nearby land: sea lions, gulls, and floating vegetation.

On August 29, they spied a cluster of five smaller islands with what appeared to be a mainland on the horizon, and they steered closer to look for a safe place to land. By noon they sailed in and anchored in the lee on the east side of Nagai Island, one of the largest of the Shumagin Islands at around thirty miles long. The Shumagin chain contains around fifty islands of varying sizes. The weather was perfect for a shore expedition, low winds and clear sky, and in the afternoon Waxell sent Yushin off toward the island in the small boat to search for a good anchorage. At around eight in the evening, they decided to move the *St. Peter* to a point midway between Nagai Island and a small nearby island called Near Island to keep it "secure from many winds." They found themselves surrounded by a cluster of small islands, in a body of water that is now aptly named Bay of Islands. Later that night, Khitrov spied in the distance a fire burning on a small island about eight miles to the northwest (now called Turner Island).

In the morning Waxell organized two parties, one led by Khitrov to go and investigate the site of the previous night's fire on Turner Island and the other led by Hesselberg to go to nearby Nagai Island to search for a freshwater spring. Bering offered that Steller could go with Hesselberg, and Steller accepted "very kindly." The relations between Steller and the others had not improved, and he suspected that Bering's offer was to distract him "in order that the naval officers might have the honor of the expected discovery" of native peoples on the other island. Although Steller was curious to meet native peoples, he hoped that "both parties might find something useful." Hesselberg led his ten crew, plus Steller, Plenisner, and Steller's servant, Lepekhin, to a sheltered cove below a cliff. According to Steller, the island was "bare and wretched," spattered with lime from generations of seabirds, and covered in twisted skeletal shrubs, crooked and interwoven, clawing a hold into the stony earth. Nowhere could he find a stick more than two feet long.

Steller and his two companions set off immediately inland toward the rocky and mountainous interior and discovered several clear springs. He was appalled when he returned to discover that Hesselberg had found a small lake or pond about two hundred yards from the shore and that "the sailors had chosen the first and nearest stagnant puddle and already started operations." Steller tested the water and found it to be alkaline and brackish, spat it out, and sent back an urgent appeal to Waxell on the ship, noting that with such stagnant water, "the scurvy would quickly increase and that, because of its lime content, the people would become dried up and lose strength and that this water, after a short while in the vessel, would even increase in salinity from day to day and finally through standing become salt water." He sent aboard a sample of the water he had discovered and claimed that it was much better than Hesselberg's and urged Waxell to sample both. Although he had found a much better spring farther inland, owing to the manner of his suggestion and the bad blood, he was refused.

The sailors continued to fill up at their "beloved salty puddle" and row the barrels of brine back to the ship. They should have heeded Steller's advice not to slake their thirst on tainted water. As the ship's surgeon, Steller claimed he was ignored out of "the old overbearing habit of contradicting," which is entirely possible, given the low level of relations between him and the officers and since he had been wrong on so many previous occasions. Although in this case Steller was attempting to "preserve the life of my fellow beings as well as my own," the answer was "Why, what is the matter with this water? The water is good, fill up with it!" Disgusted, Steller and his party set off inland and discovered a large lake nearly two miles long and a mile wide, and he then asked Hesselberg to use this lake water, which would involve an additional mile of rowing, but having received his reply from Waxell, Hesselberg declined. Waxell later acknowledged his error in not being diligent about the water quality, allowing himself to be goaded into a poor decision by Steller's irritating personality. "The water was good," he wrote of the two samples, "but although taken from a lake there was, nevertheless, some sea water in it, brought by the tide which sometimes inundated the island. Afterwards we felt disastrous effects from its use in sickness and the loss of several of our men, who died." But, he continued, "such water was always better than nothing, for we could at any rate use it for cooking."

Waxell's excuse was that they had no time for delays and that he thought any water, however imperfect, was better than none. "Our ship was not lying at all safely. Where she was, almost any southerly wind could pounce down upon us without us being able to run for shelter anywhere. That is why we wished to replenish our supplies of water with haste, so that we might sail out back into the open sea." Waxell's words seem more like justification after the fact, since they spent two days in the Bay of Islands and could have easily gotten freshwater from Steller's spring or lake. While the sick sailors were brought from the ship and rowed ashore for some fresh air, Steller carried his surly mood with him when stalking about the barren hump of land. When he came upon a small black fox barking at him, he hoisted his rifle and fired a shot, hoping to keep it as "evidence." But he was a poor marksman, and it fled before he could reload. He also encountered several red foxes but was likewise unable to obtain a specimen for his collection.

WHILE STELLER EXPLORED NAGAI ISLAND and Hesselberg supervised the collection and stowing of the tainted water, Khitrov was exploring the island where they had seen a fire the night before. At first Waxell, who was in command, did not want Khitrov to take the smaller jolly boat for his investigations because of the *St. Peter*'s exposed anchorage and the large distance between the ship and the island, fearing that they could become lost and never regain the ship if a storm blew in or the wind changed. Khitrov, echoing Steller's and Chirikov's complaints against Bering, railed against what he believed was Waxell's preoccupation with safety. Khitrov insisted that Waxell's refusal to let him take the smaller boat be entered into the logbook, and so Waxell relented, "preferring to avoid the possibility of being made answerable in the future for not investigating it," and went into the great cabin to discuss the matter with Bering. Bering roused himself and said that Khitrov should be allowed to go with a small crew to investigate. All consultations complete and the papers signed, Khitrov chose five men to accompany him, including a Chukchi interpreter. They were armed with guns and a selection of gifts. Bering gave them instructions on what to do in various situations but above all instructed them "to be kind." They rowed to the island in the afternoon and hiked to where the fire had been seen.

The men discovered the still-smoldering fire pit, but no people. When he spied an approaching storm, Khitrov and the five others rushed down from the hills and tried to make their boat ready to return to the *St. Peter*. But by the time they got the small boat in the water, the waves had grown so enormous that they were nearly swamped and flooded, and Khitrov steered the boat toward Nagai Island, which was much closer than the ship, to a place near where the others had recently disembarked. The surf ground the boat against the stones of the beach, damaging it and stranding them. They rushed about collecting all the driftwood they could easily find and built a huge bonfire to signal the ship and to keep themselves from hypothermia, as they were freezing and wet. When Khitrov and his men failed to return to the ship due to the storm, Steller, who had a particular dislike of him, wrote that "I now thanked God that through the cunning plots of the naval men I had been kept away from his company." The storm raged, "and we were exposed to all the wildness of the sea" until the evening of September 2, when Waxell could send the longboat to rescue them. It was not until September 3 that Khitrov and his men regained the *St. Peter*, abandoning the damaged jolly boat.

Khitrov was not popular, and Steller wrote that "if he had not gone at all or if, on not meeting anybody, he had returned betimes and thereby had not delayed the watering by depriving us of the yawl, we could have gotten out with the fair gale and been more than a hundred miles further on our course. . . . Everyone grumbled because whatever this man had touched from Okhotsk on until the return voyage, had gone wrong and had brought misfortune." If not for Khitrov's delay by the storm, his third misfortune in a series that had affected the timing of the expedition—events that cannot really be blamed on his competence as a mariner or officer, it should be noted—the *St. Peter* would have been at sea heading west for many days instead of remaining anchored off of Nagai Island, waiting for another storm to pass. It is often said that an enterprise is doomed seldom by a single misfortune, but by an accumulation of small mistakes and timely accidents.

While this latest delay was to have profound repercussions, it also produced a curious and fascinating encounter, unexpected at this point of the voyage.

LATE IN THE AFTERNOON of September 5, the worried mariners were roused from their torpor by the sound of people yelling from the high grassy hills above the steep, rocky cliffs of Bird Island. Soon, two small skin boats (which Steller correctly compared to the kayaks of Greenlanders) paddled out toward the ship, each with a person in the middle. When they were in voice range, the two men began a long speech in a language unknown to either of the Kamchadal interpreters, Tchuktchi or Koriak. These were the first Americans they had encountered, and Steller was quivering with excitement, "eagerness and full of wonder." When they shouted back, the men pointed to their ears. They then rummaged around their boats and produced a stick with a hawk's wing affixed to it and tossed it toward the ship. Taking this as a sign of friendship, Bering ordered a board to be lowered on which were piled gifts: red cloth, mirrors, copper bells, iron beads, and five knives. They rowed closer and offered the gifts, which the "Americans received with great pleasure." The kayakers then tossed over two thin rods with falcon feathers and claws on them. Steller wrote that "I cannot tell whether it was meant as a sacrifice or a sign of good friendship." Then they paddled back to shore and shouted and gesticulated for the mariners to follow them and made motions of eating and drinking. Bering ordered Waxell to ready the sole remaining shore boat and take more presents and some Russian vodka. The party consisted of nine armed sailors, the Kamchadal interpreter, and Steller—"lances, sabres and guns all covered in canvas so as to not rouse suspicion."

Waxell anchored the boat a stone's throw from the rocky and treacherous shore. Two Russian sailors and the Kamchadal interpreter stripped off their clothes and leaped over the side, plunged into the freezing water up to their armpits. They were unarmed, and Waxell ordered them to stay within sight and not to do anything quickly or in an intimidating manner. They clambered ashore and walked over to a small group of Americans, who were "full of wonder and friendliness" and kept pointing over the hills to the far side of the island, perhaps indicating that they lived on the other side. The Russians offered them more presents, which were refused. The Americans then took the newcomers by the arms "quite deferentially," eased them back to their nearby encampment, and seated them and offered them whale blubber. They were "mostly young or middle aged people, they are of medium stature, strong and stocky yet fairly well proportioned," with long black hair and slightly flat noses and dark eyes. They wore "whale-gut shirts with sleeves, very neatly sewed together." Many of them had bone piercings on their faces and bodies.

A man grabbed his kayak under his arm, carried it to the shore, seated himself in it at the edge of the water, and paddled out to the *St. Peter*. "He was evidently the eldest," Waxell wrote, "and I am sure the most eminent of them all." Waxell then produced vodka and tobacco, against Steller's pleadings, and after several Russians downed cups handed a full cup to the man. The American was none too pleased, spitting out the vodka and looking sour and ill, and "turning to his fellows screeched most horribly." Then as Steller recounts, the Russians proclaimed that "the Americans had the stomachs of sailors" and, "intending to neutralize the first displease with a new one," passed over a lighted pipe of tobacco and indicated how to use it. The man coughed and paddled away, looking a bit disgusted. "The smartest European," mused Steller in one of his oddly forward-thinking speculations, "would have done just the same if he had been treated to fly mushroom or rotted fish soup and willow bark, which the Kamchadals, however, consider such delicacies."

While the men onshore continued their mutual inspection, Waxell tried to coax more people to paddle out to the *St. Peter* in their kayaks. He got out a book he had kept for just this type of meeting, an English translation of French military officer Louis Armand, Baron de Lahontan's account of his time in America and his observations of native tribes. Waxell read off various "American" words (Huron and Algonquin) in alphabetical order, for such things as wood, food, and water and became convinced that these people understood his communications. Probably it was the gesticulations that accompanied the words that had more to do with the perceived understanding, since the languages and cultures of the Algonquin and Huron in eastern North America have nothing in common with the men, who were probably Aleuts. The Aleuts, native inhabitants of the Alaskan Peninsula and the Aleutian Islands, are ethnically related to the Yupik and Inuit.

The surf was now threatening the safety of the shore boat, and Waxell called to the men to return and wade back to the boat. While the two Russians began to walk back toward the boat, nine of the American men grabbed the interpreter by the arms and held him while he struggled in vain and yelled out to Waxell not to abandon him. Since he looked similar to the Americans, Waxell and Steller both speculated that perhaps they felt he belonged with the locals rather than on the boat. Waxell yelled and made motions to let him go, but they "pretended not to see me." Then some men grasped the rope of the boat and began to haul it ashore through the rocks, "perhaps not with evil design, but from sheer thoughtlessness, not realizing our danger, to haul the boat with its occupants ashore, where it would have been wrecked on the rocks." Both sides were yelling, and no one understood each other. Waxell ordered two muskets to be fired in the air, and after the explosion and the echo from the cliffs, "they became so frightened that they all fell down on the ground as if hit by thunder, letting go of everything in their hands." The Kamchadal interpreter ran into the water and climbed into the small boat, while Waxell made ready to cast off. But the anchor was stuck in the rocks. He hauled on it fruitlessly, and then he cut the rope, abandoning it, and they rowed quickly back to the ship. It was dark and nearly eight in the evening. Another storm from the south buffeted the ship during the night with pounding rain. On the shore they could see a mighty bonfire burning all night, which, Steller wrote, "kept us pondering on what had happened." This first expression of the power of gunpowder foreshadowed a not too distant time when Russian invaders wielded explosive technology to domineer and subjugate people throughout coastal Alaska.

The next day, as they readied the *St. Peter* for sea, seven men paddled out from the island to meet them. Two of the men steered their kayaks close to the ship, and Bering gave them gifts of an iron kettle and some needles and thread, while in turn they presented the Russians with two bark hats, one adorned with a carved ivory decoration resembling a person. All the kayaks paddled back to shore, and then the men began yelling or chanting around the big fire. Waxell suggested to Bering that he could have captured them, or at least some of them, but Bering disapproved, and Waxell "was given written instructions not to carry it out and ordered not to use force against them in any way whatever." Steller, who wrote descriptions of everything he saw, including clothing, tools, equipment, and personal appearance, saw similarities between the Americans and the people of Kamchatka and was convinced, though they spoke different languages, that they were related. He only regretted that he had not had enough time to prove his theories with greater research. "I have no doubt that I would have been able to give perfect proof of this thesis, if I had been allowed to act according to my own judgement, but this the nostalgia of the naval men would not permit." Any further communication or exchange between peoples was deterred by the changing weather and the shifting wind, which allowed the *St. Peter* to head to sea again before dark. As it happens, the eight days they spent in the Shumagin Islands may have sealed their fate. By the time they hoisted sails and set off for the West, the autumn gales were about to begin.

CHAPTER 9

THE SCOURGE OF THE SEA

O N August 31, the day after Khitrov had departed to investigate the fire, the first mariner who had been brought to
Nagai Island for fresh air had died, probably from scurvy, and a
grave was made with a wooden cross. The man's name was Nikita
Shumagin, and they named the island after him (now the whole
chain is named the Shumagin Islands, and the specific island has
been renamed Nagai). On the morning of September 1, the rest of
the sick men had been returned to the ship from the island, and all
fifty-two water casks filled with brine were loaded and lashed, with
the longboat, to the deck. The storm that had blown in unexpectedly increased in severity. It produced such terrific wind and waves
that many believed that Bering or Waxell would order the anchor
cable cut in an attempt to get away from land, abandoning Khitrov
but perhaps dooming them all because, as Steller opined, "we surely
would have drifted on the rocks and been wrecked."

By this time, Bering himself was barely able to leave his cabin,
and twelve other crew were on the sick list with the advancing signs
of scurvy. Steller, who had studied medicine but never practiced for
long, shared the surgeon's duties and noted the increasing numbers

of men on the sick roster. Steller even commented on some strange lethargy in his own disposition, writing that his own constitution had "fallen under a foreign power." This was a reference to a general weakness in the limbs. Suspecting the beginnings of a scurvy epidemic, Steller rummaged in the ship's medical chest in search of anything to use against the ailment but noted that the chest was "mostly filled with plasters, ointments, oils, and other surgical remedies enough for four or five hundred men in case of a battle but had none whatever of the medicines most needed on sea voyages and serviceable against scurvy and asthma, our commonest cases."

When Steller asked Waxell for "a detail of several men for the purpose of collecting such quantity of antiscorbutic herbs as would be enough for all," he was roughly turned down and ordered to collect them himself if he felt that it was important. Waxell was irritated by Steller's manner and approach and now believed anything he said to be little more than the whining of a foreign academic, an arrogant man who looked down on the others and who pronounced his evident superiority with every suggestion he uttered. Steller was evidently maddening to be around. To listen to his claims (many of which were obviously without merit to anyone used to life at sea) was to lose face and admit Steller's superiority. Now, even when Steller had sensible advice, he was brushed away, as one would an irritating insect. When Steller writes that he was "coarsely" contradicted by Waxell and other officers, as he was when he again raised the issue of the briny water, the response was likely something along the lines of "Shut up and get out of our way. We're doing useful work here."

When Steller realized bleakly that relations had deteriorated to the point that his opinion and "this important work, which affected the health and lives of all, was not considered worth the labor of a few sailors, I repented of my good intentions and resolved that in the future I would only look after the preservation of my own self without wasting another word." Steller and Plenisner had spent their time on Nagai Island collecting, and eating, as many fresh plants as they could—gentian, spoonwort, lingonberries, crow-berries, "and other cresslike plants." He later learned that the offi-cers, "from fear of death," had belatedly listened to his alarm about the briny water and had sent two barrels ashore to be filled with spring water "for their own consumption," but in the haste to get the sick on board the ship before the advancing storm, they were left behind on the beach.

With barrels of briny water and only a small personal supply of medicinal fresh plants, which Steller began prescribing to Bering and the twelve other sick mariners, the united crew of the *St. Peter* was ready to resume its journey home. Meanwhile, Bering and the other mariners who had been taking Steller's prescription of fresh plants began to show signs of improvement. Bering was back on deck, and many of the sailors were taken off the sick list, their teeth firm and their energy returned. "My ministrations, under divine grace, very clearly caught their attention," he wrote. If only they had listened earlier and collected more of these plants and fed all the mariners.

ONE OF THE MOST vivid and grim descriptions of the ravages of scurvy can be found in *A Voyage Round the World in the Years 1740–1744* by George Anson of the British Royal Navy in the same year the *St. Peter* and the *St. Paul* sailed from Asia to Alaska. Famed for plundering the Spanish treasure galleon, and a fabulously rich na-tional hero, Anson's joy was not celebrated by most of the mariners who disembarked with him from England. Most of them had died; only around two hundred of the original two thousand mariners, and only one of five ships, the mighty sixty-gun *Centurion*, returned from circumnavigating the world. The others perished miserably, mostly from scurvy. Only a handful died from other causes.

Although the ships had actually been crammed with extra men for the voyage in anticipation of a high death rate, they were soon undermanned by sick men with the usual shipboard illnesses of dysentery or typhus. But scurvy quickly became the greatest problem. Just when the storms raged and the ships were in peril, when the men needed their strength the most, they grew morose, their limbs leaden and their thoughts clouded. A third of the sailors lay moaning in their hammocks, too enfeebled to come up on deck and save themselves. Old war wounds began to open and bleed again, once-broken bones again separated, gums became swollen and brown, aching and oozing blood, while teeth became wobbly and fell out. "Some lost their Senses, some had their sinews contracted in such a Manner as to draw their limbs close to their Thyghs, and some rotted away."

There were no men well enough to clean the lower decks, so the putrid slime of body fluids sloshed back and forth as the ships rolled with the monstrous waves. The men began to die, whimpering and crying in agony as the mysterious malady took hold. Their stiff and rigid corpses pitched to the floor. One of Anson's ships threw "two-thirds of their complement, and of those that remained alive scarcely any were capable of doing duty, except the officers and their servants." When they did finally reach shore, with a skeleton crew of men barely able to stand, they found "almost all the vegetables esteemed for the cure of scorbutic disorders. . . . These vegetables with the fish and the flesh we found here, were most salutary for recovering our sick, and of no mean service to us who were well, in destroying the lurking seeds of scurvy and in restoring us to our wonted strength."

DURING THE AGE OF SAIL, scurvy was indirectly responsible for more deaths at sea than storms, combat, shipwreck, and all other diseases combined and was in fact the cause of shipwrecks when men who were too ill and weakened to haul the ropes or climb the rigging allowed a ship to be driven on the rocks or to founder and be swamped in mighty waves. From those of Jacques Cartier, Vasco da Gama, and Francis Drake to Ferdinand Magellan, James Cook, and Louis-Antoine, comte de Bougainville, scurvy appeared on nearly every lengthy voyage of discovery during the Age of Sail. It was the scourge of the seas. The problem was that no one knew exactly what caused the dreaded disease. One of Anson's lieutenants, Philip Saumarez, expressed his own weary summation of the disease. Scurvy, he wrote, "expresses itself in such dreadful symptoms as are scarce credible. . . . Nor can all the physicians, with their *materia medica*, find a remedy for it. But I could plainly observe that there is a certain *je ne sais quoi* in the frame of the human system that cannot be renewed . . . without the assistance of certain earthly particles, or in plain English, that the land is man's proper element, and vegetables and fruit his only physic."

Using the humoral theory as a foundation, physicians from numerous countries studied the disease and tried to formulate their own specific theories to explain scurvy. Dozens of tracts were written on scurvy, claiming such disparate causes of the disease as foul vapors, dampness, an excess of black bile, laziness, copper poisoning, heredity, or blocked perspiration. Cures that would bring the humors back into balance included purging with saltwater, bloodletting, putting hydrochloric acid in drinking water, smearing mercury paste on open sores, drinking dealcoholized beer, and other ineffectual but politically palatable or economically feasible solutions. On some ships, physical beatings of afflicted mariners were promoted, on the assumption that the condition was really just laziness disguised, that the scorbutic mariners were merely shirkers. The cure could occasionally be as deadly as the disease.

It was Scottish physician James Lind, aboard the ship HMS *Salisbury* in 1747, who conducted what is considered to be the first controlled trial in medical history. He selected twelve scorbutic sailors with symptoms "as similar as I could have them. . . . They all in general had putrid gums, the spots and lassitude, with weakness of their knees." He hung their hammocks in pairs in a separate enclosure in the dank and dark forecastle of the ship and "provided one diet common to all," except that he treated them with different accepted scurvy remedies, such as "elixir of vitriol"; vinegar; cider; seawater, "half a pint every day, and sometimes more or less as it operated, by way of a general physic"; and a thrice-daily "electuary" paste "the bigness of a nutmeg" that consisted of garlic, mustard seed, dried radish root, balsam, or Peru and gum myrrh, washed down with barley water. The final lucky pair was fed two oranges and one lemon daily, which they "ate greedily," for six days, when the supply of the southern fruits was depleted. Not surprisingly, the sailors fed oranges and lemons, the only ones who were fed anything fresh, recovered quickly and returned to duty. But Lind was baffled by his discovery. These fruits were scarce and difficult to obtain in northern countries, and in his attempts to concentrate the citrus liquid through boiling it into something more easily transported and stored, Lind destroyed the active ingredient and delayed the implementation of a true scurvy cure for decades. It was the preservation techniques then used for all foods on sea voyages— drying and salting—that were the real causes of scurvy.

Of course, we now know that it is lack of fresh food containing vitamin C that is the primary cause of scurvy, a deficiency disease where the body's connective tissue degenerates: from bone to cartilage to blood vessels, the body essentially coming apart. A reliable portable cure for the disease, other than acquiring fresh fruits and vegetables, was not discovered until forty years later. It wasn't until the dawn of the Napoleonic Wars in the 1790s that physician Sir Gilbert Blane convinced the Royal Navy to introduce a daily dose of lime juice to all British mariners mixed with their rum.

Steller, ahead of his time, had his own ideas about scurvy based on his discussions with the native peoples of Kamchatka and his observation that they did not get it throughout the long winter, though some of the Russians seemed to be prone to it. As far as he could tell, the Kamchadals did not do anything in particular to prevent scurvy, so he concluded that it must be related to their diet, the one thing that differentiated them from the Russians. Steller took this hypothesis and tied it to the consumption of fresh plants, sometimes bitter or unpleasant ones that would not normally be part of a diet if flavor were the only consideration. The Russians, interlopers in the region, mostly ate travel rations augmented sporadically with wild game. Scurvy was a condition that would not have been as common in the Russian Navy as it was in the British, Spanish, and French Navies, whose services had a much longer history of lengthy sea voyages and spent more time at sea, crossing oceans. By contrast, the Russian Navy was mostly stationed in the Baltic or Black Sea and was never quite as far from port where fresher foods would have been available. In any case, the precautions Steller took in the fall of 1741 and his inquisitive mind and ability to experiment were the only things working in favor of the mariners aboard the *St. Peter*.

NEAR THE END OF SEPTEMBER, after sailing generally west through rainy, overcast weather for two weeks, the *St. Peter* was still hundreds of miles from Avacha Bay, only 40 percent of the way home. Steller's journal entries contain reports of the occasional sea otter or clump of drifting seaweed, owls or gulls and their direction of flight. A sighting of whales on one day foreshadowed a brief storm on the next, while porpoises following the ship foreordained another short storm. In general, though, the westerlies prevailed, rushing them toward their destination. But with the sun and stars mostly hidden because of the perpetual cloud, they were cruising west generally blind, hoping that the direct route they had chosen through these unknown waters would also be the safest and fastest path and would not be blocked by hidden reefs or fogbound islands. "Thus," Waxell reported, "for two or three weeks we never had sight of the sun, and at night we were unable to see the stars," which made navigation impossible. "We had to sail along without knowing what was what and that in an unknown ocean, like blind people who do not know whether they are going too quickly or too slowly." There was a general anxiety among the entire crew. Not knowing their location or the location of land or deadly obstacles, with possible disaster lurking behind every cloud bank or veil of mist, the stress was building, and sleep was anxiety ridden and unrefreshing. "We did not know what obstacles might lie ahead of us," Waxell wrote, "and so had to count with the possibility that any moment something might come to finish us off." They were sailing by dead reckoning, and so, without knowing it, they were slowly drifting south as they progressed west.

September 21, at last, was a clear and calm day. The swells eased, and the wind was a refreshing northwesterly. Men came on the deck and basked in the sun and hoped for the future. But by afternoon the wind began to shift, first to the southwest, and then, increasing in velocity, it became erratic. It was the beginning of more than two weeks of vicious storms, storms that blew them fifty miles south and east while working to a crescendo in early October. The log tells the story: "stormy," "wind comes in gusts," "waves running high," "squally and rainy," "flashes of lightning," "heavy storm," "strong gale blowing," "heavy sea running," "terrific storm and great waves," "heavy squalls and high seas," "squalls, rain, snow," "thick clouds," "altogether exhausted from scurvy." Steller wrote that "every now and then we could hear the wind rush as if out of a narrow passage, with such terrible whistling, raging, and blustering that we were every minute in danger of losing masts or rudder or else of seeing the vessel itself damaged by the force of the waves, which pounded it as when cannons are fired, so that we were expecting every moment the last stroke and death."

As the storm increased in severity beyond the wildest imaginings of the crew, a storm more violent than any could ever recall during their combined decades at sea, the tainted water supply turned brackish and undrinkable. The steady diet of salt beef, hardtack, groats, and peas began to take a toll on the mariners' health. Steller had already used up his meager supply of scurvy grass and sour dock in the first week after leaving the Shumagin Islands. The ship contained nothing else to alleviate the spread of scurvy. Morale was low, and a dark lassitude hung over the ship. Steller wrote that "the unwholesome water lessened the number of healthy men from day to day and very many were heard to complain of hitherto unwonted disorders." Sailors began to express doubt that they would ever reach home this season and began to mutter and suggest that the captain and officers should plan to winter in Japan or America.

With the minds of the men smothered by despondency and gloom, the physical manifestations of scurvy increased. Soon, a third of them lay ill, swaying in their hammocks in the reeking hold of the ship as it pitched and plunged through the rising waves. The floor was awash with sickly fluid, and men lay prostrate in the slime, sluicing about as the ship danced and leaped to the tune of the gale. Waxell wrote that "they were attacked by scurvy so violently that most of them were unable to move either their hands or their feet, let alone use them." The teeth of the remaining sailors were wobbly, and their gums were turning black and bloody. Although Steller had revived Bering briefly with his antiscorbutic herbs, the commander returned to his previous state of morose indifference as soon as Steller's supplies ran low, unable or unwilling to raise himself from his bed.

The storm became ferocious, coming now from the southwest instead the north, Steller recorded, "with such redoubled violence as we never have experienced before or since; we could not imagine that it could be greater or that we should be able to stand it out." Sometimes the wind was so fierce that the clouds "with incredible swiftness shot like arrows past our eyes and even met and crossed each other with equal rapidity, often from opposite directions." Winds tore at the rigging from erratic angles, purple and black clouds made navigation impossible, and ragged froth was whipped across the deck. "Every moment we expected the destruction of our vessel," Steller wrote, "and no one could lie down, or sit up or stand. Nobody was able to remain at his post; we were drifting under the might of God wither [*sic*] the angry heavens willed to send us. Half our crew lay sick and weak, the other half . . . were quite crazed and maddened from the terrifying motion of the ship. There was much praying to be sure, but the curses piled up during ten years in Siberia prevented any response." Occasionally, Steller or others claimed to see land, but, unable to control the ship, this was just another source of worry and danger over which they had no control. Waxell later remembered that "I can truthfully say that I did not get many hours sleep during the five months I was away on that voyage, and never seeing known land. I was in a continual state of uneasiness, always in danger and uncertainty."

Squalls tore the sails into tatters. The ship was spun about uncontrollably, teetering on the precipice of a curling tongue of sea before plunging into the trough between the monstrous waves, with timbers shuddering. Near the end of September, a chill descended from the North, turning the rain to snow, hail, and freezing rain. Ice crusted on the rigging and froze the hatches, while the wind moaned during the dark, brooding days and the even longer nights. Men were either mad with terror or debilitated beyond the point of caring. Yet as the provisions ran low, their appetites increased. "God knows, we were very short," wrote Waxell, especially when there was nothing wholesome to eat other than biscuits. The bucking and heaving of the ship made cooking impossible. Even worse, the liquor supply also dwindled and ran dry on October 16. Waxell lamented, "Nor had there been much gin left for several weeks now. As long as it had lasted, it had kept the men in fairly good fettle."

Gin or vodka was utterly useless in treating scurvy, unless they had orange juice to mix it with, but it may have had a salubrious effect of numbing the men to their horrible and seemingly hopeless predicament. "Their only wish," Waxell wrote, "was that a speedy death might free them from their miserable plight. They told me that they would rather die than let life drag on in that wretched fashion."

All progress west from the Shumagins was lost during the eighteen days of storms, as the *St. Peter* was blown back east an astonishing 304 miles. On October 12, when the *St. Paul* was limping into Petropavlovsk, the *St. Peter* was still being blown about the wind-whipped ocean and was again more than 1,000 nautical miles east of Kamchatka and three degrees of latitude south of where the ship had been one month earlier on September 13.

By mid-October, most of the men were sick or weak. Once at sea again the sailors had started dying on September 24, when "by the will of God died of scurvy the grenadier Andrei Tretyakov." The next recorded death was Nikita Kharitonov on October 20, but from then on sailors routinely expired in the dim, fetid hold where their bunks were strung up. "Not only did the sick die off," Steller reported, "but those who according to their own assertion were well, on being relieved at their posts, dropped dead from exhaustion. The small allowance of water, the lack of biscuits and brandy, the cold, dampness, nakedness, vermin, fright, and terror were not the least important causes." Soon after Tretyakov's death, Waxell announced that merely fifteen barrels of water remained, and three of them were damaged and had leaked. Day by day, mariners perished with agony frozen on their ghastly countenances, and the living hauled the stiff corpses above deck and hove their erstwhile companions overboard. Bering was feverish and insensible; his skin was like stained leather and his eyes unfocused as he lay in his cabin. "The most eloquent pen," Steller wrote, "would find itself too weak to describe our misery." The voyage was now one of "misery and death," with little else on anyone's mind and little hope for the future.

On October 28, the skies momentarily cleared of snow and hail, and, to their astonishment, they spied through the mist a low, flat, and sandy-beached island not more than a mile directly in front of them. "For the second time," Steller wrote, "we had here occasion to see plainly God's gracious help, as we should have been done for without fail if we had come into this situation a couple of hours sooner and in the dark of night, or if God, even now, had not driven the fog away. We might well conclude that, in addition to the islands seen, there must have been many others here and there along our course, which we may have sailed past at night and in foggy weather." Steller, the pious catechist, not yet fully under the baleful influence of scurvy, alone retained his gracious acceptance of what fate placed before them and hung on to the possibility of survival. The crew rushed to turn the ship from being driven onto the rocks or beaches and steered it back into the frothy gray waves of the unknown sea. They now knew that America did not extend directly west from the Shumagin Islands, but instead curved gently southwest—the direct line home was not only not the quickest, but not even possible. Khitrov suggested that they should lower a boat and row ashore to see if any freshwater was available. Steller wrote how relieved he was when the "unfortunate proposition" of going ashore for water was overturned by the other officers, because "only ten feeble persons were left, who, though able to lend a hand, were yet in no condition to hoist the anchor again from the bottom." In any event, another storm soon rolled in, and had they been caught trying to row ashore, they "would assuredly all together have found our graves in the waves."

Waxell, along with Steller, somehow kept his strength, but he was one of the few who did. The sails were mostly torn and tattered. He could seldom locate a sailor well enough to climb the ropes. Soon there was no one strong enough to hold the great wheel and steer the ship, which was "like a piece of dead wood, with none to direct it; we had to drift hither and thither at the whim of the winds and waves." Waxell continued, "Indeed, when it came to a man's turn at the helm, he was dragged to it by two other of the invalids who were still able to walk a little, and set down at the wheel. There he had to sit and steer as well as he could, and when he could sit no more, he had to be replaced by another in no better case than he." Perhaps the strangest development was Steller's transformation from a gentleman into a laborer. As the scurvy epidemic raged, when there were scarcely four men lucid and vigorous enough to sail the ship, Waxell "tearfully begged [Steller] to help and assist," which Steller did with "bare hands" to the utmost of his "strength and means, although it was not my office and my services had always been scorned before the disaster." He set aside his acerbic tongue and, for the first time on the voyage, conformed himself to naval hierarchy, accepting orders from the officers he had disdained for so long and doing work that he had considered beneath him, manual labor.

Waxell's strength also soon began to wane. "I myself was scarcely able to move about the deck without holding on to something," he lamented. He tried to raise the morale of the dying scorbutic men by begging them not to despair: "With God's help," he shouted, "we shall soon sight land again; that will save our lives, whatever the land is like, perhaps we shall there find the means to continue our voyage." But the ship drifted, and they had no means to direct their course or control their destiny. "To put it bluntly," Waxell wrote, "we were utterly wretched."

THE *ST. PAUL* HAD suffered the same misfortunes and accidents as the *St. Peter*. By September, no one had had a satisfying drink of water in six weeks. Their mouths were pasty, and they dreamed of cool refreshment. The winds were against them, coasts and islands appeared through the fog, and storms buffeted the ship as they raced west to Kamchatka. Since departing Takanis Bay on August 27 and cruising west along the same latitude as Avacha Bay, Chirikov had ordered a strict rationing of water. Water for all was limited to survival levels. Without any shore boats left, the ship could not land to replenish the water or obtain any fresh foods. Chirikov reported that "when it rained the crew set buckets and other vessels to catch the water from the sails; and although it was bitterish and tasted of tar, yet the men drank it gladly and said that it was good for the health and that the tar bitterness cured them of scurvy." This "cure," however, proved temporary. The daily meal consisted of cooked kasha, or buckwheat mush, with a mug of wine, with a bonus second daily meal every third day. As August passed and the sailing was skittish and slow, Chirikov noted with alarm how quickly the barrels were emptied. Kasha would now be served only every other day, and on the day in between the men lived on dry biscuit and rancid butter, augmented with salt meat cooked in seawater. All the salt would have burned their lips as they ate. Soon kasha was served only once per week, as there was hardly any water with which to cook it.

"These privations began to tell," wrote Chirikov. Soon the *St. Paul* was having its own battle with scurvy, around the same time, and oddly on the same route home, as the *St. Peter*. "Officers and men did their work under great difficulties," and soon some became too weak to climb up on deck and lay moaning in their bunks. "I began to fear that the worst might happen," Chirikov recalled, "and ordered that the members of the crew should have daily two cups of wine." It was undoubtedly a pleasant diversion from the monotony of their diet, but unfortunately no panacea for scurvy. The ship limped west through storms, while the men weakened and grew despondent and fearful in the unknown seas and unknown land. They could never seem to catch sight of land, despite the abundant evidence of its proximity—birds, sea otters, and floating vegetation along with the occasion glimpse of spectral outlines in the distance to the north.

On the foggy morning of September 9, with visibility severely impaired, Chirikov ordered the *St. Paul* to put out an anchor cable in twenty-four fathoms of water. They could faintly hear the pounding of surf on rocks, but the heavy fog blinded them and Chirikov did not want to go farther. A few hours later, when the fog dispersed, land was revealed a few hundred yards from the ship, a place now called Adak Island. There were high mountains shrouded in tendrils of mist, with grass-covered and treeless slopes and cliffs right to the shore in many places. The waves broke dangerously over protruding rocks a stone's throw from the path of the *St. Paul*. Had Chirikov not called a halt to the ship, they would have run aground. Without shore boats, the men of the *St. Paul* were trapped onboard their ship, looking at the land and dreaming of the wealth of freshwater it contained, their lips burning from the salt in their food and the insatiable craving for a clean drink from the clear creek that descended through the rocks and washed into the small bay.

The *St. Paul* was so close to shore that two people could be seen walking along the beach. The crew began yelling through the speaking trumpet in Russian and in the "Kamchadal language," telling the walkers to come aboard the ship. "A little while later," Chirikov reported, "we heard human voices calling to us, but the breaking of the surf made so much noise that we could not make out what was said." A few hours later, they heard more shouting from the shore, and then seven men in skin kayaks paddled out toward the ship. They began a ceremonial chanting that Chirikov believed was "praying that no harm might come to them from us." They then paddled together and conversed in a cluster, and Chirikov made his men look pleasant, bowing and waving their hands for the natives to come aboard. Most of the Russians were hidden below with their guns primed and ready in case of attack, with only a few on deck. Chirikov noted that "they made a gesture with their hands as if drawing a bow, which showed that they were afraid we might attack them."

Chirikov and his men increased their striving, pressing their hands to their hearts and trying to look friendly. Chirikov then tossed them a cup "as a mark of friendship." A man examined it and then tossed it into the water, where it promptly sank. Chirikov next produced some damask cloth, which they also tossed away disdainfully. Then "I gave the order to bring up the different things we had to give as presents—small boxes, small bells, needles, Chinese tobacco, pipes—and, holding them up, I invited them to come near." All to no avail, as the kayakers would not come closer. The Aleuts were cautious. Finally, Chirikov tried to make them understand that he needed water by displaying an empty barrel. One man paddled closer, and Chirikov gave him a pipe and some tobacco, placing it on the deck of his kayak. Soon another paddled closer as well, eager to see what his more audacious comrade had obtained. Chirikov and a few of his men distributed the small gifts, which were "received rather indifferently." After a while, "we noticed several who raised one hand to their mouth and with the other hand made a quick motion as if cutting something near the mouth. This gave us the idea that they wanted knives," because of the Kamchadal custom of cutting meat near the mouth while eating.

When Chirikov gave the man a knife, he was overjoyed, and when he produced an empty barrel and motioned toward the nearby stream, they understood quickly but chose to paddle over and back with bladders rather than an unwieldy barrel. "One of them held up a bladder and indicated that he wished to have a knife in payment. This was given to him. But instead of handing over the bladder, he passed it to the second man, who also demanded a knife. When he got it, he passed the bladder to the third man, who equally insisted on a knife." The trading game went on for a while, exchanging certain roots and grasses for sea biscuits, some form of strange mineral wrapped in seaweed and some arrows, and a bark hat for a "dull axe, which they received gladly." They handed back a copper kettle as being useless for unknown reasons and then paddled ashore.

Later in the afternoon, fourteen men paddled close and also made the cutting motion with their hands that indicated knives. By now Chirikov was not amused, and the water they could obtain this way was insufficient to help them. "This act," he sniffed, "as well as some other things they did, proves that their conscience is not highly developed."

Erratic winds began to blow, and, "trusting to God's help, we attempted to get away from where we stood before it was too late." While the ship drifted dangerously close to the reef, and Chirikov feared even more submerged rocks, he ordered the anchor cable cut at the "hawse hole," and he put on full sail to try to free themselves from the rocky bay. "It was a narrow escape, for a strong wind blew off the mountains and from all directions." The men heaved a sigh of relief after they cleared the reef-riddled bay and made open ocean again. They still had insufficient water, but now at least the wind was in their favor and they headed west. As the days passed, Chirikov wrote his opinion that they were paralleling the American continent, as land appeared intermittently to the north through the fog as they sailed. They kept a detailed ship's log daily despite the hardships, noting such things as "All during the day we saw sea cabbage and floating grass, the kind that grows near the shore; the color of the water was green, unlike the color of sea water."

On September 20, Chirikov lay in his bunk, unable to move from scurvy, "expecting death at any moment." Despite being unable to move, he worked out calculations for the ship's course from the logbooks. He passed the instructions to his mate Ivan Yelagin, who steered the ship. "Thanks to God my mind did not leave me," Chirikov wrote. Soon, dozens of men were unable to leave their bunks. The first man died on September 26, and quickly thereafter a total of six, including three officers, Constable Joseph Kachikov, Lieutenant Chikhachev, and Lieutenant Plautin, "were snatched away." On October 8, the distant forested peaks of Kamchatka came into view, and a day later they entered Avacha Bay and fired five guns as a signal for help. Soon smaller boats came to help them. They had two barrels of brackish and salty water remaining. Professor Croyère, who had been sick for weeks, begged to come ashore, but when he was brought up into the light on the deck and breathed fresh air, he suddenly died. The others had to be helped from the hold of the ship and nursed back to health ashore. By the time they reached home, a total of twenty-one men had died out of the original ship's complement of seventy-six: fifteen were abandoned to an unknown fate in Alaska, and six succumbed to scurvy in the final two weeks of the voyage.

Chirikov began writing a detailed report of the voyage, including all the meticulously documented instances when the officers agreed on any deviation from their official orders. He also collected the many items of natural history and culture they had obtained during the voyage. He explained his actions when the storm separated the two ships early in the voyage, how they had lost the men and shore boats, how the low water made a more detailed investigation of Bolshaya Zemlya impossible, how the storms deterred their progress, and how scurvy nearly destroyed them. Chirikov also apologized for not returning with one or more live Americans, as "we could not persuade them to come, and to force them against their will without special instructions was dangerous. . . . It is not likely they will come aboard willingly, and I do not suppose Her Imperial Majesty would have us use force. For that purpose a larger crew is necessary." One wonders what fate might have befallen any Tlingit or Aleut who had been daring enough to board the ship. In previous centuries, English, Spanish, French, and Dutch kidnapping of natives from the Americas had been common on the Atlantic and Caribbean coasts.

By December, Chirikov had finished his report and had a messenger sent along the tortuous route across Asia to St. Petersburg. In the official orders for the expedition, the report was supposed to be delivered personally by one of the senior officers of the ship, but Chirikov apologized that this was not possible, "as the officers are dead." "As to myself," he admitted, "I am quite unfit for sea duty. The scurvy is asleep in my system, and it is difficult to shake off because of the heavy atmosphere and especially because of the poor and insufficient food. . . . By God's mercy I am just able to sit up; my feet are drawn up and full of spots, and my teeth are loose in my gums." As for the drugs available in Kamchatka for treating scurvy, they "are so old that they are worthless. A similar state of ill-health exists among the crew." With all the deaths, they were shorthanded, many unfit for service, and there was only one man still alive trained in navigation other than Chirikov. The *St. Paul*, he reported, was in little better shape than its crew, with broken parts, missing cables and anchors, while "the ship's rigging is in bad condition," with no means to easily replace or repair any of the deficiencies in Petropavlovsk. Chirikov's health was permanently broken by the unbearable suffering and the medical distress of the scurvy epidemic on the final stretch of the voyage. The once bold and ambitious officer straining at the restraints placed upon him by Bering was at the end of his career as an explorer.

While the surviving crew of the *St. Paul* recuperated at the primitive outpost, and as fall turned into winter and the season for safe sailing drew to a close, there was still no sign of their sister ship. Chirikov and his men were left with worry and questions about their old traveling companions and Commander Bering. Were they stuck overwintering in Alaska? Did the *St. Peter* founder in a storm? Did they perish miserably from scurvy? The fate of their comrades was unknown.

PART FOUR

NOWHERE

This illustration from a 1753 German edition of Georg Steller's *Beasts of the Sea* depicts the creatures of Bering Island that both fascinated Steller and made survival possible in 1741–1742.

The *St. Peter* is driven onto the rocks in this dramatic but fanciful nineteenth-century reimagining of the wreck on Bering Island.

Bering stares from the deck of the *St. Peter* toward Mount St. Elias in this Soviet-era stamp issued to commemorate the 250th anniversary of Bering and Chirikov's voyage across the Pacific Ocean to Alaska.

Bering is found dead and covered in sand in this stylized and not completely accurate depiction of the events of December 8, 1741, in a Russian book from the 1890s.

Seals litter the beach in this contemporary photo of Bering Island. Hunting these animals and others that populated the uninhabited island enabled the mariners to survive the winter of 1741–1742.

CHAPTER 10

ISLAND OF THE BLUE FOXES

NAVIGATION TECHNOLOGY WAS IN its infancy in the mid-eighteenth century, subject to poor knowledge of global geography and imprecise instruments that worked only in ideal conditions. Calculating latitude, the north-south measurement, was a much simpler process than calculating longitude, the east-west measurement. Whether on land or sea, latitude was calculated by measuring the angle of altitude of the sun at noon, or sometimes of a known star at midnight, using a mariner's astrolabe (or later a sextant), designed to work on ships in moderate seas or winds. An officer trained in navigation would hold the instrument from a ring at the top and let the circular form of heavy brass dangle. Once it had settled, the navigator would level it to the horizon, to determine the angle of the sun. Then he would consult a set of tables to get the measurement and mark the position on a map. It was never perfect, but it did provide reasonably accurate determination of a ship's north-south position, the obvious drawback being that it was essentially useless in rough weather or in poor visibility, which is what the *St. Peter* endured for many weeks in the fall of 1741.

The calculation of longitude, by contrast, was fraught with potential errors and technical challenges, and the problem of its accurate calculation was not solved for many decades after Bering's voyages. Longitude represented the distance, east or west, from a standard meridian of longitude. Several standards had been set over time, but by the 1740s the north-south line running through Greenwich in London, England, was the baseline. The earth is always rotating at a set speed, and so each hour of time difference between local time and the set time at Greenwich is equivalent to fifteen degrees east or west. The solution would later be to carry an accurate chronometer, or clock, set to Greenwich time so as to compare the time difference between Greenwich and local time at high noon. In this way, mariners could calculate their distance across the surface of the globe. One of the first accurate marine chronometers was the prototype chronometer used by British mariner Captain James Cook on his famous voyages in the 1760s.

In the 1740s, however, Bering and Waxell had to rely on a far more time-consuming and delicate means for calculating longitude, involving the observation of celestial bodies. Since the earth, moon, and stars of the solar system all move in relation to each other at a set rate, longitude could be determined by a complicated set of mathematical calculations. Navigators of their time would have stood on the ship's deck, squinting into a telescope to record the moment of the eclipse of one of Jupiter's moons at local time. Then they would have gone into the cabin and consulted a standard set of tables that indicated when the same eclipse was predicted to have occurred at Greenwich. The time difference between the same eclipse seen from two locations was then calculated into degrees of longitude. When the moons of Jupiter were not visible, obscured by clouds, they would have had to measure the angle of the moon against two fixed stars and then consult a standard set of astronomical tables or star charts. Each of these methods required many hours of observations and mathematical calculations and could be performed only by certain senior officers with rigorous training and a clear mind. When determining their course, they would also have been responsible for calculating compass variation, or magnetic declination, the difference between true North and magnetic North. Navigators had to have a solid foundation in mathematics and spent countless hours taking measurements and then using equations to determine their position.

After several weeks of storms during which the sun and stars were mostly hidden, and with other more pressing concerns with which to occupy themselves, such as storms and the scurvy epidemic, Waxell and other officers whose job it was to calculate the ship's location on the vast swath of open water of the North Pacific Ocean had a nearly impossible task. Their estimate of the ship's position was little more than an educated guess. They certainly hoped they were nearing Kamchatka, but they really had little idea how close they were or whether other geographical obstacles lay in their path.

IN LATE OCTOBER, THE wind turned in the *St. Peter*'s favor, shifting to the west, and the ship began to claw back lost miles as it sailed west and north. Occasionally, the sun peeked out between "fast flying" clouds, only to be veiled again when fog and drizzle descended. They had no real idea of how far south the ship had drifted during the weeks of storms. Dead reckoning, estimating speed and direction, was all but useless after the terrible battering of the storm, and the fog and clouds made it difficult to take a reading from the sun or stars to determine latitude or longitude, let alone do the calculations. Waxell urged Bering, now unable to rise from his bunk but still alert enough to assert his command, to search for a site to overwinter before they all perished, but Bering was firmly against it; he wanted to make it to Avacha Bay. In a brief burst of energy, he ordered that coins be collected from all hands and made a vow to donate the money equally between two churches, the newly founded Russian Orthodox church in Avacha Bay and the Lutheran church in his town of Viborg. There was much praying, promising, and soul-searching.

The ship sailed on through the final days of October, some days covering as much as a hundred nautical miles in twelve hours, occasionally nearing small islands through the mist and drizzle. They sailed at a good speed, despite the lack of healthy sailors and the damaged sails, rigging, and masts. Steller wrote that "on November 1, 2, and 3, nothing unusual occurred except that our patients were dying off very rapidly and many at a time, so that it was scarcely possible to manage the ship or make any change in the sails." The daily deaths from scurvy were now so routine that they were rated as "nothing unusual." The ship's log for November 4 alone records deaths matter-of-factly as they occurred throughout the day, the bodies wrapped in dirty cloth and lowered into the ocean: At one in the morning, drummer Osip Chentsov "of the Siberian garrison" died. At one in the afternoon, "by the will of God," Siberian soldier Ivan Davidov perished. At four it was the grenadier Alexei Popov. There were now twelve dead from scurvy, while thirty-three sailors and several officers were unable to leave their bunks under any circumstances, and most of the others were weakened and feeble. They all knew the ship would founder if they encountered another storm.

On the fourth of November, the drizzle abated, and the skies momentarily cleared. The remaining mariners stood at the railing and wept and stared in disbelief at a distant outcropping of land, with a snow-covered mountain range rising in the distance. In the ship's log, Waxell wrote optimistically that "we think this land is Kamchatka." Steller wrote that "it is impossible to describe how great and extraordinary was the joy of everybody at this sight. The half dead crawled up to see it, and all thanked God heartily for this great mercy." Even Bering became excited. "The Captain Commander, who was a very sick man, became not a little aroused, and all talked of how, after having suffered such terrible misery, they were going to care for their health and take a rest." Waxell assured the crew that, according to his calculations, this land was Kamchatka, and he urged Bering to sail toward it. Steller, like many others, was astonished and relieved. "Even if there had been a thousand navigators," he wrote, "they could not have hit it off to a hair like this in their reckoning; we are not half a mile off." The men went and dug out all their remaining liquor, long concealed for a moment such as this, and passed small cups around, toasting their deliverance. The officers collected charts and brought them on deck and scrutinized them, comparing the sketches to the land that lay mist enshrouded on the horizon. All agreed the outline of the coast matched that of Kamchatka, and they positively identified prominent capes in the distance, the lighthouse, and the mouth of the harbor of Avacha Bay. But Steller soon began to have doubts. "It might have been known from dead reckoning," he surmised, "that we were at the very least on the 55th parallel, while Avacha is two degrees farther south."

The next day, Bering convened a meeting of the officers in his cabin. It was an open-door meeting, and the crew was allowed to listen to the discussion. The ship's log reports that the main points of discussion were that "we had few men to manage the ship. . . . [W]e have little fresh water." Waxell added that the rigging and sails were all severely damaged, with no one in condition to repair them, and that it was late fall in a northern latitude—if they departed the coast, they could not expect to reach anywhere safe in their present condition. Khitrov wrote similar sentiments in his journal: "We could not go on because we had no able bodied men, our rigging was rotten, and our provisions and water were gone." Bering said that he wanted to push on to where they believed Avacha to be, but Waxell and Khitrov firmly opposed him with arguments that were well rehearsed. They insisted on landing in any nearby bay and then sending a messenger overland to Lower Kamchatka Post for horses.

Waxell and Khitrov persuaded the petty officers and crew of their proposition, but many of them agreed to sign the proffered document only on condition that they were assured that the land was indeed Kamchatka, since they were not experts, whereupon Khitrov proclaimed that "if this were not Kamchatka, he would let his head be cut off." Despite the drama, the two had persuasive arguments—essentially that it was not just about suffering or perseverance; men were dying daily, the rigging and sails were rotten, and there were not enough men to sail the ship in anything but perfect weather—the sort of weather that would become more elusive as fall turned to winter. Still, some joined with Bering in wanting to continue on. Dmitry Ovtsin, his adjutant and demoted former lieutenant, was one. But he may have found it difficult to go publicly against his master and commander. Waxell and Khitrov apparently shouted at him for his loyalty to Bering, called him a dog and a scoundrel, and forced him out of the cabin. They then turned and asked Steller to sign the document of agreement, but the testy German naturalist demurred. "I have never been consulted in anything from the beginning," he boldly announced, "nor will my advice be taken if it doesn't agree with what is wanted; besides, the gentlemen themselves say that I am not a sailor; therefore I would rather not say anything." Steller did agree to prepare a document attesting to the poor health of the crew, which he considered to be within his duties as surgeon. This satisfied Waxell and Khitrov, as the report could only bolster their opinion that they lacked healthy men to properly sail the ship.

Waxell and Khitrov won the day, the official sea council had made its position clear, and the *St. Peter* did not try to sail up the coast in an attempt to reach Petropavlovsk. Instead, they would "take advantage of the wind and steer for the shore in sight in order to save the ship and men." They were in such a dire situation that they would try to go ashore right away rather than attempt to ease the ship into a sheltered bay they spied to the west. "Perhaps God would also help us to keep the ship," Waxell mused. It may have been the lesser of two evils to have sailed on as Bering wished, but with men perishing daily from scurvy and the ship damaged, with torn sails dangling from snapped masts, this was not obvious at the time. As they sailed northwest toward what is now known as Copper Island and the land features became more clear, doubts and despair began to form in their minds: Where were the distinctive volcanic cones to the south around Avacha Bay?

After rounding the cape, they steered the *St. Peter* toward what appeared to be an inlet. It was then that the clouds opened and the navigator was able to take a reading on the sun, which showed that the ship's latitude was actually more than one hundred nautical miles north of the entrance to Avacha Bay. Waxell later explained away their error by noting that "these were parts unknown not only to us but to the whole world besides. . . . [W]e were unable to put a name to the land we sighted, not least because we had been five months at sea without setting eyes on a single known or observed land with the help of which we might have been able to correct our journals and dead reckoning. We had no sea-chart we could follow, but must proceed like the blind, not knowing whither their fumbling will lead them." Waxell was still cursing the false map of Gama Land that led them astray.

But who among them could have provided logical, sober judgment while suffering from scurvy, as they were, and fearing for the soundness of the ship while lost near unknown shores in the wild North Pacific in November? Later that day, they steered the near wreck of a ship toward the land to get a closer appreciation of the terrain. Once the decision had been made to seek a landing as soon as possible, the sick and dying mariners collapsed from exhaustion or relief, and everyone lay down in their places below deck and went to sleep to regain some semblance of their strength. At about four in the afternoon, Steller found himself on deck watching as the ghost ship slowly headed toward the inlet and bay, now scarcely a mile away, with no officers present. Both Waxell and Khitrov were "gently and sweetly" sleeping below (but also, it should be mentioned, dazed by scurvy). The ship seemed to be sailing unmanned directly onto the land. Steller rushed to the cabin to inform Bering, who, once roused, issued orders for Waxell and Khitrov to get on deck and take charge. Waxell and Khitrov groggily roused themselves and then stood observing the land approach until sundown. When they were close to shore, they hove out an anchor in view of a sandy beach with no apparent rocks or breakers.

During the night, the moon shone brightly under clear skies and a gentle breeze. But without warning, the waters grew turbulent and powerful. The receding tide exposed a hidden reef of jagged rocks, and "the ship was tossed about like a ball and threatened to strike against the bottom." The anchor cable snapped, and the ship was "swept away by huge powerful waves that were breaking over a rock and time after time swept across the ship with such force that it quivered from bow to stern, and we thought that the deck would be stove in. . . . [T]wice the ship bumped on rocks." Sailors rushed to drop a spare anchor, but within moments it too was lost, the cable snapped by the twisting current that dragged the ship around "and was as much help as we had never dropped it." Only one anchor remained, and the few able-bodied men struggled to get it into place as tide and storm dragged the *St. Peter* toward the reef. Panic-stricken men dashed about, shouting and crying questions like children as the hull ground sickeningly upon the jagged rocks. In the chaos and panic, "no one knew who should give or who should take orders," as they were "seized with the fear of death." One yelled, "Oh, God! It is all over with us! Oh, God, our ship! A disaster has befallen our ship!" A group of seamen ran and grabbed the corpses of two men who had died from scurvy and were waiting a burial ashore and pitched them overboard, "without ceremony, neck and heels into the sea," believing the corpses were cursed and were the cause of the disaster. Steller "could not refrain from laughing" as one bewildered mariner asked "whether the water was very salty . . . as if death in fresh water would be more delightful!" If the hull tore asunder, they all knew they would be sucked to their doom in the frigid waters or battered on the rocks as the ship went down. It seemed inevitable.

And then, only moments from destruction, a huge wave lifted the battered ship over the reef and deposited it in a shallow lagoon near the shore, "as in a placid lake all at once quiet and delivered from all fear of stranding." It was suddenly calm, and when the sailors dropped the final remaining anchor overboard, it stuck in four fathoms of water with a sandy bottom, approximately six hundred yards from shore. The reef was behind them, locking the ship into the small bay. Steller noted how his nemesis Khitrov seemed to shrink from the responsibility and the terror: "He who until now had been the greatest talker and advice-giver" slunk belowdeck until the danger had passed and then emerged and "began valiantly to preach courage to the men, though he himself was as pale as a corpse." Nevertheless, it was now calm, the danger had passed, the night was again pleasant, and the sailors, wasted by scurvy and believing they were somewhere in Kamchatka, collapsed into slumber.

THE BEACH WAS NARROW and bounded by bluffs. Grass-covered dunes stretched back to a base of low snow-covered mountains. This was the view that greeted the sailors when they woke the next day and stared from the deck of the ship toward land. So far, twelve men had died from scurvy, and forty-nine out of sixty-six survivors were officially on the sick list. No one was at full strength, except perhaps Steller, his friend Plenisner, and his servant, Lepekhin. These three were free from scurvy only because of the antiscorbutic herbs collected on Shumagin Island. The *St. Peter* was now safely in calm water, but it was trapped between the shore and the reef. November was the storm season in a stormy part of the world. The next spell of rough weather was inevitable, and it would either push the ship ashore or drag it onto the reef. Waxell called their placement in this tiny patch of safe water "God's miraculous, merciful assistance."

On the morning of November 7, the sea was so strong that it was eleven o'clock before they could get the longboat lowered to go ashore and inspect the land for a place to set up a camp, get freshwater to replace the brackish water remaining in the six barrels on board, hunt for fresh meat, and search for antiscorbutic plants. Steller, Plenisner, Lepekhin, Waxell, and his young son, Laurentz, along with three sailors and several of the sick, were the first party to be rowed ashore to explore. They brought along some sundry equipment and a large sail to be used as a tent. One of the first "strange and disquieting" things that Steller noted as they closed on the beach was a cluster of sea otters slowly approaching them curiously and a line of small foxes on the bluff—why were these animals on shore in such numbers, and why were they so seemingly unafraid of the boatload of armed men?

Once ashore they split up. The oarsmen stayed with the sick on the beach near the boat; Plenisner went off hunting along the beach in one direction, the three sailors in the other. Steller, Waxell, Lepekhin, and Waxell's son hiked toward a nearby stream that was not ice covered and discovered it to be good, clear freshwater suitable for drinking. They saw no trees and no bushes, nothing that could be used for fuel, other than a scattering of driftwood that was difficult to see under the blanket of light snow that covered the beach. They searched for a suitable place for a settlement and found one in a series of sand dunes near the mouth of the stream and the bluff. The pits between the dunes could be used as the foundation of a camp to shelter the sick until a rescue party could arrive. The sand could be built up into walls for protection from the wind, and a sail could be stretched over them to keep off the snow and rain. Perhaps some driftwood could be collected to build up the sides and roof. An added bonus was that the urine from sick men unable to move would drain away easily through the sand.

While Waxell and his son returned to the longboat to help the first batch of sick mariners move to their new home, Steller and Lep-ekhin wandered farther into the dunes to inspect the local flora for possible antiscorbutics. Steller collected some small plants that were commonly used in salads in northern Europe: bachbung, American brooklime, nasturtium-like herbs, and other crucifers still collect-ible beneath the snow. He then returned to help Waxell, whom he found "very weak and faint," still waiting at the boat by the water's edge. As they huddled on the beach below the treeless dunes, clasp-ing cups of warm tea, Steller remarked, "God only knows if this is Kamchatka." Waxell replied briskly, "What else would it be? We will soon send for post-horses and will have the ship taken to the mouth of the Kamchatka River by Cossacks. The most important thing now is to save the men." Soon after this conversation, Plenis-ner strolled down the beach, clutching six large ptarmigan that he had shot. Waxell rowed back to the ship with several of the birds and Steller's salad, specifically intended for Bering, while Steller made a soup from the remaining birds, boiled in a large pot. As it grew dark, the three other sailors returned, dragging two sea otters and two seals, "news which appeared quite remarkable to us." It was easy to hunt here. The shore party slept that first night huddled under a sail propped up by some driftwood, while most of the men still lay suffering from scurvy on the ship.

The next few days were filled with drizzle and snow. The shore party continued their investigations of the land and hunted animals for food, while the men on the *St. Peter* worked to secure the ship for the winter and tend to the sick. Over the next weeks, the few reasonably able-bodied men began ferrying the sick and supplies to the stony, mist-enshrouded shore and to enlarge the pits in the sand dunes so that they could be used as the foundation for tents. Getting the dozens of sick from the ship to the shore was the first priority. Many of the mariners who hovered at death's door passed quietly away as soon as they were brought from the befouled interior of the ship into the clean air, others died on the boat ride to the beach, and others perished once they set foot on land. Waxell recorded that sailor Ivan Emelianov, cannoneer Ilya Dergachev, and Siberian soldier Vasili Popkov died on board before they could be moved ashore, while sailor Seliverst Tarakanov died as he was being landed. One man, upon being told he was going ashore in the next boat, became so excited he got up, dressed himself, and proclaimed, "God be praised that we are going ashore; there we will be able to manage better and even do something to help our own recovery." He then dropped over on the deck, dead. Savin Stepanov, Nikita Ostvin, Mark Antipin, Andreyan Eselberg—the ship's log records the near-daily deaths from scurvy, some on board the ship, others in the growing tent colony. Because all the men were enfeebled, the work of unloading the sick men and supplies from the ship progressed achingly slowly, especially when the rough water and unruly waves made rowing the longboat dangerous.

Meanwhile, Steller, Plenisner, Lepekhin, and several other sailors continued to hunt and explore the new land, the land where they all now knew they would be spending the winter. Behind the beach beyond the bluffs, there was a stony scrub-covered slope with low snowy mountains extending in the distance. Steller began to have serious doubts that they had reached Kamchatka. His view was based primarily on observations of the natural world. The plants he collected were similar to those found on Kamchatka, but some were of the type he had seen and collected in Alaska during the summer. There were no trees and no familiar shrubs. Most tellingly, the animals seemed to have no experience with humans. The ptarmigan could be easily caught at close range; the sea otters floated close to shore and were easily shot, as were seals.

Along the shore, he and Plenisner spied the huge slow-moving back of a whalelike animal that lingered offshore and undulated up every few minutes for a great breath of air that sounded like a horse snorting. Steller had never seen or heard of such an animal. It was not a whale and was much too large to be any other marine mammal he had ever seen or read about. His servant, Lepekhin, likewise concurred that no such creature existed in Kamchatka. "I began to doubt that this was Kamchatka," Steller wrote, "especially as the sea sky overhead in the south indicated sufficiently that we were on an island surrounded by the sea." It was the "water sky" common in the Arctic, where the open water could be seen darkly reflected in the bottom of clouds. When he quietly raised his suspicions with others, he was met not with the scorn that had often been directed his way before, but with denial. He again brooded on "the unjust conduct of various persons," by whom he meant Waxell and especially Khitrov, his tormentor. Even his friend Plenisner would not accept the truth of their situation. Perhaps it was too awful to contemplate. If they were not on Kamchatka, then they were not anywhere known, not on any chart or map, and there would be no aid from nearby Russian outposts, not now, not ever.

Steller suspected that they might not just be the only people on the island but perhaps the only people ever to have visited it. This time Steller's speculations were correct. They had landed on what would later be known as Bering Island. The small bay was the only safe place a ship could have come ashore along the 140-mile coastline of the island. The entire island is surrounded by the shelving rocks of an encircling reef, except for this one inlet. Waxell wrote that "the place to which we had come was so narrow that had we been but 20 fathoms farther to the north or south, we would have become hung up on a shelf of rock and from there not one of us would have escaped."

THE SECOND NIGHT ASHORE, Steller, Plenisner, and Lepekhin had their first encounter with one creature that not only confirmed Steller's theory that the local animals had not had contact with humans before, but would also be a defining presence of their winter: the blue foxes, a subspecies of the Arctic fox, *Vulpes beringensis*. There appeared to be unlimited numbers of them, and they weren't shy. The two men shot eight of them right away, and Steller noted that "the number and fatness of which as well as the fact that they were not shy astonished me exceedingly." As the three men sat around a small fire nursing cups of tea after a meal of ptarmigan soup, a blue fox brazenly strolled up and snatched away two ptarmigan "right before our eyes."

Within days of the mariners shambling up the beach to make camp in the dunes, they all became intimately familiar with the blue foxes of the island. When the men set about constructing shelter against the approaching winter by enlarging the series of burrows Steller and Waxell had found near the dunes and the river, a pack of snarling blue foxes rushed up and began tearing at the cloth of sailors' pants and had to be driven away with kicks and shouts. Without knowing it, the sailors had chosen a contested spot for their camp: the dunes had been the temporary or seasonal burrows of the foxes. Having lived undisturbed for ages, the animals fought for their territory. This battle of the species was most violent and cruel in the first few weeks and dragged on for months. Steller later reported that the foxes had other dwelling places, and in the summer "they especially like to have their lairs up in the mountains or on the edges of the mountains." For most of November and December, however, they were particularly drawn to the human camp in the sand dunes.

The sailors dug out and enlarged the burrows and banged together a rude framework of driftwood to which they affixed fox hides and the remnants of the tattered sails. But the work progressed slowly, as even those who could rouse themselves could barely stand, let alone do heavy work. Men continued to die routinely, and there was no room in the makeshift shelters to house the corpses. Hordes of foxes swarmed about the makeshift camp, drawn down from the snow-covered hills by the scent of food. Becoming increasingly aggressive, they stole clothing and blankets and dragged away tools and utensils. In one three-hour period, Steller and Plenisner killed sixty, stabbing them and hacking at them with an ax, and used their dead frozen bodies to shore up the walls of the huts. The foxes "crowded into our dwellings and stole everything they could carry away, including articles that were of no use to them, like knives, sticks, bags, shoes, socks, caps. . . . While skinning animals it often happened that we stabbed two or three with our knives because they wanted to tear the meat from our hands." They also came during the night, ripping clothes from the helpless sick, pulling at their boots until driven away. "One night when a sailor on his knees wanted to urinate out of the door of the hut, a fox snapped at the exposed part and, in spite of his cries, did not soon want to let go. No one could relieve himself without a stick in his hand, and they immediately ate up the excrement as eagerly as pigs." The foxes would creep into the camp at any hour and defecate or urinate on garments or provisions, befouling them, or attempt the same on sleeping men. Most disturbing was Waxell's report that the foxes "ate the hands and feet of the corpses before we had time to bury them."

To preserve themselves, the mariners were driven to mindless slaughter, bashing and hacking at the kits as well as the adults, torturing them when possible. "Every morning," Steller wrote, "we dragged by their tails for execution before the Barracks our prisoners who had been captured alive, where some were beheaded, others had their legs broken or one leg and the tail hacked off. Of some we gouged out the eyes; others were strung up alive in pairs by their feet so they would bite each other to death. Some were singed, others flogged to death with the cat-o'-nine tails." Nevertheless, the foxes persisted throughout the months, even returning after their torture, limping on three legs behind their comrades, snarling and barking just as loudly as the rest. The men sometimes skinned a dead fox and tossed it into a nearby ditch, whereupon dozens of others would rush in to devour their fallen comrade and then be clubbed to death themselves. Although Steller was usually very particular and specific in his observations of the natural world, when the subject of the pestiferous blue foxes comes up, a slight taint of disrespect creeps into his writing. "They stink much worse than the red foxes," he stated. "In rutting time they buck day and night and like dogs bite each other cruelly for jealousy. Copulation itself takes place amid much caterwauling like cats."

But they dared not exterminate them, if indeed that would have been possible in their pitiful state, in case it should prove necessary to eat them later if the sea otters or seals disappeared. They all dreaded the "necessity of eating the stinking, disgusting, and hated foxes."

By mid-November, Steller had observed that the men ashore were dying less frequently than the ones on ship, recovering slowly on a diet that included some native plants as a salad and the fresh soup of sea otters and seals and ptarmigan. Shipboard, while Waxell and Khitrov continued to supervise the transfer of men and equipment and supplies ashore and worked to secure the ship to weather the winter, men were still dying nearly daily. The situation looked dire, with work progressing slowly, the weather getting more fierce, and the attacks of the foxes unrelenting.

The quasi-military discipline that had structured relationships for the past years was weakened in the great hardships. Orders were not forcefully bellowed; there were no prompt salutes to authority or hierarchy. Mutiny may have been in the air, or at the very least efforts at self-preservation. But the officers were still the best managers and able to marshal whatever natural authority they possessed.

Junior officers such Aleksei Ivanov, the boatswain's mate, and Luka Alekseyev, the quartermaster, rose in estimation by force of character, while the authority of Khitrov and to a lesser extent Waxell diminished, as did the artificial authority of naval command. Waxell called Ivanov "a tower of strength when we were in trouble." And although Waxell gave no specific example of this strength, or indeed any other information about the man, Ivanov may have been good at comforting and reassuring the sick and dying and organizing parties to build and maintain shelter and hunt and collect driftwood.

Steller's servant, Lepekhin, who was growing weak and sick with scurvy during the first week ashore, upbraided his erstwhile master for bringing him on the voyage and leading him to this miserable fate. Taken aback, Steller wisely chose a diplomatic response, what he called "the first step to our future companionship." Instead of growing angry, he calmly said, "Be of good cheer. God will help. Even if this is not our country we still have hope of getting there; you will not starve; if you cannot work and wait on me, I will do it for you. I know your upright nature and what you have done for me—all that I have belongs to you also; only ask and I will divide with you equally until God helps." This wisdom and insight during the shipwreck were at odds with his caustic manners during the voyage. But Lepekhin was bitter and living in fear of scurvy. "Good enough," he claimed slowly. "I will gladly serve Their Majesties, but you have brought me into this misery. Who compelled you to go with these people? Could you not have enjoyed the good times on the Bolshaya River?" Steller laughed at this show of disobedience or insubordination. "We are both alive!" he exclaimed and then assured Lepekhin that he could not have known the disaster would befall them and that he in any event now had a lifelong friend in Steller. "My intentions were good Thomas, so let yours be good also. You do not know what might have happened to you at home."

This conversation, previously unthinkable under the old regime where a servant never questioned a master, opened Steller's eyes to something not fully apparent to everyone. In the face of starvation and death, nothing was the same, no one could expect special treatment, and no life was more valuable than another. He realized that "rank, learning, and other distinctions would be of no sustenance; therefore before being driven to it by shame or necessity, we ourselves decided to work with what strength we still had left, so as not to be laughed at afterward or wait until we were ordered."

The dozens of men now on the beach certainly had a shared purpose and goal: to survive. But with so many sick and no clear or obvious means of achieving this objective, Steller knew smaller groups could better respond to the needs of their members. Soon after landing, he had formed a small communal group with Plenisner and Lepekhin, and they invited the assistant surgeon, Berge, to join them. They pledged to share a dwelling and work toward their joint survival. The original group agreed to share everything, including survival tasks such as hunting and cooking. Their group soon grew by three Cossacks and two of Bering's servants, with all decisions of the semi-independent band being made jointly. They began to call each other "more politely by their patronymics and given name," in an effort to solidify group loyalty and help sustain their "miserable existence." Soon, other members of the former ship's company also organized themselves into distinct groups.

Steller's keen observation took note of how quickly the value system of shipboard life was replaced by something more prosaic. Although they all knew that sea-otter pelts were valuable and would normally have been hoarded, they now tossed them aside for the foxes, considering them a burden. Items to which they had never before given particular thought and may not have even bothered to pick up had they been dropped, items certainly worth less than a sea-otter pelt, were now considered "treasures." These included axes, knives, awls, needles, thread, shoe twine, shoes, shirts, socks, sticks, and strings. Nothing from their previous life, the life aboard the *St. Peter*, retained the same value.

Some of the animosities from shipboard life continued, how-ever, to ripple through camp. With disrupted naval discipline and far from home, grumblings toward the officers for past grievances and perceived slights and wrongs were amplified. Steller heard men occasionally "calling down God's judgement for revenge on the authors of their misfortune." Many in formerly high positions now glanced around apprehensively at the suffering men looking for someone to blame. Khitrov in particular was unpopular with the crew and feared for his life. For a few days near the end of No-vember, Khitrov maintained a desire to stay on the ship through the winter, arguing with Waxell that it would be more comfortable and free from the wind. He clung to the structure of life and the authority that the navy afforded him. Perhaps he feared the mis-ery, destitution, and squalor of the shore camp; perhaps he thought that the men, once freed from the ironbound strictures of the navy and with idle time, might turn their memories to incidents of past discipline and harsh words, to cruel jokes played upon them, to rough commands and punishments meted out. Khitrov no doubt recalled his claims and assurances to the men that they were per-fectly safe and to his proclamation that he would allow his own head to be cut off if it proved that this landing was not Kamchatka. Many blamed the disaster on Khitrov and to a lesser extent the other officers. Steller recorded that "day and night," when he passed by or lay down to rest, Khitrov heard barely concealed "reproaches and threats for past doings." He approached Steller and his mates and "implored us for God's sake" to accept him into their group. Steller was adamant. Their dwelling was already full, he said, and they had unanimously agreed on this. Khitrov had at one point or another during the voyage insulted all in Steller's band, and they all believed that he "was the chief author of our misfortune." They "refused him absolutely." And so Khitrov crept back to sleep among the men in a large dwelling called "the Barracks," where the sick were being transferred from the ship, ignoring the lidded glances and pretending not to hear the "wailing and lamenting" and the calls for justice.

COMMANDER BERING WAS ROWED ashore on November 9, with four men carrying him on an improvised stretcher made with poles and coiled rope. They placed him in a hollow in a choice location of what was becoming the shore village in the dunes. The men joked about the "grave" they were digging for themselves in the sand. Steller was astonished at how much his commander's health had deteriorated but was "amazed at his composure and strange contentment." Once Bering was settled, Steller crouched out of the wind under the tent, and they had a private conversation. Bering wanted to know what Steller thought of their situation. Had they reached Kamchatka? Steller replied that "to me," it did not look like Kamchatka and then quietly explained his observations on the nature of the plants and how he did not think it was far from Kamchatka, since the flora did not correspond to the plants he had seen in Alaska, either. Steller had also recently found some debris washed up on the beach that evidenced Russian workmanship. He showed Bering part of a broken fox trap, also found washed up on the beach. It was of a similar design to the traps made by the Itelmans of Kamchatka, but was fitted with a sharpened shell rather than with iron. This suggested that it had washed ashore from Alaska, where the natives did not have access to iron. Without making the claim, Steller proposed that they were probably somewhere in between the two continents. Bering looked pensive and replied, "The vessel can probably not be saved, may God at least spare our longboat."

As November progressed, the storms grew worse. The *St. Peter*'s rigging was ice encrusted. Snow covered everything, and waves pounded the ship, occasionally crashing over the deck and pouring into the hold. The high waves further slowed the transfer of men to the shore by making the boat trip to the ship treacherous. The men were exhausted from wading into the freezing surf, rowing back and forth between shore and the dilapidated ship. Waxell and four others were still trapped aboard working when another storm blew in on November 17. Waxell fired guns to call the longboat, but no open boat could make the journey during four days of violent storms. They had run out of water and had begun drinking mouthfuls of brackish fluid from the dregs of the barrels until it snowed and they could crawl on deck, scooping snow and melting it. While they waited, they pitched several more dead bodies overboard, so that they wouldn't have to share the ship with them.

In his own account, Waxell boldly describes the precautions he took to secure his own life. He covered himself up and protected himself with blankets, to shield his face from the change in air between inside and outside. During the past couple of weeks, he had "seen how many of our men had died like mice as soon as their heads had topped the hatch." He had ensconced himself far from the hold and its noxious smells and damp dark spaces. The galley at least was lighter and warmer, and he could keep a small fire burning. He mused that he might be better off here than "burrowing in the snow ashore." But he was mistaken, and "the bad air and filth found its way even there from the holds where so many had been lying ill for two or even three months, attending to the needs of nature where they lay." He soon was so afflicted by "this evil, unhealthy stench" that he was unable to move his hands or feet or his jaw. He was nearly dead when they found him on November 21, insensate and slumped in the galley, unable to take two steps without being held up by someone under each arm. The last to leave the ship, Waxell fainted several times getting into the longboat and he was carried along the shore to the camp, where he was placed in the Barracks.

Once on shore, Waxell soon became "so ravaged by scurvy that we abandoned all hope for his life." Steller, "without a thought for former treatment," rushed to Waxell's aid with some fresh food and a salad that he had collected from the withered roots and grasses behind the beach. Waxell lay, unable to rise, crammed into the Barracks with the other mariners, fending off advances from the foxes, until a smaller tent was made ready for him. Steller devoted extra effort to Waxell's care for a motive not entirely altruistic—anxiety over what should happen if Waxell died. The next in command was the near-universally despised Khitrov. Steller feared that "the universal hatred would destroy all discipline and delay or even prevent, the enterprises necessary for our deliverance." Under Steller's care, Waxell began a slow and painful recovery, much to the relief of many who also feared Khitrov's actions. Part of the problem for Waxell was that his son Laurentz was not officially on the ship's roster and so was not entitled to a ration from the ship's stores. He and his father shared a single meager allotment of rye flour between them.

On November 22, Bering was still prostrate and lying in the same sandpit in which he had been placed when first brought ashore more than a week earlier. He quietly spoke a command to Waxell to convene a meeting of the surviving officers and devise a plan to save the ship. A day later, the officers prepared the "Report on Saving the Ship" and presented it to Bering. The weather remained stormy and rough for days, and everyone was too weak to do anything about these orders, as it was impossible to row out to the ship, which was unmanned and tethered to the shore with every remaining anchor and the grapnel hooks. The report was signed by Waxell, Khitrov, and the remaining junior officers, Kharlam Yushin, Nikita Khotyaintsov, Boris Roselius, and Alexei Ivanov. It begins: "As you know, the ship lies out in the open sea and if a strong wind should come up from the east, southeast, west or northwest, one anchor would not hold. On the east, north and west there are rocky reefs. If a strong wind should blow up from the south, or from between south and west, the ship would be driven out to sea." They proposed sailing the ship onto the beach and tethering it as tightly as possible and then securing the supplies. And then in the spring, they hope-fully would be able to resail the vessel. In any case, they believed that if they did nothing, the ship would surely be destroyed or lost during the winter.

On November 26, Khitrov was the only senior officer still stand-ing, but he too was now very weak, reporting in the log that he could "barely stand on my feet." He tried to inspire some men to implement Bering's orders to beach the ship, but he could only round up five able-bodied men with any strength to do the job. They tried to get the longboat into the surf, but the men became soaked in the freezing water and had to hobble back to the tents. With this small number of men, Khitrov knew that they probably would not even have the strength to weigh the anchor, let alone set the sails and steer the ship ashore—most likely they would have cracked against the reef, destroying the ship and killing themselves. He called off the operation and reported his failed attempt to Ber-ing, with a written statement to protect himself in case of later re-percussions. The next day, Khitrov was too sick to leave his tent, although Steller somewhat uncharitably, considering everyone was down with scurvy, suggested that Khitrov was more lazy than sick. In any event, their plans were overtaken by events. A mighty storm blew in on the twenty-eighth, snapped the anchor and all the ca-bles, and spun the ship around. Then, incredibly, the currents and winds took the *St. Peter* and drove it not toward the reefs, but to-ward the beach, "on the spot where we had planned to lay her up," near the small river below the camp. Steller was astonished that the storm had done the job "in a better way than perhaps might ever have been done by human effort."

The *St. Peter* now lay tilted and aground, just offshore, and it slowly settled into the loose sand of the bay to a depth of eight feet, up to the gunwales, and filled with the sea. The ship would never sail again. The wreck was only two hundred meters from the camp, a constantly visible reminder of their woeful predicament.

Whenever the weather briefly calmed, men continued to ferry the remaining food stores ashore, rowing slowly back and forth in the single longboat. It was now a much easier job since they could get to the ship without rowing through the big waves and open sea. The food stores that could be saved consisted mostly of rye flour and groats that were stored in large leather sacks. Unfortunately, the sacks had been soaked by seawater in the hold of the ship. Waxell set a monthly allotment of these food items of thirty pounds of rye flour, later reduced to fifteen and finally to none; five pounds of sogged groats; and a half pound of salt. The food was equally divided among the men with no preference for rank or social standing, and it went a long way toward smoothing the tensions between the officers and the sailors. Eating the flour wasn't much of a pleasure, though. The salty groats had to be fried in seal or sea-otter fat to be palatable. "Until we got used to it our bodies became distended like drums from flatulence." The remaining gunpowder was also damp with saltwater and mostly ruined—a devastating and gloomy disaster greater than any that had befallen them so far. How could they continue to hunt for food all winter without gunpowder?

When the men looked at one another, they saw writ on each other's visages the evidence of their own deprivation and suffering. "Had a stranger somehow been able suddenly to come among us," Waxell wrote, "some nobleman, for example, with his servants, or an officer with his men, and had seen how we were living, he would assuredly have been unable to distinguish master from man or the commander from his lowliest subordinate, for we were all in the same situation, master as man, sailor as officer, and alike in both regard to standing and work, food and clothing."

CHAPTER 11

DEATH AND PLAYING CARDS

WITH THE *ST. PETER* sunk crookedly into the sand of the bay, deserted and battered, everyone's focus and attention was on their new life ashore. There was no more talk about sailing on to Avacha Bay, no talk about anything other than immediate survival. Once Waxell and the last mariners were taken ashore, the camp had grown to accommodate the entire company. It settled into the form that would remain throughout the winter—a cluster of dirty, ill-shaped domes of ragged, flapping sailcloth draped over mounds of frozen sand roughly bolstered with stiff fox corpses and driftwood, encircling a small smoldering campfire. Each cluster of dugout huts was organized into the smaller units first conceived by Steller, tending to their own immediate daily needs without central authority. Since most of the men were either prostrate with scurvy, dying, or already dead, there was little movement about the primitive village. The near-constant wind drowned out the low moaning of the sick.

"Everywhere on shore there was nothing but pitiful and terrifying sights," wrote Steller. "Some of the sick cried because they were so cold, others because hungry and thirsty, since the mouths of many

were so miserably affected by the scurvy that they could not eat because of the great pain, as the gums were so miserably swollen like
a sponge, brown-black, grown over the teeth and covering them."
Waxell wrote that "men were continually dying." And the dead had
to lie for a "considerable" time among the living, "for there was none
able to drag the corpses away, nor were those who still lived capable
of moving away from the dead." Moaning and staring glassy-eyed,
the living could scarcely be distinguished from the dead. "We became more and more depressed mentally," Waxell recalled.

> Those who allowed themselves to be overwhelmed by this first
> stage of the disease experienced it thereafter as a general asthmatic
> condition, which made them unable to get their breath. This was
> soon followed by stiffness in the limbs, swelling of the feet and legs,
> while the face became yellow. The whole mouth, and especially the
> gums, bled and the teeth became loose . . . and having got to this
> state it is already all up with the patient and he might just as well
> remain lying where he is. Nor will he, as a rule, make any effort to
> save himself, but becomes so depressed that he would far rather die
> than live.

Men were wracked by violent fever, unexplained rashes, stabbing
pains, delusions, and constipation. They were utterly defenseless
and helpless, even to fend off the nips of hungry foxes. "Truly,"
Steller confirmed, "the sight was so pitiful that even the bravest
might lose courage."

The mariners were reduced to such a miserable state that the
old antagonisms and mutual contempt receded. Steller could not
long remain indifferent to the suffering and labored tirelessly to
minister to the sick, concocting antiscorbutic broth from herbs and
roots he chipped from the frozen earth. In his eyes they soon became not his Russian tormentors, but human beings in need of his

care. The barbed sarcasm disappears from his journal, and so, one imagines, might his voice have lost its imperial twang. With Bering near death, Khitrov universally disliked, and Waxell succumbing to scurvy, Steller became the unofficial leader of the shore camp. Virtually alone in being unaffected by scurvy, he found himself in a position of unexpected power over his erstwhile antagonists. Yet it seems that he took no advantage of the situation and that his character turned in a different way, toward being a comforter and doctor. Surprisingly, he also took over cooking duties. Steller was an admirably adaptable man who, for whatever reason, was able to instantly shed the cultural trappings of his former life—the privilege he enjoyed as an educated gentleman, the creature comforts bestowed by a higher rank, and the authority over a personal manservant. He took on menial chores without complaint and earned the respect of many. Steller never entirely lost his acid tongue, but now he kept it quietly relocated to his journal—and for his critique of those he felt incompetent or disrespectful.

While Steller might have devoted extra effort to nursing Waxell back to health simply for the benefit of the expedition, others he saved out of friendship or respect. When the old and experienced mate Andreyan Hesselberg, a Dane who had served at sea for more than fifty years and was now probably more than seventy years old, was brought low by scurvy, Steller was particularly saddened. Hesselberg had always been friendly toward Steller and had sided with him on some of the controversial decisions made on the voyage. Steller bitterly recounted the injustice that he should "suffer the misfortune now to be treated as a silly child and idiot by men scarcely half his age and one-third his skill." When the Dane died, Steller wrote that Hesselberg "discharged his duties always in such a way that he carried to his grave the reputation of a pre-eminently useful man whose disregarded advice might perhaps have saved us earlier."

Steller became not just a physician but a minister, comforting the dying and saying words over the dead. His role in tending to the sick and dying, his tireless collecting of any antiscorbutic plants he could locate and organizing others to do the same, and his instructions to prepare broths and soups from freshly killed animals likely saved dozens of men. Yet he who usually filled his journal with details and stories is silent on his own actions in dealing with the scurvy epidemic—his decisive actions were reported by others afterward. Müller, the historian who later wrote of the expedition, relying on interviews with survivors, said that "men could not lose heart because they had Steller with them. Steller was a doctor who at the same time administered to the spirit. He cheered everyone with his lively and agreeable company." Steller was respected as a doctor as he never had been as a naturalist. His ambition for science and recognition was slowly replaced with patience and compassion. It is also worth noting that Steller's personality shift came along with the change of circumstances, at a time when he had real practical knowledge and skills to share, but it also corresponded to a reduction or exhaustion of the liquor supply.

On December 1, Bering decided to send off a small exploratory expedition into the interior of the mysterious land, the first of several such missions. The three men, led by sailor Timofei Anchugov, were among the least affected by scurvy. They struggled up windlashed, rocky slopes, across "tall mountains and untrodden paths," for about seven miles to the top of a barren hill, from which they could see open water to the west and the coastline ringed in frothy surf. Their journey lasted nearly four weeks, as they trudged through the rough interior of what they soon determined was most likely an island. Later exploration confirmed that the camp was situated on the east coast, about a third of the way from the southern tip of the island, which runs generally southeast to northwest and is around ten to fifteen miles wide and forty miles long. When they eventually returned with this news, it was a sobering blow. "We now saw ourselves threatened with certain destruction," Waxell recalled, "being on an unknown deserted island without a ship or timber with which to build a new one, and at the same time with little or no provisions. Our people were very sick and we had no medicines or drugs of any description. Nor were we even decently quartered, but lodged, so to speak, under the open sky. The whole ground was covered in snow and we quailed at the thought of the long winter and the fierce cold that would descend upon us here, where there was no sign of fuel." This news sent many into "utter despair" and to "abandon hope of ever being rescued." They were on their own.

BERING HAD BEEN GROWING steadily weaker in the month since leaving the ship. Once ashore, he never rose from his place in the sandpit under a makeshift tent. He suffered from more than just scurvy. Under Steller's care, he had recovered from scurvy twice during the voyage. Four of his teeth had fallen out from puffed, darkly swollen gums earlier on the voyage, but his gums were firm on December 8. Steller claimed that Bering suffered from a collection of unclear maladies and that he "perished rather from hunger, thirst, cold, vermin and grief" more than any specific disease. His feet were swollen, he was feverish, and "internal gangrene" had caused "inflammation of the lower abdomen." He had been refusing Steller's attempts to broaden his shore diet. Once when Steller brought back to the cluster of huts a still suckling sea otter and pleaded with Bering "in every way and manner" to let Steller prepare it specially for him, he was rebuffed. Bering looked away and muttered, "I wonder at your taste." Steller did not take offense. He looked around him at the huts and the snow-covered beach with the wreck of the ship in the background, and he replied that he adapted his taste "to the circumstances." But Bering would eat only boiled ptarmigan.

Bering was wracked by worry and stress, constantly preoccupied with the survival of his men, and brooding over the failures of the expedition. He confessed to Steller that his strength was not what it had been. A powerfully built man, Bering was referring not just to physical strength but to his will to bring order to the expedition. He complained to Steller that the expedition had been made far more complex and extensive than he had ever imagined and that "at his age he could have wished to have the whole task taken out of his hands and put into those of a young and active man."

The voyage planned by Bering was to have been a quick and fruitful excursion that would make his career and fortune. He would cross the Pacific, which was believed to be much smaller than it was, even without the wasted search for Gama Land; roughly chart the coast; hope for friendly encounters with people in safe harbors with freshwater; lay claim to a vast new world and an even greater frontier for imperial Russia; and burnish his and Russia's international reputations for scientific discovery and the advancement of knowledge. Then he would return to Petropavlovsk and the long trek west across Siberia to St. Petersburg, to Anna and his children. It would be capped off with a respectable and wealthy retirement, perhaps with some prestigious ceremonial appointments. Now here he was weakened and withering on a deserted and frozen beach, the expedition and his dreams in tatters, with one ship lost and the other shattered and destroyed in the nearby lagoon, his men starving and scurvy ridden on this barren island in the middle of nowhere. He would never see his family again. There was little to be enthusiastic about, even had he been in good health. He spoke to Steller frequently about how he had had incredible luck in his life and career until about two months earlier, when the first bout of scurvy attacked him. Steller was convinced that had he been able to bring the commander back to Kamchatka, he would have lived, that Bering was broken in spirit if not completely in body. At sixty years old, Bering was just too weakened and dispirited to recover.

He died at five in the morning, before daybreak, on December 8. That night a strong wind was blowing sand around the encampment. It trickled into the pit where Bering lay with his legs partially covered in sand. "Let me be," he told Waxell and Steller, to forestall any further medical help in his final hours. "The deeper in the ground I lie, the warmer I am; only the part of me that is above ground suffers from the cold." Steller wrote in his published account of the expedition that Bering had "composure and an earnest preparation for death," with full possession of reason and speech. But later in a private letter to a colleague at the Academy of Sciences, he also wrote that Bering "died miserably under the open sky . . . almost eaten up by lice."

The next day, Bering's body was taken about fifty feet from the camp, where a grave was dug in the sand next to Hesselberg's, marked by a wooden cross. Some of the men banged together a primitive coffin, which although too small for his body and requiring him to be bent to fit, was certainly a sign of respect. The planks of wood, scavenged from the ship, were extremely valuable, and no other person was given such a distinction. Many of the men and the officers retained a great respect for their commander, and Waxell led a brief service in the Lutheran tradition.

Though Bering was honored with a burial ceremony, Steller was annoyed at the choice of sermon: "He died like a rich man and was buried like the ungodly." Bering, after all, was the supreme commander of not just the voyage but the entire expedition from St. Petersburg. He was a wealthy man and a man of high status in a culture that prized hierarchy and social standing. In all of Siberia, Bering could outrank any local governor or official in matters related to the expedition. He traveled in style, with an entourage, inhabiting the trappings of his office as the czar's representative. He looked and lived as the imperial symbol. Even on shipboard he inhabited the role of the noble, with nine sea chests of ornaments and fancy, impractical attire. But in the dramatic shift in the social situation following the wreck, he dropped from his rarefied position of authority and respect to at best first among equals. Waxell's sermon probably captures Bering's situation. In the suffering and chaos on the beach, symbolic attire and social rank were valueless compared to the skill of skinning an animal, tending the sick, or starting a fire. Bering was buried in a primitive, or ungodly, land, unable to adapt to the new reality of their predicament.

Although Waxell's sermon was undoubtedly given in respect and honor, Steller was rankled because of the implication that Bering was flawed. He groused that "in the slimy environs of Okhotsk and Kamchatka he [Bering] tried to lift out and up everybody who had fallen into the mire, they leaned so heavily on him that he himself must sink." Steller felt that Bering "took with him to his grave everyone's receipted bill." Steller's opinion was that "the only blame which can be laid against this excellent man is that by his too lenient command he did as much harm as his subordinates by their too impetuous and often thoughtless action." In the sort of eulogy he wrote for Bering in his journal, Steller did allow that Bering was not known for quick, decisive action and wondered whether "more fire and heat" would have better overcome the dangers and challenges of the expedition.

Despite his clashes with Bering during the voyage, Steller had great respect for the commander for piloting the expedition and laid blame for the voyage's failures at the hands of the other officers—in fact, Steller contrived to believe that all of Bering's failures were the result of the undue influence of these officers, who eventually became too conceited and "looked with contempt on all those near them." And Steller reserved, as usual, a particular ire for Khitrov, whom he felt should have shown loyalty to Bering because Bering had promoted him to lieutenant, instead of challenging his commander at the sea council that resulted in their shipwreck. Khitrov, Steller wrote, owed Bering a particular debt but afterward "contradicted him in everything, became the author of our misfortune, and after Bering's death his greatest accuser."

While Steller resented Bering's choice of certain officers, particularly Khitrov, he also respected Bering for living his life as "a righteous and devout Christian whose conduct was that of a man of good manners, kind, quiet and universally liked by the whole command, both high and low." The officers and sailors decided to name the island in Bering's honor, despite the fact that it was Bering who wanted to sail on, while it was Waxell and Khitrov who overruled him and sailed the *St. Peter* toward the beach.

IN THE ARCTIC LATITUDE of Bering Island, December and January have as little as seven hours a day of light, and even then it felt gloomy on the numerous overcast days. But the ocean moderated the temperature, and it was much warmer on the island than it would have been at a corresponding latitude in Siberia, with an average temperature of 6–8 degrees Celsius (17–21 degrees Fahrenheit). Unfortunately, late fall and winter were also the seasons with the most precipitation. It was a miserable and deadly time of year to be shipwrecked without proper shelter and food, huddled in pits dug into frozen sand, with tattered sails for a roof and frozen fox corpses for walls. The primitive dwellings deteriorated throughout the winter, frayed by wind, snow, and rain.

"From the sea came thick mists and dampness that caused the sails to rot," Waxell recalled, "until they were no longer able to withstand the violence of the storms, but were blown away on the first gust, leaving us lying under the open sky." Savage winter gales pried through the cracks in the huts, tearing off the roofs and dumping sleet inside. After each storm, the able-bodied stood up and shook off the snow, swept their dugouts as best as they could, and readied themselves for the next storm. There was no "great, penetrating cold," but there were frequent hurricanes and "stormy winds with thick snow." The snow depth inland varied between six and nine feet. "The storms were so violent that on several occasions people getting out of their hollows to relieve nature were whirled away and would undoubtedly have been blown out to sea had they not flung themselves on the ground and clung to a stone or anything else that they were able to seize." Once Waxell was uplifted and nearly sucked out of his tent. He hung on by his hands while his legs flapped in the wind, and he was saved only when two companions each grabbed an arm and hauled him back in. Undoubtedly, the men's generalized weakness contributed to the perceived violence of the wind and storms, but it surely was not pleasant.

Throughout December and early January, the terrible scurvy plague continued once the snow covered everything. Steller could not find enough fresh herbs to fully drive away the disease. The monotonous diet consisted of fox, sea otter, and fried rye flour. The cooks took the salted rye flour, added water to it, and put it in a bowl for several days until it began to ferment and then fried it in seal oil. Although unpalatable, it filled empty stomachs. "Altogether, want, nakedness, cold, dampness, exhaustion, illness, impatience, and despair were the daily guests," Steller recalled. But at least the plague of foxes had subsided. As December wore on, many had been killed and others had grown wary. Outside of each dwelling pit, at Steller's urging, they placed barrels for food storage and constructed wooden racks three to four feet off the ground for hanging items and drying clothes when the wind was calm. Both of these strategies prevented fox attacks, since there was now no loose food lying about nor any personal item worth defiling or stealing.

After Bering died, the command of the expedition passed to the next in command, Lieutenant Waxell, even though he was still unable to rise from his place in the Barracks. Waxell, like Steller, proved to be a man of good cheer in the face of disaster, and he sought to bring up the spirits of the others, despite the grim situation. Also like Steller, he recognized the new social reality of the beach camp. "I considered it most advisable," he wrote, "to carry [orders] out with the greatest possible mildness and calmness. That was no place for exerting one's power and authority. Severity would have been quite pointless." He retained his position as leader, but he no longer commanded as a ranking naval officer. Either his appreciation of the circumstances or his own weakness and lethargy allowed for a decentralized authority and a general disregard for rules that he never would have permitted onboard the ship.

The general laxness, however, caused its own problems within the band of despairing and dying men. Of the five communal dugouts—which they variously referred to as pits, graves, yurts, or huts—four were clustered near each other in the original spot selected by Steller and Plenisner, while one camp was conspicuously positioned farther upstream along a sandy ridge. Here dwelled twelve men, mostly regular sailors. Their unofficial leader was Dmitry Ovtsin, the lieutenant who had been demoted to regular sailor prior to the voyage, ostensibly for having relations with a political exile during his explorations in Siberia. Bering had recognized Ovtsin's abilities and had given him the responsible position as his adjutant, but when Bering died Waxell did not want him in this role, and, according to navy protocol at least, he was again demoted to regular sailor. Ovtsin harbored a grudge, and Waxell feared a challenge to his leadership would come from this quarter. Ovtsin was a leader of the discontented, waiting for an opportunity to exploit weakness or incompetence, to wedge some authority for himself, or to increase his standing. Although Waxell was the commander, he was still so weak that he relied on others to nurse him back to health and to carry out his few orders. Waxell was not secure in his command or even convinced that he would live for long.

Among the rules that Waxell relaxed were the standard naval regulations regarding cards and gambling. The games started slowly and innocuously, and when Steller, with his pious upbringing, frowned on all forms of gambling, complained to Waxell, Waxell defended the practice, claiming that not only was he in too weak a position to be issuing commands, but he was in favor of the gaming. "The regulations or ukase against playing cards had been made without any thought of this deserted island," he replied, "because at that time it had not yet been discovered. If they had had any inkling then of our men's card-playing and of our pitiable circumstances, I was sure that they would have introduced a special paragraph giving permission for all suitable pastimes." Not only did Waxell not disapprove, but he actually had in his personal luggage many decks of cards that he gave or sold to the men. Since in December most of the men were still immobilized with scurvy or very weak, Waxell thought it a good way for them to pass the time. They could become despondent dwelling on their dire circumstances, and he hoped the games would distract them and help them to "overcome the melancholy" and to redirect them from searching about for someone on whom to pin the blame. He told Steller his opinions and reasoning and said that "as long as I remain in command," he would stick to his decision. After he died, however, he said that "my successors could deal with matters as they liked, for all I cared."

But Steller, true to his character, was not easily mollified when he thought he was in the right. He pointed out to Waxell the serious problems he observed that were caused by the "wretched gambling with cards." Though one hopes he did so in a more diplomatic manner than the way he wrote about it in his journal, this is unlikely to have been the case. Steller cast his critical eye about the sprawling camp and fumed that "whole days and nights nothing but card playing was to be seen in the dwellings. . . . In the morning, at inspection, no other topic of conversation was heard than: this one has won a hundred rubles or more, and that one has lost so and so much." Both Waxell and Steller had valid points—most of the men could hardly move, so playing cards was one of the only things they could do other than stare at the flapping tent walls and listen to the snow or hail pelting down or the ripping wind or, worse, the mumbled prayers or insensible groans of the sick and dying. They were desperately bored without work or recreation. Over time, rather than solving problems, however, the gambling created more. Steller claimed that the officers were using their better skills to win all the money and furs from the sailors. He meant Khitrov in particular and suggested that the real reason Waxell, and the other officers, allowed gambling was because they liked it and were winning. Some of the men lost so much that they began stealing otter pelts from others to pay their debts, and soon "hate, quarrels and strife were disseminated through all the quarters."

As December passed and some of the men regained a semblance of their former strength, the plague of scurvy was indeed supplanted by a plague of gambling that caused discord rather than unity. By then Waxell, Khitrov, and the other officers were too afraid of the men, at least some of them, to remove their one pastime. It could provoke a rebellion. And any discontent among the men would likely coalesce around Ovtsin, himself an already discontented former officer.

When Waxell refused even to acknowledge any of these legitimate concerns, Steller secretly began buying up the decks of cards and removing them from circulation. Waxell later discovered that most of the decks of cards he had sold or given to the sailors were in Steller's possession—a dangerous gambit to halt the gaming. Steller was nothing if not a man of conviction and principle. Nevertheless, it reveals how his stubbornness led to poor judgment, since he assumed the men would see the error of their ways and accept that it was all for the better once, like a parent punishing recalcitrant children, he had removed their toys. Waxell, in contrast, seemed to have a healthy appreciation of the possibilities for discord and the limits of power, perhaps stemming from his naval training and experience—once the gambling had started, he probably would not have commanded the authority to stop it. Why risk it and have his authority challenged over something he hoped would just go away on its own?

Another problem brought about by the gambling was overhunting of the one resource that was sustaining their waning lives: the sea otters. The gambling was "at first for money," Steller wrote. But eventually, money was "held in low esteem, and when this was gambled away, the fine sea otters had to offer up their costly skins." They all knew that the pelts were worth a fortune as trade items, particularly with the Chinese. Many sea-otter skins had been tossed to foxes in the first weeks ashore, but when the mariners' health had improved even a little, a new use was found for the pelts in the gambling bouts enthralling the camp, and they suddenly soared in value. Steller frowned when an individual "who had totally ruined himself tried to recoup himself through the poor sea otters, which were slaughtered without necessity and consideration only for their skins, their meat being thrown away."

To obtain sea-otter pelts, some of the men went "raging among the animals, without discipline and order, often only going to amuse each other," soon driving the animals from all the nearby spots where they had previously lived. Hunting was already made difficult by the lack of gunpowder, so it had to be done with sticks or clubs. The men would sneak up on sleeping or unsuspecting animals, pounce upon them, and club them, sometimes working in teams, one to herd, the other to do the clubbing. Soon the otters became attuned to this new predator, man, and became wary of approaching humans. It even seemed to Steller that a herd of them would post a guard to wake the others on the beach when they detected intruders. When otters came ashore, they would turn about with their noses in the air, sniffing for a whiff of the new smell that meant danger. Steller even thought that he saw blue foxes sneaking ahead of hunting parties, running along the beach and barking to wake the sleeping otters before they could be hunted. Nature, he fancied, was turning against them for the sin of gambling. The easy hunting of the early days soon became very challenging. The men had to organize nocturnal scouting expeditions even through ferocious and unpredictable snowstorms to get close enough to attack beached otters. Before the year was over, they had to hike four to six miles to get enough food, and by February 1742 they had to hike as far as twenty miles down the beach.

The depletion of resources around the camp also applied to fire-wood. So much wood was needed for the continuous fire in the center of the camp and the other smaller cooking fires that men were now obliged to walk for many miles along the beach to collect it, squinting at the horizon for lumps under the snow after storms, digging to retrieve the wood and carry it back to camp, strapped to their backs. For weakened sailors, these walks were agonizing affairs that took all day in foul weather. This increased travel to obtain animals and firewood fortunately paralleled the recovery of their strength.

Yet as the weeks went by, food was less and less plentiful. At dinner there were days when "the portions were sometimes so small that the entrails were not thrown away, not even the intestines, but cooked for the sick to eat, which they did, all of it, with great appetite." For some, who were dying or were the most ravaged by scurvy, it was difficult to open their ruined mouths to swallow sinewy strands of boiled sea otter. Waxell described their daily meal: "Even if you can perhaps endure the smell of sea otter meat, it is extremely hard and as tough as sole-leather and full of sinews, so that however much you chew at it, you have to swallow it in large lumps." Disgusting as sea-otter meat tasted, it was better than foxes.

Sometime on an unspecified date early in January, the carcass of an enormous whale washed ashore, several miles from camp. Although the blubber was "slightly rank" and it "must have been drifting dead about the sea for some considerable time," they soon came to rely on it during the period of scarcity before the arrival of spring. They called it "the provision store," and the partially butchered carcass remained on the beach for use whenever no other animals could be obtained for food. A group of men would hike to the location and flense large cubes of the blubber, load it into packs, and carry it back to camp, where they would cut it into small squares and fill a pot to boil the fat away so that the unpalatable "liquid train oil" could be discarded. What remained after straining were the nerves and sinews, which they cut into pieces and swallowed whole, without chewing. "It was easy to get the pieces down," Waxell recalled, "as we were never able to get all the oil out of them." The meat supply was also augmented by the discovery of other sources. The men killed a sea lion and butchered its enormous body on the beach and dragged quivering chunks of meat back to camp. It was a welcome respite from the monotony of sea otter and the occasional seal. They roasted it over fires, and Steller approvingly declared that "the meat was found to be of such exceptional quality and taste that we only wished soon to get hold of more. The fat was like beef-marrow, and the meat almost like veal." It was certainly better than visiting "the provision store" for rancid whale blubber.

All this meat contained vitamin C, and, since it was fresh and lightly cooked in soups as suggested by Steller, it slowly but surely brought an end to the scurvy epidemic. The meat and animal broths were nowhere as potent as specific fresh plants, but they were sufficient to slowly nourish the men back to health. Steller also had teams of men scrabbling at the snow-covered ground to locate crakeberry bushes that they boiled into tea. Six more men died in December, but only two died in January. On January 8, 1742, Ivan Lagunov was the last man to die of the scurvy epidemic. He, like the dozens who died on Bering Island, is a man for whom history records nothing other than his name and his job, sailor, and the date of his death. He merely had the dubious distinction of being the last to die in this way. Thirty-one of the seventy-seven men aboard the *St. Peter* had died of scurvy before Steller's herbal broths and sea-otter soups worked their effect. Only fourteen had proper burials on Bering Island, in a row adjacent to the camp and the river. The others had been pitched overboard into the ocean or carried away; many had been gnawed on by blue foxes. There were forty-six survivors in the camp, and by mid-January most of the survivors could, with effort, hobble about.

STELLER AND WAXELL ORGANIZED celebrations at regular intervals to help give structure to everyone's lives and to give the men something to look forward to, reminders of their previous lives that might help sustain their spirits through the darkest days of winter. They celebrated every Sunday and official national holidays, including "holy Christmas," as if we "were in the proper place and home." Nonetheless, Christmas had been a miserable affair, passed in darkness and cold. Steller invited the officers over, and all were entertained with "pleasant speeches" and toasts over cups of tea, "for lack of any other kinds of drink." Oddly, the one thing they had in plenty was tobacco. For whatever reason, the tobacco supply had not been damaged by the saltwater, and Steller made pipes from the wing bones of black albatrosses; they puffed away on pipes in the rustic squalor of their new community.

There had been little to celebrate for the first month on Bering Island, but by the end of December, the deaths had slowed, the camp had been built, and a basic unspoken organization had evolved. It was an equality-based system given order by the officers and Steller, in sort of first-among-equals roles. All their ceremonial clothes such as uniforms and "Sunday clothes" were repurposed into work clothes and distributed according to need. They all knew their jobs, and "consequently everyone at all times knew his business and duty without having to be reminded of it, and it made life flow without anxiety and resulted in cheerfulness and good feeling among us." Everyone was permitted to voice opinions at any meeting, and these opinions were evaluated without consideration for the person's former rank.

The year 1742 brought a new optimism. The days were slowly getting longer, and although the weather was as stormy and cold as ever, and hunting animals increasingly difficult, there was a sense that if they had made it this far, they could survive until spring. Once the beast of scurvy had been tamed, and nearly all the men could at least hobble about, the collective perspective on life once again changed. With the men slowly recovering from the disease, and with minds now cleared and able to focus on things other than immediate survival, the question of what to do with the ship and how to get off the island became daily topics. Whenever they exited their dugouts and stared across the beach, the first thing they saw was the sunken hulk of the *St. Peter* tilted and buried in the sand with waves slapping against the seaward side. It was a constant reminder of their doom, but as the new year began it also became the first problem that had to be addressed before any other considerations: What condition was the ship in, and would it ever float again? It had been all but confirmed that they were marooned on a deserted island, and their only hope of escape lay in some manner with the wreck of the *St. Peter*.

On January 18, 1742, Waxell went around the ramshackle village and informed the sailors and officers that he was convening a formal ship's council to go out to inspect the wreck and then to decide what should be done. It was his first important job as commander, other than allowing the men to gamble with cards. Since the ship did not look in good condition, and Waxell and Khitrov had already declared it unfit to sail, some felt the inspection was a mere formality. But the *St. Peter* was a government ship, and any decision to deliberately damage it would be scrutinized by imperial bureaucrats in St. Petersburg. Careers, and perhaps even lives, could be at stake. Also, while it was a navy ship and the officers were still in the Russian Navy, Waxell understood that the new social order that ruled the beach camp was not a purely naval order. Everyone should be consulted, since this was how things had been done since November and this approach had staved off internal dissent so far. It was probably still the best plan for keeping everyone optimistic and focused on getting home. Naval hierarchy and custom would have to wait until they were again at sea.

Waxell also knew that consensus was strategically the best route to avoid reprisals and punishment for himself afterward. By putting everything down in writing, there could be no later claims of disagreement, and if there was any disagreement on the best course of action now, he could prepare a written counterargument if needed. Certainly, there would be an accounting, an official inquiry into the death of so many men, including the commander, and the destruction of her imperial majesty's ship. Waxell was going to be scrutinized, and he wanted everything in writing to better defend himself against claims of professional or personal misconduct. So the men all came from their encampment and crossed the beach to the wreck. Some of the stronger ones scrambled aboard and delved down into the hold, while others inspected the masts and rigging. Waxell brought them together and made it clear that they had to come to a unanimous decision, that everyone had a right to voice their questions and ideas, and that he required as much input as possible. He then proclaimed, "God would give it His blessing, for He helps all who help themselves." Many suggestions were discussed, such as digging a trench to allow the ship to slide back out into water, or placing rollers under the hull and pushing it out into the bay. But in the end, it became obvious that no other timber was to be found on the island, so to construct anything, the materials would have to be cannibalized from the ship itself.

Over the next few days, Waxell wrote up an official document highlighting the general assessment of the ship. He called it "Statement on the Condition of the Ship," and it was a sobering list of damage and problems. There were no anchors left and no hope that they could recover one; the rudder had been destroyed and carried out to sea; the hull, keel, and sternpost were all damaged; the rigging, shrouds, and cables were rotted, torn, and unreliable; and, most important, the ship was buried up to a depth of eight feet in the water and sand and was therefore impossible to move. The *St. Peter*, Waxell concluded, "was not fit for a continuation of our voyage." Once the statement was written, Waxell read it aloud to the gathering and instructed all to sign the document. Only Dmitry

Ovtsin declined to do so. And so Waxell told him to put his objections in writing, which he presented to Waxell five days later. Ovtsin was perhaps showing his discontent against the officers for being shunned by that group or attempting to manufacture a division in the group, something to exploit. Perhaps he simply feared for his career and wanted to record his opposition to the destruction of the ship.

On January 27, Ovtsin presented his "Counterstatement by the Sailor Dmitry Ovtsin," which he addressed, probably mockingly, "To His Highness Lieutenant Waxell." It was a numbered listing of the original points made by Waxell, along with Ovtsin's brief and overly optimistic assessment of the ship's condition. He stated that the rigging could be repaired, the conditions in the spring might be good for refloating the ship, they might be able to dredge the sand for the lost anchors, and that timber for repairing the hull and rudder "could probably be found." In spite of these bold statements, he was well aware that none of the expeditions sent out to investigate the island or any of the hunters had seen a single tree that could be used for this purpose. Ovtsin concluded that "at present it is difficult to say how badly damaged the bottom is; and even if it were, it could be repaired." It was too early, he claimed, with too much snow and ice, to determine the fate of the ship.

Waxell and Khitrov read his claims; consulted with all the crew, the officers, and Steller; and built a consensus against the claims. Then they wrote an official "Rebuttal" on January 29, "after listening to his statement and reasons they were rejected by all who were present, because on January 18, they had examined the ship and found it unseaworthy." They reiterated the fact that they had no timber and none had been found on the island, they had no materials to repair sails and rigging for such a large ship, and they did not have enough men to sail it even if it were repaired. Waxell and Khitrov agreed to one final inspection in the spring or when the water was drained from the hold during a low tide, to confirm what they suspected, but that barring any new information, the *St. Peter* should be broken up and "out of the wreck some kind of small vessel should be made to take us to Kamchatka." It was a difficult and emotional decision—the *St. Peter* had been their home for many months, and even the wreck, looming always through the mist on the beach, was a beacon of stability and their only hope of escape.

The *St. Peter* was stoutly constructed with iron bands and nails, and it was hard to be certain of the success of breaking up the ship to construct something new. "I did not want the entire blame heaped upon myself," Waxell wrote. If things went wrong, "there would be as many proposals as heads," and he feared being told afterward that "if only we had acted upon this or that, or on any of the other forty suggestions, it would have been all right." Waxell was also worried for his life, not just from the unpredictable directives from St. Petersburg but from the men closer at hand, who might blame him and turn on him if things went badly. He still believed that breaking up the ship was their best hope of escape and survival.

The decision to cut up and dismantle the ship sat heavily on everyone's mind, even when they knew it was the only way forward, but the decision was made easier to accept only a day into February, during what Steller called a "violent northwest gale and a very high tide." During the mighty storm, enormous waves and a heavy tide pounded against the *St. Peter* and lifted it in the surf and drove it farther onto the sandy beach. The wreck now listed well above the regular high-tide line. At first there was excitement when they climbed aboard and noticed that the hold was filled with water— this indicated that perhaps the hull had not been breached. But this elation was short-lived. It wasn't just water sloshing in the hold of the ship. It was still nearly filled with sand, and there were cracks in the hull. There would be no relaunching it.

Early February was still the height of winter. Winds blew ferociously, snow smothered the land, and the skies were gray and overcast nearly every day. It was too early to begin the process of breaking up the *St. Peter*. They would have to wait for spring and warmer weather and for the men to be further along on their long, painful climb back to strength. The months passed slowly, with regular camp routine, hunting expeditions, and firewood expeditions taking up most of their energy and most of their waking hours. On one noteworthy day, February 7, it was clear and bright and pleasant, the first fine day they could remember and a harbinger of milder weather. In the afternoon there was a strong wind from the west, followed by "a violent hissing and roaring—ever stronger the closer it came to us." It was the foreshock of an earthquake that rattled the island for six minutes. It knocked down the walls of their dwellings, and sand poured into the pits, covering resting and still recovering men. Steller rushed out to inspect the ocean but saw no telltale surge in water that might precede a tidal wave. All was clear and sunny. Far from discouraging the men for the extra work repairing the camp, or frightening them with the winds and rumbling, the earthquake roused spirits all around—earthquakes and volcanic eruptions were common in Kamchatka, and so, they reasoned, they must be within easy sailing distance of home. They just needed a vessel to sail.

CHAPTER 12

A NEW *ST. PETER*

O NLY WHEN THE FIRST tentative, tender green shoots poked through the snow in March did Waxell and Steller truly believe that they would survive. Although the deaths had ended in January and the men had regained their ability to get up and move and provide for themselves, it would be these early "herbs and plants" that secured their survival. Steller scoured the snow-covered dunes inland from the beach and located several plants he deemed antiscorbutic and helped others locate them in the slowly melting landscape. Waxell praised Steller for giving "excellent assistance, for he was a good botanist. He collected and showed us many green herbs, some for drinking, some for eating, and by taking them we found health noticeably improved. From my own experience I can assert that none of us became well or recovered his strength completely before we began eating something green."

With spring came lighter days, warmer temperatures, and less rain, but it was often still stormy and overcast. Everything was damp, and cloth and leather had weathered the winter poorly. But as the vestiges of scurvy retreated and vitality returned to the men's limbs, Waxell was eager for more information on their location.

They believed they were on an island to the east of the Kamchatka coast, but how big was this island? Did it have any other resources in the more distant quarters? Without accurate knowledge of their location, Waxell knew they couldn't make good decisions about the future. Hunting for food was becoming an ever-greater challenge, as the increasingly wary animals became difficult to catch in numbers sufficient to sustain the appetites of the forty-six hungry men. The mere sight of a man in the distance drove sea otters into a frenzy, and they would rush to the water.

So, on February 24, Assistant Navigator Kharlam Yushin took four men on an expedition north "to make a careful observation of the country," but his party was thwarted by the weather after one week of trudging through the slushy snow along the base of huge cliffs that extended into the sea. They traveled only sixty versts (thirty-seven miles) from camp through this dramatic terrain before they returned. Yushin reported that they had seen an island to the east, which was an inaccurate observation, perhaps a distant cloud bank. Other men had been hunting sea otters in faraway regions, but they brought back no new information about the island. On March 10, Waxell called for a gathering and then proposed another expedition south across the country, following a different route, this time to be led by the boatswain, Alexei Ivanov, a man universally respected for his competence. Ivanov and four men departed on March 15, and they returned after only several days of strenuous climbing over hills and mountains and reported having seen the sea on the western coast. They brought back pieces of a small boat that had washed ashore. One of the men, Ivanov Akulov, definitively identified the wreckage as part of a boat he himself had constructed in Kamchatka the previous year. And most important, Ivanov excitedly described a new animal that lived in profusion along the beaches of the western coast, one that he called a "sea bear" but that Steller identified as a fur seal.

This news was so electrifying—a new source of food—that Ivanov and his men were quickly sent out again, accompanied by Steller and three others. They had instructions to go until they "came to some mainland or the end of the island." If they should spy the mainland, perhaps along a connecting pier of land, two men were to keep going and report to Avacha Bay, while the others were to return with the good news. Waxell still desperately hoped that they were situated on a spit of land connected to Kamchatka, despite all the evidence to the contrary. The certain discovery, though, was the confirmation of a new food source. As the weather was warmer now, this new route became the standard twelve-mile trek for hunting parties. The route was not only exhausting but also dangerous, due to fast-approaching storms that could trap men where there was no shelter. On April 1, a vicious storm trapped four men from a group led by Steller. "No one could keep an eye on his feet or see a step of him," he recalled. Six feet of snow fell during a short period of a few hours in the night, and they were forced to sleep out in the open. In the morning, they were entirely covered in snow, and they had to break out and stagger back to the camp, arriving "senseless and speechless, and so stiff from the cold that, like immovable machines, they could hardly move their feet." The main encampment on the eastern beach was just then digging out from under the same heavy spring snow. They rushed to strip Steller and his companions of their wet clothes and boiled tea while they shivered under blankets, nearly hypothermic. One man was snow-blind and one was missing. They sent out searchers to find the man and discovered him an hour later, stumbling about delirious and in "a pitiable condition." He had fallen into a creek, his clothes were frozen solid to his body, and his hands and feet were frostbitten. They feared he would die, but Steller revived him. Steller preferred not to take the credit himself and proclaimed that "God, however, pulled him through without harm."

Despite the need for a more secure food supply, Waxell decided to wait until the weather stabilized after this devastating storm before crossing the midisland mountains again. But hunters were not able to catch animals on the eastern beach anymore, and they quickly ran short on food. Despite the danger, another small hunting expedition, consisting of Steller, Plenisner, Lepekhin, and another man, set off along the same trail to the west on April 5, a clear and pleasant spring day. The crossing was uneventful, and on the western beach they hunted many seals and dragged them back to the base of the cliff and sat relaxing around a campfire to spend the night before returning. A midnight storm soon dumped vast piles of wet snow on them, and they could hardly keep their footing for the violent wind. They ran around in circles for hours keeping each other awake. Steller by "constantly smoking tobacco tried to keep myself warm and banish the bitterness of death." The dawning day was nearly as dark as night, and they knew they had to find shelter or they would die. Lepekhin had fallen asleep and was buried under the snow, and they rushed to dig him out and drag him to his feet. Then they all put a final effort into searching for a crevasse or cave. After many hours of fruitless wandering, they were "full of despair and half dead."

Finally, Lepekhin came across a wide crack that led into the cliff, and they all hastened into it and out of the storm. They then dragged wood and some of the meat inside. The cave proved to be roomy, with a separate storeroom to keep food "safe from the thievish and malicious foxes," which had followed them to the hunting grounds. The cave even had a natural chimney to dissipate smoke so they could cook inside without asphyxiating themselves. They huddled out of the storm for three days before it blew out. During the storm, blue foxes had crept from the hills and devoured the carcasses of the animals they had left on the beach. They had to hunt again before returning fully loaded with meat and news on April 8. They made use of the incredible cave discovery for many months into the summer as a hunting base and called it Steller's Cave. For the next two months, the western beach and Steller's Cave were a common destination and the fur seals the primary food source. But these seals were not a gourmand's treat. Waxell reported that their "flesh is revolting, because it has a very strong and very unpleasant smell, more or less like that of an old goat. The fat is yellow, the flesh hard and sinewy." They universally "loathed" it, but it was better than starving.

At the same time, another hunting party led by Yushin had gone to the north of the island and had been held up for seven days by a similar storm. They were trapped in a crevasse by high tides, without food or fire. The men at camp believed that they had been "either drowned or crushed to death by snow dashing down from the mountains," and there was great rejoicing when they saw them trudging across the beach. Yushin brought confirmation that they were on an island. Ivanov had also been on a journey and returned around the same time. They had "doubled the northern cape on the other side" of the island so that, between the members of various exploratory parties, they had all but circumnavigated the island. They still had no exact idea where the island was situated, and both Yushin and Ivanov claimed to have seen land to the east. Steller also claimed to have seen land "very clearly" to the northeast, and they agreed that they were on the westernmost stretch of the American continent. Actually, there is no land within sight of Bering Island in any direction. Steller believed they lay marooned closer to America than Kamchatka. Waxell and Steller disagreed about how great the distance was between Kamchatka and Alaska. Steller thought the distance could be sailed in three or four days from Avacha Bay, while Waxell maintained it would take up to eight days at sea. Both were outrageously off in their estimates. The previous spring, it had taken them six weeks to cross the Pacific to Alaska, and it would take future ships sailing along the safest and most efficient route about three weeks.

On April 9, Waxell convened a meeting of all the men to share the newly agreed-upon geographical information and to confirm plans for the *St. Peter*. Yushin and Ivanov presented the story of their discoveries, and then Waxell rose to speak as commander. "The time has come to consider how we [will] escape from this wretched spot," he announced. He asked each person to give his opinion clearly, as "our plight is the same for one and all." He wrote that "the lowest seaman longed for deliverance just as much as the first officer; therefore we should all stand together as one man." During the gathering, there emerged three main ideas for the planned escape.

The first idea, put forth yet again by Ovtsin, the ex-lieutenant who had opposed the initial proposal of breaking up the *St. Peter* back in February, was to make a great effort to repair and raise the *St. Peter*, even if it took all the resources of the men and most of the summer, in the hope that they would be successful in launching it before the storm season. Waxell had long given up on this plan. But to placate the handful of men who advocated it, he outlined again why it was a poor option. The hull had such serious and large breaks in it that the water level inside the ship was always exactly the same as the level of the water outside in the bay. They had not the men or the equipment to undertake this type or scale of repair. Dredging a canal to drag the ship out into deeper water off the beach was impossible because the surf and tides replenished the sand as quickly as the limited number of men could dig. "We could have gone on digging for all eternity without making any progress," he stated. The most convincing argument against this plan was that if they devoted the summer to it and failed, which was likely given the condition of the wrecked ship, then they would be stuck on the island for another winter—a dreaded prospect. They needed a different plan, and the only feasible option was to break up the *St. Peter* and construct a smaller ship. But the shape, style, and size of the new vessel were not immediately obvious. It would have to be much smaller to be sailed by a smaller crew, yet it would still have to withstand a potentially rough ocean voyage.

After Ovtsin's proposal, the next suggestion was to do a little work quickly on the longboat, strap some sailcloth over it to make a primitive "deck" so it would have a chance of crossing to Kamchatka without foundering, and choose about six men to sail away and report the location of the island to the garrison at Petropavlovsk and hope that a rescue ship would arrive before the end of summer. Waxell did not immediately dismiss this idea, but he had serious reservations that he enumerated to the men: Because they did not know how far they were from Kamchatka, the small "boat would not be able to withstand the least bad weather but would incontestably founder, and all aboard her would be lost." The majority of the men would be left to fend on the island, living in a state of "anxiety and doubt," waiting passively to see if they would be rescued or if they would have to spend another winter somehow surviving on the rapidly diminishing number of easily hunted animals. This plan was "unreasonable and dangerous," Waxell stated, but could be revisited if nothing else worked out since it required little work—just a great deal of bravery for the chosen few and a great deal of patience and anxiety for the remaining forty. Waxell concluded his speech with the claim that "it would be a great relief and comfort for us if we who had survived so many sufferings should find consolation together" and that if any further disaster befell them, they could all endure it together. Likewise, if they reached home, their "deliverance" would be as a group.

In the end, Waxell persuaded all of the men, even Ovtsin, to go with the third option: dismantle the *St. Peter* and build a new vessel about half the size from the scavenged wood and materials. After the meeting, they all signed a document titled "Decision Made on Determination That Land Is an Island," which also included the conclusion that the *St. Peter* should be broken up, as there was no way to return except by sea and the *St. Peter* could not be floated or repaired. The document also provided some details on who would be working on the ship and who would be responsible for hunting for the entire group. They decided that the remaining salty groats and rye flour would be reserved for use on the return voyage, which would take place later in the summer. On May 2, Waxell, Khitrov, and several other officers searched for a suitable place to begin laying the foundations for the new ship and conveniently agreed that the best spot was "on the beach directly in front of the ship."

As the weather warmed throughout April and into May, the island came alive with plants and birds. Three weeks were spent unloading everything from the wreck, prying the wood planks from the frame, carrying it all to the beach, and placing it in ordered piles. All the tools were prepared, laid out in order, and a small forge was constructed to make new specialized tools such as hammers and crowbars. This was fired by making charcoal from all the new driftwood that had washed ashore throughout the winter and was visible on the sandy beach now that the snow had melted. "Grindstones were dressed and placed in troughs, tools were cleaned of rust and sharpened, and a smithy erected, crowbars, iron wedges and large hammers forged." It was tedious and exhausting work and not very exciting, since it was only preparation for the main task ahead.

There were twelve men skilled in using axes or who had shipbuilding or carpentry experience. These men were to work continuously on the dismantling and reconstruction of the new ship. All of the others, with the exception of Waxell, Khitrov, and Steller, were to be placed on a constantly rotating three-day duty roster—a day of hunting (which involved hiking many hours across the island), followed by a day of camp duty, followed by a day of assisting the carpenters in whatever needed doing. All the meat was to be brought to the camp each morning and then distributed by one of the petty officers to the designated cook of each of the five camps. This routine, with minor exceptions, went on for months throughout the spring and summer. The remaining flour was strictly rationed for the home voyage; each person's monthly allotment was reduced to twenty pounds, so that by Steller's calculation, each person would have twenty pounds of flour for the home voyage. There was only one skilled shipbuilder who had survived, a Siberian Cossack named

Sava Starodubstov, who had worked on several ships, including the *St. Peter*, with Spangberg while at Okhotsk. Starodubstov told Waxell that if he was given "the proportions of the ship he would build her so solid that, with God's help, we should be able to put to sea in her without risk." So great was his work that Waxell admitted they never could have made the new ship without his knowledge, and, after they returned, he petitioned the provincial chancellery in Yeniseisk for the man to be promoted into the ranks of the minor nobility of Siberia.

The work gave the entire group of increasingly ragged-looking survivors a focus, something to unify their dreams and prevent despair and infighting. Waxell rose in stature as a leader, while Steller earned the men's respect for his role in preserving everyone's lives as a scientist and physician and for his tender care and spiritual council of the sick. But it was Waxell who would get the men off the island. Like Steller, who buoyed spirits with his optimism and appeals to the divine, Waxell maintained a hearty and cheerful persona and kept up his courage. He never complained aloud and strove to highlight anything good that happened, even if it was to note a change in diet or to appreciate a mild day. Waxell, as much as Steller, became a guiding symbol of survival and hope. During the difficult months, once scurvy had been defeated and the foxes driven off and the scourge of gambling abated, the quarreling factions, for the most part, settled into a harmonious pattern that had not existed on the ship. Rank and privilege all but disappeared, and work was shared equally and without complaint; they all knew that their lives depended upon it. The few "malcontents" who shied away from work were frowned upon by their comrades, and Waxell regained most of the authority as a naval commander that he had lost during the first few months ashore, when survival trumped social order. Now that there was a clear objective to unify the unruly band, Waxell asserted his command when he saw shirkers failing to contribute. "I used my authority to force them to work," he wrote.

The actual construction of the new ship began on May 6 with the "erecting of the stern and the sternpost." It was planned to be thirty-six feet long, with a twelve-foot beam and a depth of five feet and three inches. The men took the excess timber from the old ship, the timbers and boards deemed unsuitable or unneeded for the new ship, and quickly used them to build better dwellings that were aboveground—the spring runoff from the melting snow combined with rain was routinely flooding the pits. The first day that the skeleton of the new ship took shape on the beach was a day of great joy and hope. At the day's end, Waxell invited the whole community, apart from the absent hunters, to join him in a celebratory toast. They all brought their own mugs, bowls, or cups "or whatever they had." As a special treat, Waxell had supervised the boiling, in the great cauldron over a fire, of a Siberian drink called *saturnan*. It was customarily made by frying wheat in fresh butter and then blending it with hot brewed tea until it "becomes as thick as cooked chocolate." But Waxell, "not having any of these ingredients," improvised with "train [seal or whale] oil instead of butter, musty rye-flour in place of wheat flour, and crakeberry plants instead of tea." Nevertheless, the drink passed muster, and they all became "quite gay and cheerful, without anyone becoming intoxicated." Steller wrote, "We enjoyed ourselves pretty well."

After that date, the work progressed slowly because of insufficient food for the workers. There had been just barely enough food to keep everyone fed, if not fully satiated. Hunting the animals without guns and the challenge of hauling the meat from the other side of the island meant that it was never abundant. By now most of the men wore tattered shirts and had no shoes. Walking barefoot over the mountains and returning to the camp over the passes with great chunks of meat strapped to themselves front and back was damaging their feet. The diet now consisted of great quantities of the repulsive "sea bears," or fur seals, but at least at this time of the year, it was the females and young that proliferated on the beach and not just the vomit-inducing old bulls they had first subsisted upon. According to Khitrov, even the females and the young were still "quite savage and attack people." Steller, ever precise in his descriptions, conveyed the brutality of the hunt. "The beasts are so tenacious of life that two or three men beating only their heads with clubs could scarcely kill them with two hundred blows, and frequently would have to rest and refresh themselves two or three times. . . . When the cranium is broken into little bits and almost all the brains have gushed out and all the teeth have been broken, the beast still attacks the men with his flippers and keeps on fighting."

At the end of May, a one-hundred-foot whale carcass washed ashore about four miles from the camp. As it was "quite fresh," it provided them with blubber for many months, which they stored in barrels and made available for everyone's use. The blubber kept them from starving, though it wasn't very appetizing. And always, just offshore, like sleepy sea monsters, ponderously and unselfconsciously rising and sinking beneath the waves as they feasted upon seaweeds, were enormous whalelike mammals that none of them had ever seen before. They all knew that a single one of these mysterious beasts would solve their hunger for weeks, since the animals were so huge. They dreamed of killing one as May progressed, but it would be a dangerous undertaking.

ONCE THE INITIAL NIGHTMARE of scurvy had abated and the men and officers were busy dismantling the old *St. Peter* to construct the smaller ship, Steller was freed from immediate responsibility and had time to devote to his great passion, the study of the natural world—the reason he had crossed Russia to Siberia and sailed to Alaska in the first place. Much of his posthumous fame is a result of these observations, however unscientific they may be by modern standards. Steller spent months observing the behavior, migration

patterns, diet, life cycle, and life history of several of the most
prominent and unique creatures that were endemic to either Bering
Island, the Aleutian Islands, or coastal Alaska. Although the sea
otters were his personal favorites, he also described in detail the sea
lions (a species later named Steller's sea lion) and fur seals, which
"covered the whole beach to such an extent that it was not possible
to pass without danger to life and limb." Even the blue foxes, which
much to the relief of all, had retreated into the hills for spring mating received their share of his time. He also prepared a catalog of
plants found on the island.

Steller noted and studied three species of birds not found in Europe or Asia: a "white sea raven . . . impossible to reach because it
only alights singly on the cliffs facing the sea" that has never been
found by a naturalist since; "a special sea eagle with a white head
and tail" that today is known as Steller's sea eagle, one of the three
types of American eagles now believed to be extinct; and "a special
kind of large sea raven with a callow white ring around the eyes
and red skin about the beak." The spectacled cormorant, as it is
now known, was a flightless penguin-like bird that was as large as
a goose. It was easy to catch and was hunted to extinction in the
coming years despite being, according to Steller, plentiful during
the winter of 1741–1742. A single bird, he noted, "was sufficient for
three starving men." Steller was the first and only naturalist to see
the bird before it disappeared. He also wrote about countless other
migratory birds that visited the island for brief periods of time.

The most populous creature that Steller studied was the sea otter,
a friendly communal animal that he observed throughout the voyage whenever the ship approached land. They were playful creatures
that offered welcome enjoyment to all the mariners until someone
remembered, during the winter gambling spree over the winter, that
their skins were extremely valuable. The furs of these creatures were
highly sought in China, and throughout the later winter and spring
hundreds, perhaps thousands, were killed and stripped of their skins.

Steller was outraged by the wanton slaughter. The men, hardened by years of harsh life in Kamchatka and the dreadful sufferings of the past winter, saw the otters as their ticket to a life of ease. They set upon the animals ferociously, clubbing them, drowning them, and stabbing them until the large herds were all but absent from the entire eastern side of the island. By late spring, it became very difficult to kill the remaining few because the intelligent creatures sent out sentries to warn of approaching hunters. Many men began collecting and hoarding the pelts, anticipating selling them for profit upon their return. A prime pelt could be worth twenty rubles in Kamchatka, two or three times that farther west in Siberia, but as much as one hundred rubles at the Chinese frontier.

Steller spent weeks making mental notes of sea-otter behavior for his treatise and then scratched out the text in his damp notebook at camp. He observed:

> If they have the luck to escape, they begin, as soon as they are in the water, to mock their pursuers in such a manner that one cannot look on without particular pleasure. Now they stand upright in the water like a man and jump up and down with the waves and sometimes hold the forefoot above the eyes as if they wanted to scrutinize you closely in the sun. . . . If a sea otter is overtaken and sees nowhere any escape it blows and hisses like an angry cat. When struck it prepares itself for death by turning on the side, draws up the hind feet, and covers the eyes with the forefeet. When dead it lies like a person, with the front feet crossed over the breast.

During countless hours of observation, including one six-day excursion to the south of the island to study them, Steller recorded, among other things, their preferred foods, playful games, size and skeletal structure, mating practices, and intense attachment to their young.

He believed that the sea otters, more than any other creature he encountered on the voyage, deserved the greatest respect, although he also thought they were lazy. He wrote:

Altogether in life it is a beautiful and pleasing animal, cunning and amusing in its habits. . . . Seen when they are running, the gloss of their hair surpasses the blackest velvet. They prefer to lie together in families, the male with its mate, the half-grown young and the very young sucklings all together. The male caresses the female by stroking her, using the forefeet as hands, and places himself over her; she, however, often pushes him away from her for fun and in simulated coyness, as it were, and plays with her offspring like the fondest mother. Their love for their young is so intense that they expose themselves to the most manifest danger of death. When their young are taken away from them, they cry bitterly, like a small child, and grieve so much that, as I came to know on several occasions, after ten to fourteen days they grow as lean as a skeleton, become sick and feeble, and will not leave the shore.

Perhaps Steller's greatest scientific contribution, however, was his classic description of the northern manatee, the giant Steller's sea cow. His description is the only account of this fabulous creature, whose appearance is between a whale and a seal. As with the spectacled cormorant, Steller was the only naturalist ever to see a Steller's sea cow and study it. The huge whalelike beasts grew to more than thirty feet in length, traveled in large clusters, and fed voraciously on the great strands of seaweed in the sheltered coves of the island. They never left the water, but their backs were exposed to the air while they fed. Underfed men with a constant hunger cast their eyes from their jobs as they toiled away on the carcass of the old ship and observed the beasts languidly passing by within a stone's throw of the beach. By Steller's estimate, each of the largest sea cows weighed more than seven thousand pounds, around four tons—a lot of meat for hungry men.

On May 21, Waxell gave the men a break from hammering and sawing and set out to try to hunt a sea cow. The previous day, he had the smith forge a huge iron hook weighing fifteen to eighteen pounds and secured it to a thick ship's cable. Five men got into the longboat with the hook and rowed quietly out to where the closest sea cows grazed with their heads angled downward, focused on the sea grasses. The strongest man leaned over and rammed the sharp hook between the animal's ribs, and then the forty or so men ashore hauled on the cable. But the sea cow was too strong. Seemingly unperturbed by the hook, the beast slowly moseyed farther from shore, dragging all the men with it into the surf until they let go. Several times they tried this strategy and always lost the tug-of-war. They snapped cables, lost hooks, and became disconsolate to see their time and energy wasted, as the sea cows escaped time after time.

Steller came up with a better plan, but it required two boats, which meant repairing the small yawl, which had been damaged during the shipwreck. It took until near the end of June for the repairs to be completed. By this time, the men were working on planking the hull of the new vessel. On the day of the hunt, the two small boats rowed in tandem into the herd of grazing sea cows, one filled with men armed with spears, the other filled with rowers and a man with a large sharp harpoon, with a rope attached that was held by the men ashore. When they were near the beast, the harpooner plunged the hook into its hide, and the men on the beach hauled on the cable. The armed men, meanwhile, rowed close and began stabbing and plunging into its back until,

> tired and completely motionless, it was attacked with bayonets, knives and other weapons and pulled up on the beach. Immense slices were cut from the still living animal, but all it did was shake its tail furiously and make such resistance with its forelimbs that big

strips of the cuticle were torn off. In addition it breathed heavily, as if sighing. From the wounds on its back the blood spurted upward like a fountain. As long as the head was under water no blood flowed, but as soon as it raised the head up to breathe the blood gushed forth anew.

They butchered it on shore and hauled the meat back to their dwelling, "rejoicing" at their good fortune. Some blubber was eaten fresh. After being cured for a few days, it was "as agreeably yellow as the best Holland butter" and when boiled "surpasses in sweetness and taste the best beef fat." It was the color of fresh olive oil. The taste, like "sweet almond oil," was so good that they drank it by the cupful and was a welcome break from the monotony of their diet. Even the meat, though somewhat tough in texture, was indistinguishable from beef in flavor. Of particular noteworthiness, for a large quantity of meat in a camp without refrigeration, was that it survived two full weeks "without becoming offensive, in spite of its being so defiled by the blowflies as to be covered with worms all over." Now that they had figured out how to do it, they killed a sea cow approximately every two weeks until July 31, when they killed eight of them and salted the meat for the return voyage. Waxell claimed that "of all the foods we ate during our time on the island, the manatee was the best. . . . Eating it, we felt considerably better and became quite active." Without the sea cows as food, they never could have fed themselves while working on the new ship.

Although the sea cows became easy to catch, tasted delicious, and were a much-needed source of nourishment, Steller did more than just eat them. He recorded all he could of their behavior during different seasons, their mating rituals and rearing of their young, and other living patterns. He dissected one large specimen and was astonished that the heart alone weighed thirty-six and a half pounds. The stomach was six feet long and five feet wide, so swollen with seaweed that he and three helpers strained their backs hauling it from the carcass at the end of a long rope. He wrote down, in perfect Latin, a full description of every portion of the beast from its eyes, skin, and feet to joints, muscles, bone structure, breasts, and mouth. And he commissioned a draftsman, probably Plenisner, to sketch six precise drawings to scale, depicting his dissection. Unfortunately, all the drawings were later lost somewhere in Siberia.

One of Steller's most subtle observations was that the huge beasts appeared to be monogamous, perhaps mating for life. After one large female was hauled ashore, he was startled by the behavior of the male. "It is a most remarkable proof of their conjugal affection," he wrote, "that the male, after having tried with all his might, although in vain, to free the female caught by the hook, and in spite of the beating we gave him, nevertheless followed her ashore, and that several times, even after she was dead, he shot unexpectedly up to her like a speeding arrow. Early next morning, when we came to cut up the meat and bring it to the dugout, we found the male again standing by the female, and the same I observed once more on the third day when I went there myself." The Steller's sea cow was hunted to extinction for food in the following years as the Russian Empire expanded east to Alaska.

Steller's opportunity to study the marine creatures of the fog-bound Aleutian Islands was unparalleled, and he knew it. His description of Bering Island includes a discussion of the habits and anatomy of nearly every creature that frequented the island, including observations of their seasonal activities and their behavior. He also wrote about dozens of plants, including flowers, shrubs, and others that formed a thick and dense tangle over most of the low places inland apart from the dunes near the camp. His descriptions were precise and insightful, and he engaged his friend Plenisner to sketch dozens of illustrations to accompany them. As an afterthought, to fulfill his obligations as set out in his orders, Steller also reported to Waxell that during his rambles and investigations of the island, he "had prospected the island for metals and minerals and had found none."

With the sea-cow hunt relieving anxiety over food and freeing up labor, the work on the new ship proceeded rapidly. By mid-July the hull was fully planked. The design of the new vessel confirms necessity as the mother of invention. Wooden structures were adapted for new purposes. "For the keel," Waxell recalled, "we used the old ship's mainmast which was sawed off three feet above the deck. . . . The remaining stump had to serve as the new vessel's prow. The sternpost we made from a capstan we had had on the old ship." Other masts could be transferred, because even though most were broken, the new ship was smaller and needed shorter masts and spars. Since the hull on the old *St. Peter* proved to be more damaged than they had estimated, the new hull was completed with old deck planks. "These were full of nail and bolt holes and much splintered and cracked from being wrenched loose." The most damaged pieces were used for a second layer of interior planking, secured with giant spikes. They built a small cabin in the rear just large enough for the principal leaders, Waxell, his son, Khitrov, and Steller. The galley was built in the front, and sleeping room for the crew was in the hold, below the single deck. It was clear to all that the ship would be small and crowded for the number of men.

As August approached and the ship took form, there was a palpable excitement. Any who had worked reluctantly or slowly, urged to action under Waxell's scrutiny, now moved with vigor and purpose, without exhortations or commands. Men rowed into the bay to search for the anchors and found the small grappling, others picked apart old ropes and heated the segments to melt the tar and then used it to caulk the hull, while still more repaired barrels for fresh-water or hunted and salted sea cows. On August 1, Waxell again called a meeting of all the men on the beach in front of the ship. He announced, "Our ship with God's help will be soon finished." He then began a discussion of the future. It was obvious that all of the equipment, supplies, and materials from the old *St. Peter* would never fit in the new ship. Much would have to be left on the island if all the men were to sail away in the new ship. Even though Khitrov had inventoried everything and certified that most of it was "worth-less and rotten," it was still government property and had value. The nearly two thousand pounds of items slated for abandonment on the island included all the artillery and associated equipment; all the axes, crowbars, hammers, saws, and other tools; surplus naviga-tional items such as compasses, lanterns, and sounding cables; flags; copper cooking pots and utensils; and surplus tobacco. Even during all their months of smoking ashore, it still hadn't been consumed.

No one wanted to be left behind to guard these items, no matter how valuable, and they all concluded that it would be "dangerous," since there was no food apart from what could be hunted. "If we should leave a guard, we should have to come after him next year. There is no harbor here, nothing but rocks and reefs and the open sea, and there is great danger in wrecking the vessel." Therefore, "taking these arguments into consideration," they unanimously agreed to leave no one behind on the island. Once again, they all signed the agreement to spread the blame, should any be forth-coming. There was no real intention to leave anyone behind, and it is hard to imagine their actually doing so, waving good-bye to the lone stranger as the rest sailed away, but Waxell and Khitrov wanted a written record of all of their decisions, showing the una-nimity of the crew. They planned to construct a storehouse out of scrap wood to protect the material from the continual fog and rain, on the off chance a future expedition was shipwrecked. Room was made in the new ship for nearly nine hundred sea-otter pelts, apportioned to each person according to rank. Somehow Steller ended up with more than three hundred, perhaps as gifts for his services as pastor and physician.

IN THE FINAL WEEKS before the departure, everyone was busy preparing food and making piles on the beach. "No one wanted to be idle, because everyone was exceedingly anxious for deliverance from this desert island." They had to launch the ship before they could load it and had constructed wooden runnels or a sliding bilge block, leading from the beach out into the water. This was a mighty construction, as it needed to be 150 feet long (45 meters) to get the ship clear off the sandy beach. Waxell was nervous because once the ship was afloat, it would essentially be unprotected from the open sea, and a storm or strong offshore wind could drive the vessel ashore again and deprive them "of our last hope of rescue." On August 8, a typical overcast day with sporadic rain and wind, Waxell judged the time right to catch a high tide and launch the ship into the water. After a quick prayer and a toast to the new ship with *burda*, the drink made from fermented or soured flour paste boiled in water and seal oil, they began winching the ship along the runners. The ship was too heavy. The runners pressed into the sand, and the ship became stuck. A wave of horror washed over everyone. They rushed about, trying to lift the ship higher and hauling on ropes, to no avail. The tide receded, leaving the ship stuck lopsided in the sand. Waxell rallied everyone with good cheer, and they spent the day jacking the ship higher by wedging planks under the runners. The next day, they hauled on the ropes again, and the ship slowly slid into the water and was moored in eighteen feet, tethered to the shore with ropes. They named the ship after the old one, a new

St. Peter, only it was now called a "hooker," the term for a smaller single-masted ship. The ship later remained in use for many years as a transport vessel between Okhotsk and Kamchatka.

Now the race was on. The weather was calm and breezy, good sailing weather, but no one knew how long these conditions would last. Using the two small boats, they all began working day and night, loading the ship with everything for the voyage, stopping only when exhausted. Since they had no idea how long they might be at sea, they needed a great deal of food and water in addition to all the regular materials for running the ship, including the ballast. Men hastened to set the masts, hang the anchor, and set the rigging. After days of constant activity, the men were nearing collapse, but the ship was ready for sea. Last to be loaded on was the men's personal baggage. On this issue, Steller fell to quarreling with the mariners. They felt there was no room for him to bring aboard all his collected specimens from Alaska, the Aleutians, and Bering Island, despite the fact that each mariner had stuffed the hold with bales of dried sea-otter skins. Steller had to be content with his notebooks and a few choice items. He had a large collection of preserved plants, of which he was permitted only the seeds, and he had painstakingly prepared the skeletons and skins of many mammals, including a young sea cow and a Steller's sea lion, stuffed with grass. But there were no exceptions, and Steller grumbled and fumed until he reluctantly abandoned his specimens.

At four in the afternoon on August 13, 1742, the men emerged from their dwellings for the final time, feeling "much inner emotion," according to Steller. They stood around the nearby graves, remembering. They hammered into the sand a wooden cross where Bering lay, hung their heads, and then ferried out to the ship in groups. It was only then that they truly appreciated just how crowded they would be, crammed in among the baggage and food. As they began to row over the reefs and out to sea with the tide, they looked back and saw that blue foxes had already swarmed their abandoned camp, scavenging "with the greatest glee" for scraps of meat and fat and other interesting items left behind.

THE NEW *ST. PETER*, riding low in the water, set sail and slowly headed south around the headland before steering west to where they surmised Kamchatka would be, hopefully not too far away. The weather was unusually "clear with passing clouds." They set their course and prayed to avoid any early autumn storms. The ship coasted along, and the men looked one final time ashore to the island, "on which we knew every mountain and valley which with much toil we had climbed so often in search of food . . . and to which we had given names." Steller, the unofficial spiritual leader and counselor, wrote of their final longing: the island was a place of struggle, misery, and death when they arrived, yet he marveled "how wonderfully we were fed, and how in spite of astounding toil we steadily gained in health and became more and more hardened and strengthened, and the more we gazed at it in parting the plainer it appeared to us, as in a mirror, God's wonderful and loving guidance." Soon the island was gone from view entirely, and they again faced the unknown ocean.

The wind increased the next day, and the seas became so choppy that they had to cut adrift the ship's yawl, which was dragging against a headwind. By midnight, someone noticed that the ship seemed to be steering sluggishly, and when they looked below they beheld a sickening sight: the hold was awash in water. Water was filling the ship faster than they could bail or pump it out. Waxell called for reduced sail, and they began heaving overboard anything they didn't immediately need, including all the cannonballs and other lead shot. Men frantically scampered about belowdeck, moving barrels and bales around, searching for the problem. Once the ship was lightened and floating higher in the water, at around three in the morning, the carpenter Starodubstov discovered the hole: an open gap between planks where the caulking had fallen out. They caulked it again and then nailed planks over the gap from the inside, and this stemmed most of the water from flooding the ship. With constant pumping, they could keep the water level steady as the ship slowly continued west.

Two days later, on August 17, they spied to the west through the fog and drizzle high snowcapped mountains, and they steered south to follow the coast to Avacha Bay, which they calculated was about thirty miles farther south. It took them eight days of struggle against contrary winds and calms, including a period when they rowed for twenty-four hours continuously, before they entered the bay on August 25. As they passed the rudimentary lighthouse at the entrance to the bay, a Kamchadal rowed out to them in a canoe. To his astonishment, he found that he was talking to survivors of the American expedition sailing in a new vessel made from the remnants of Bering's old ship. They had all been presumed dead, he said, and according to long-standing custom, their "property which we had left behind had fallen into the hands of strangers and had mostly been carried away." The news produced scarcely a ripple of discontent among the survivors, so accustomed were they to "misery and sorrow." Stoic and filled with relief, they "regarded the present circumstances as in a dream."

The new *St. Peter* cruised on to Petropavlovsk and arrived at two in the afternoon of August 26, 1742, thirteen days after leaving Bering Island and ten years after the expedition began. The weary men clambered ashore in bewilderment, filled with joy and delight, tinged with disbelief. "From uttermost misery and distress," Waxell recalled, "we were plunged into veritable superabundance," where anything could be had from storehouses full of provisions, where there was plenty of room in comfortable, dry, and warm quarters. They were surrounded by things commonplace in their past lives but that they hadn't seen for what seemed a lifetime. Despite the elation at being home again after fifteen months, the men soon realized that they now had nothing, no money and no possessions, and no physical reminders of their prior life. They walked around stunned, wondering what to do. The "sense of contrast [was] so overwhelming that it just cannot be expressed in words," Waxell wrote. When he was alive, Bering had made a request to the officers and men that if they returned safely, they should all go together, whether Russian Orthodox or Lutheran, and make a contribution to the chapel for a common prayer service and to place there a memorial plaque with an image of the apostles Peter and Paul and an inscription offering thanks for their escape from the deserted island. In honor of their commander, they did so. It was their final act together before going their separate ways.

EPILOGUE:
RUSSIAN AMERICA

O N APRIL 25, 1742, just as the survivors on Bering Island were recovering from scurvy and debating plans for their escape, a new empress was crowned: Elizabeth I, cousin to Anna and daughter of Peter the Great. Although Empress Elizabeth never executed anyone during her long reign and remained an enthusiastic supporter of the sciences and arts, she came to power in a coup that cleared the court of non-Russians, specifically Germans, and her reign was open to few foreigners in positions of authority. The expedition remained officially in operation for the next year, but it had lost its luster as a celebration of Russian sophistication. On September 25, 1743, after reading the reports from Waxell and Chirikov and hearing of Bering's death, the senate disbanded the expedition. All members were eventually recalled and their contracts terminated. The monumentally expensive and hugely ambitious Great Northern Expedition was officially over.

Although little is known about the fate of many of the mariners who sailed on the *St. Peter* and the *St. Paul*, beyond their names, occupations, and dates of death, several of the officers who had prominent roles in the expedition basked in the historical limelight. Steller and Waxell wrote memoirs that keep this extraordinary tale alive.

AFTER WAITING OUT THE winter in Petropavlovsk and recovering from scurvy, while wondering about the fate of his comrades on the *St. Peter*, Chirikov repaired the *St. Paul* and led a brief search for the *St. Peter* in June 1742. On June 22, he sailed close enough to Bering Island to name it St. Julien. He observed fur seals and snowcapped mountains but approached from the south and never saw or was seen by the shipwrecked comrades, who were building the new smaller *St. Peter* on the beach. Chirikov's men were still in poor health and the ship was not in perfect shape, so after discovering Attu Island, the voyagers soon returned to Petropavlovsk. By mid-July the *St. Paul* sailed for Okhotsk to await further orders from St. Petersburg.

With the presumed death of Bering and the loss of the *St. Peter*, Chirikov was proclaimed new leader of the Second Kamchatka Expedition, so he headed inland to Yeniseisk to make his report. He continued to manage the affairs of the expedition, including working on the final map of the Russian discoveries. But his health was broken from the privations of the American voyage. He who had so often been impatient to get going on an adventure, and a little disdainful of Bering's caution and prudence, had lost his own zeal for bold and uncertain undertakings. In 1746 Chirikov was ordered back to St. Petersburg, where he was promoted to captain-commander and placed in charge of the Naval Academy. Still suffering bouts of ill health, he died in November 1748, leaving a wife and four children.

WAXELL DID NOT REMAIN long in Petropavlovsk after the astonishing return from Bering Island in August 1742. He learned that Chirikov had returned from America the previous October with his men dying of scurvy and had sailed for Okhotsk barely a month before the return of the new *St. Peter*. He had a great desire to catch up with his new commander and make a report, so he quickly readied the ship, recaulked planks, and used the naval store of supplies in Petropavlovsk to make other repairs. By early September, he was at sea, but when, not long after, the ship soon proved unseaworthy with multiple leaks, he returned to spend the winter in Petropavlovsk. He sailed west to Siberia the following spring.

Waxell continued to serve in Yeniseisk for several years finalizing the expedition's business, during which time he fought for compensation for his men. He argued that the government should give them their contracted ration supply for the time they had spent on Bering Island. Rations were part of their pay and obviously were never delivered. He sent a report to Chirikov, who forwarded it to the Admiralty Council. Waxell described the "privations and wretched conditions" of the men's lives on Bering Island and explained the reasoning for his impertinence: "I am only doing what I owe to my subordinates," he wrote in his six-page submission, "for those under me could complain to God and supplicate Him for vengeance upon me were I not to stand by them and reveal the pitiable state in which they then were." He wanted the men to be paid in money for their lost ration allotment and explained in detail how the lack of rations had compelled them to "live off of all sorts of unclean beasts." He then described them, painting a graphic picture for the urban officers of the council. "If you can perhaps endure the smell of sea otter meat, it is extremely hard and tough as soleleather and full of sinews, so that however much you chew at it, you have to swallow it in large lumps." The sea bear "has a very strong and revolting smell. . . . [W]hen you have to eat them it requires a great effort." He also described eating the entrails with "gusto" in order to survive, "yet we were never able to get enough of these revolting foodstuffs to nourish us properly," and, besides, he continued, it was freezing cold and the men all suffered from scurvy and other hardships. He calculated a value on the "flour, groats and salt" for the time the men were marooned on the island and then offered detailed justification of the large total. In his journal, he included transcripts of his correspondence with the admiralty and was proud to report that his petition, and his description of their horrible conditions, resulted in each man being paid an additional one hundred rubles plus back pay at the rate of any promotions they might have received during the voyage for their "unheard-of sufferings and great distress." Waxell's petition reflected his enduring priority: while he certainly made some mistakes, he was a thoroughly honorable officer for his men.

Waxell eventually returned to St. Petersburg in 1749 and by 1756 had completed his memoirs in German. He never published them, and they became widely translated only in the twentieth century. These memoirs, along with Steller's journal, form the primary source of narrative information on the expedition and voyage. Waxell died in 1762 with the rank of captain first class, and his three sons were placed in the nobility as a recognition of his service. His son Laurentz Waxell, the only boy volunteer on the voyage, went on to a successful career as an officer in the Russian Navy.

IN THE GREATEST OF ironies, Ovtsin, the demoted former lieutenant whom Waxell and Steller hinted might have had the inclination to lead a mutinous challenge to Waxell's command while on Bering Island, discovered that his position had been restored by St. Petersburg prior to the sailing of the *St. Peter* and the *St. Paul* in the spring of 1741. The letter informing Bering and him of the news simply hadn't arrived in time. Due to his many years of service, he, rather than Waxell, had actually been the senior officer once Bering died and should have been in charge on Bering Island. Things might have turned out differently had this been known. With his rank and status restored, Ovtsin after he returned resumed his naval career, serving in the Baltic as a captain first rank and later in a senior desk position before he retired. The detailed map he had made of his Siberian coastal explorations was a secret with the Russian government until it was published many years later.

Soon after the remarkable return to Avacha Bay, Steller elected to remain in Kamchatka for more scientific investigations. He and Lepekhin set off right away, hiking thirty miles overland across Kamchatka to Bolsheretsk, where they were joined by Plenisner. Without funds (the Academy of Sciences had cut his pay when it believed he had disappeared), Steller spent the winter teaching and writing up his reports. He revised and cleaned up his field notes, sent reports to the academy, and wrote *De Bestiis Marinis; or, The Beasts of the Sea*, in which he detailed the fauna of Bering Island, including the northern fur seal, the sea otter, Steller's sea lion, Steller's sea cow, Steller's eider, and the spectacled cormorant. He also opened a school in Bolsheretsk for both Russian and Kamchadal students. The following summer, he collected botanical specimens in the north, before he reluctantly made his way west, intending to return, with uncertain prospects, to St. Petersburg. He had heard that with the change in government, many of his German associates at the academy had been dismissed or departed the city in the wake of strong antiforeigner sentiment.

A deeply religious man, Steller was saddened by what he termed, in a letter to expedition botanist Gmelin, his failure to "accomplish something worthwhile" on the voyage, "owing to the lazy and pompous conduct of the officers Waxell and Khitrov." His career was stalled, and he feared his detailed reports, painstakingly prepared on Bering Island and perfected in the following year, received no recognition at the academy. He feared they would never be properly edited or published. His dreams of world renown as a naturalist were dashed. Steller's most prescient worry was that the most significant contribution of his voyage would not be to pioneer a route to a new land for continued scientific discovery, but to unleash a swarm of rapacious fur hunters in unregulated plunder—an exploitation that would result in the destruction of the very wonders he wished to study and preserve. Steller had natural sympathies for the various native peoples he encountered and particularly the Kamchadals, whom he felt were being unjustly abused and harassed by the Russians. In a misunderstanding, he released some prisoners who had been captured and were being detained by Russians in Bolsheretsk and was accused of fomenting rebellion. Competing accounts of his actions were sent to the Russian Senate, and he was recalled to St. Petersburg. Although he was eventually exonerated of the charges, word traveled slowly, and he was put under arrest near Tobolsk and ordered to return east across Siberia to Irkutsk for a hearing. Before he got there, another courier brought news that he was freed, and he again turned west toward St. Petersburg.

Since his return from the disastrous voyage across the North Pacific to Alaska, and probably for longer, Steller had been known for overindulgence in alcohol. On his return to Europe after news of his exoneration reached him, he stopped in Tobolsk to visit his friend Archbishop Antonij Narozhnitski. Tobolsk was a hard-drinking town, and Archbishop Antonij loved to celebrate. During a three-week binge, Steller contracted a fever and then unwisely pushed on west by horse sleigh. When the sleigh driver halted at an inn east of Tyumen to warm himself on a freezing night in November 1746, Steller was left outside in the sleigh, burning with fever and barely sensate. When found, he was near death and could not be revived. He was thirty-seven years old.

De Bestiis Marinis was published posthumously in 1751. Various collections of his reports were published later in 1774, but his journal of the voyage was not made publicly available until 1793. A host of birds and sea mammals bear his name, though, as he feared, some have been slaughtered to extinction.

THE SUSPICION TOWARD FOREIGNERS that intensified under Elizabeth's two-decade reign took a toll on Bering's legacy. There was a reluctance to promote his role as commander since he was originally from Denmark. There was also the need for secrecy to protect Russian imperial interests in the new lands and commercial interests in the lucrative sea-otter trade with China. As a result, there was no grand celebratory publication highlighting the expedition's accomplishments in Siberia and Alaska, as there were for many other voyages of exploration. Many vague details of the expedition and particularly of the perilous sea voyage circulated, but they were from unreliable and inaccurate sources. It took many years for the scientific records and maps and logs to be organized and to make their way across the continent to St. Petersburg. Many more years were to pass before any of this information made it into the scientific discourse of the rest of the world.

Owing to the Russian government's desire for secrecy, the early rumors and reports of the expedition were partial and rarely accurate. Some claimed that Bering had never been across the Pacific, that his ship had been wrecked on the outward voyage and not the return voyage, that only Chirikov had reached and beheld America. Steller's brother, upon hearing of his brother's death, but being denied all information surrounding the circumstances, wrote a report in German, suspecting the Russian authorities' involvement. In 1748 the Russian government issued a truncated and vague report of the expedition to refute these claims, but omitted all interesting discoveries and provided little more than a sketchy outline of dates and events. This approach was the opposite of what Peter the Great had envisioned. He wanted to publicize the scientific and geographic findings widely, to bring prestige and respect to Russia for contributing to global knowledge, not to have it all buried in the Russian archives.

In 1752 cartographer and geographer Joseph-Nicolas Delisle, the brother of Louis Delisle de La Croyère, who died on the *St. Paul*, published maps of the voyage in contravention of his terms of employment with the Academy of Sciences once he returned to France. He praised his brother and claimed that he should have been given equal credit with Chirikov for discovering America. He also repeated the false information that Bering's ship had been wrecked before crossing the Pacific, again denying Bering any credit as primary leader of the expedition. Naturally, there was a "Russian" response. Likely written by Gerhard Friedrich Müller, the response, written in German, was based on Waxell's and Steller's unpublished accounts and included maps. It was the only official account of the expedition to be published in the eighteenth century. Bering is but a minor character in the account, and his actions are attributed not directly to him but to a passive consensus. Though Bering was never the sole undisputed leader, in particular of the most dramatic component of the Great Northern Expedition, his great contribution was in laying the foundation for the voyage and in the tedious but crucial preparation in Siberia. With his death he lost his voice, and his tale has been left to others to tell.

As a result of Russian secrecy and the trickle of tenuously accurate information that minimized Bering's role as commander and his inability to write his own account or defend himself, Bering and the incredible shipwreck and survival that were the culmination of the Great Northern Expedition were not widely known for more than a century. Bering was never celebrated in his time, and so his reputation, never great to begin with, diminished during hundreds of years in obscurity, as a sort of sideline to the achievements of his more famous contemporary explorers, like Cook, Vancouver, Bougainville, Laperouse, Malaspina, or even earlier explorers such as Columbus, Champlain, da Gama, or Magellan. Yet as the reports suggest, as a leader and explorer, Bering and the Great Northern Expedition should be placed within the pantheon of the world's great explorers and explorations.

In August 1991, a joint Danish-Russian archaeological expedition exhumed the graves of Bering and five other mariners from along the river and beach where the survivors spent the winter of 1741–1742. Their work helped to tell the tale of the survivors by confirming aspects of the recorded story and revealing some surprises as well. Forensic reconstruction of Bering's remains in Moscow recreated his facial appearance. It also revealed Bering to be a heavily muscled and lean man, not the portly, double-chinned individual typically associated with him based on the painting that for many years was believed to be his but may have been his uncle Vitus Pedersen Bering, a poet and royal historian in Denmark. Oddly, Bering did not show signs of scurvy on his teeth, so he may have recovered from that disease prior to his death, and, as Steller speculated, it may have been a combination of factors that ended Bering's life. The final or proximate cause of his death apparently was heart failure, but the ultimate cause was probably a toxic melange of problems and hardships. His wife, Anna, and children were still on their way west to St. Petersburg when he died. She eventually received a pension and proceeds from the sale of his possessions.

While Bering's fame rests on the claim that he was the first recognized explorer of the North Pacific region, it was actually a Russian Cossack named Semyon Dezhnev who in 1648 first sailed what became known as the Bering Strait. Dezhnev's story was lost and unknown for many generations, unknown to even Peter the

Great. Bering's voyage was more well known and also pioneered the long route across Siberia to get to the Pacific. Many landmarks are named after Bering, including the Bering Strait, the Bering Sea, Bering Island, Bering Glacier, and the Bering Land Bridge. Captain Cook named the Bering Strait after him three decades later during his own famous third voyage of exploration.

THE GREAT NORTHERN EXPEDITION had far-reaching ramifications for the Russian Empire and for northern Pacific America. When the mariners returned from their journey, the tales they wove of the profusion of sea otters in the Aleutians and Alaska caused great excitement in Petropavlovsk. This soon spread to Okhotsk and other Siberian towns. The following year, a shipload of hunters returned with a cargo of sixteen hundred sea-otter, two thousand fur-seal, and two thousand blue-fox skins. Soon thousands crossed the Bering Sea annually with ships loaded with beads, cotton cloth, knives, and kettles, searching to trade for sea-otter and fox pelts. Traders became rich overnight, prompting even more to enter the bonanza, financed by merchants as far away as Moscow. About half the merchant adventurers were Russians and the other half Siberian natives or men of mixed parentage. Within fourteen years, Bering Island was all but denuded of sea otters, sea lions, fur seals, and foxes, and the hunters had long since moved farther east, where they became occasionally engaged in bloody battles with the Aleuts. By the second half of the eighteenth century, the trade became more violent, as the hunters moved from island to island and along the Alaskan Peninsula, Kodiak Island, Cook Inlet, and Prince William Sound, conscripting Aleuts when they needed more labor. One expedition in 1768 returned with forty thousand fur-seal and two thousand sea-otter pelts, fifteen thousand pounds of walrus ivory, and vast quantities of whalebone. Later, the sea-otter trade drew British and American traders from the Atlantic, so great was the profit.*

The Russian merchants' quest for sea-otter pelts laid the foundation for Russian America by extending imperial Russia's reach across the Pacific Ocean. It was the realization of Peter the Great's original dream of extending his country's territory and sphere of influence, the reason he envisioned the exploration of eastern Siberia and the voyage to America, making Russia a major power on a global scale. As the expeditions progressed farther along the island chain and along the mainland of Alaska, permanent trading fortifications and depots were constructed, territory was claimed, small ships became larger, and partnerships consolidated into larger enterprises. The competing companies quarreled with each other as they expanded and fought the native peoples, attempting to enslave them and destroying their villages. In the legal and political vacuum, anarchy reigned, and practices that would have been illegal in Russia became commonplace for Russian traders and hunters. In 1763 Empress Catherine the Great issued orders to Russian subjects, admonishing them for their behavior and advising restraint and goodwill between peoples, but the situation became more chaotic and violent as the trading companies became ever larger and better financed. Although it was technically illegal for any Russian citizen to harm or abuse indigenous Alaskans, a crime punishable by death, there was no authority to observe such violence or to enforce such a law.

---

*By 1830 sea otters were extremely rare in Alaska, and the Russian government forbade the use of firearms to harvest them. After Alaska was purchased by the United States in 1867, however, the ban was lifted, and the animals were driven to near extinction again by the turn of the nineteenth century. In 1925 they were declared extinct, but from a few survivors they have begun a revival.

One aspect of Bering's original orders did come to pass: the ports of Okhotsk and Petropavlovsk grew busy as they hosted the sailors, hunters, and traders and their families as well as the shipbuilding industry. The packhorse route from Irkutsk, pioneered by Bering at such great cost and suffering, became worn and established. Traders packed and carted vast quantities of furs to the Chinese town of Kiakhta on the Mongolian border, from which Chinese merchants carried them thousands of miles south across the Gobi Desert. The region was growing, if not wealthy, and was developing a commercial economy that produced population growth and the extension of Russian culture and political control over Siberia.

The anarchy and infighting among competing Russian companies contributed to the development of a colonial-style monopoly corporation to control the fur trade and govern all settlements in what was being called Russian America. On July 8, 1799, the new czar, Paul I, issued a ukase disbanding all competing Russian companies engaged in the American fur trade, giving them a year to finalize their independent business operations, and consolidating them into the Russian American Company. The company was similar in scope and structure to that of other European powers, such as the Dutch East India Company, the English East India Company, or the Hudson's Bay Company, which blended corporate and government responsibilities. The head office of the new corporation was in St. Petersburg, to emphasize that the new entity was an appendage of government rather than an independent business and that it had obligations to promote Russian culture and the Russian Orthodox Church in the new lands. Although the permanent Russian population in Russian America did not exceed around seven hundred during that time, there now remain more than twenty thousand converts to the Russian Orthodox Church from the various indigenous peoples. Russian culture was present in the region well into the nineteenth century. During the next sixty-eight years, the Russian American Company ruled Russian America, with territory

extending to outposts in California and Hawaii. It eventually became unprofitable, owing to the severe depletion of sea otters, and
in 1867 the territory was sold to the United States for $7.2 million
and became the state of Alaska.

"THEY PUSHED INTO A trackless region of storms, fogs, mists
and rain; of strong and unknown currents; a wilderness of islands;
mountainous shores; deep waters and exposed anchorages," wrote
George Davidson, president of the Geographical Society of the Pacific, in 1901. He observed that ships like the *St. Peter* and *St. Paul*
would never have been permitted to leave port even a century ago.
The food was nearly inedible by modern standards, the ships were
crowded and filthy, and they had nothing to fight scurvy or other
sicknesses. They sailed blind into the unknown and, sometimes,
back again. It is hard to understate their bravery and determination,
their sense of adventure and curiosity. That several of them kept
records of their voyage and their plight even under the most trying
conditions is nothing short of astonishing.

Although it remains the greatest, most extensive scientific expedition in history, spanning three continents over nearly ten years,
the story of the Great Northern Expedition, and particularly its epic
Pacific voyage, is not merely a tale of imperial hubris. It is a story
of individuals faced with the power of nature, of the struggle and
triumph over disaster, a testament of human ingenuity in the face
of adversity, the failure and resurgence of leadership, fortitude in
the face of horrible suffering, and the powerful urge to persevere
and return home.

Notes

Part One. Europe

CHAPTER 1. THE GREAT EMBASSY

1 **"such as is due only among private friends":** Johann Georg Korb, *Diary of an Austrian Secretary of Legation at the Court of Tsar Peter the Great*, 155.

12 **"Confess, beast, confess!":** Ibid., 243.

13 **"crimes that lead to the common ruin":** Ibid., 180.

14 **"his character is exactly that of his country":** Sophia Charlotte, quoted in Eugene Schuyler, *Peter the Great*, 1:285.

15 **"constructed and launched a new ship":** Peter the Great, in Maritime Regulations, quoted in ibid., 265.

16 **"the Tsar wants to eat!":** Korb, *Diary of . . . Peter the Great*, 157.

26 **"made many attempts along the American coast":** Reports of Peter the Great, quoted in Frank Alfred Golder, *Russian Expansion on the Pacific, 1641–1850*, 133.

26 **"draw a chart and bring it here":** Ibid., 134.

CHAPTER 2. THE FIRST
KAMCHATKA EXPEDITION

27 **He was a handsome man in good health:** See V. N. Zviagin, "A Reconstruction of Vitus Bering Based on Skeletal Remains,"

248–262. See also Svend E. Albrethsen, "Vitus Bering's Second Kamchatka Expedition: The Journey to America and Archaeological Excavations on Bering Island," in *Vitus Bering, 1741–1991: Bicentennial Remembrance Lectures*, edited by N. Kingo Jacobsen, 75–93.

28 **"everything had come his way"**: Georg Wilhelm Steller, *Steller's Journal of the Sea Voyage from Kamchatka to America and Return on the Second Expedition, 1741–1742*, 157.

28 **"universally liked by the whole command"**: Ibid., 155.

31 **"even if your people did not bring them"**: Schuyler, *Peter the Great*, 2:458.

32 **"Bering has been in East India and knows the conditions"**: Instructions from Czar Peter Alekseevich, in Basil Dmytryshyn, E. A. P. Crownhart-Vaughan, and Thomas Vaughan, eds. and trans., *Russian Penetration of the North Pacific, 1700–1799: A Documentary Record*, 66.

32 **"It is very necessary to have"**: Ibid. See also Peter the Great's Orders, Papers of the Admiralty Council, 1724, in Frank Alfred Golder, *Bering's Voyages: An Account of the Efforts of the Russians to Determine the Relation of Asia and America*, 1:7.

36 **Wealth and status were the goals of this couple**: See Orcutt Frost, *Bering: The Russian Discovery of America*, 32; and Natasha Okhotina Lind, "The First Pianist in Okhotsk: New Information on Anna Christina Bering," in *Under Vitus Bering's Command: New Perspectives on the Russian Kamchatka Expeditions*, edited by Peter Ulf Møller and Natasha Okhotina Lind, 51–62.

37 **commanding the governor of Siberia**: Dmytryshyn, Crownhart-Vaughan, and Vaughan, *Russian Penetration of the North Pacific*, 68.

39 **"You are all swindlers and you should be hanged"**: Evgenii G. Kushnarev, *Bering's Search for the Strait: The First Kamchatka Expedition, 1725–1730*, 35.

39 **"many were lame, blind, and ridden with disease"**: Ibid., 36.

40 **"in order to keep warm during the night"**: Bering's Report, in Dmytryshyn, Crownhart-Vaughan, and Vaughan, *Russian Penetration of the North Pacific*, 83.

41 **"I cannot put into words how difficult this route is"**: Kushnarev, *Bering's Search for the Strait*, 55.

43 **"we are going straight to town [Yakutsk] and you can't stop us"**: Ibid., 67.

45 **"penetrated even under our parkas and into our baggage"**: Peter Dobell, *Travels in Kamchatka and Siberia*, 102.

45 **"then he will be covered by snow and die"**: Bering's Report, in Dmytryshyn, Crownhart-Vaughan, and Vaughan, *Russian Penetration of the North Pacific*, 84.

46 **"and are quite devoid of any good habits"**: Ibid.

46 **"out into the forest with only enough food for a week"**: Ibid.

48 **"variable winds blew from the ravines between the mountains"**: Piotr Chaplin, *The Journal of Midshipman Chaplin: A Record of Bering's First Kamchatka Expedition*, 131.

48 **"if one moves not far from here to the east"**: Ibid., 133.

49 **"covered in snow even in winter"**: Bering's Report, in Golder, *Bering's Voyages*, 1:19.

49 **"a harbor on Kamchatka where we will stay through the winter"**: Kushnarev, *Bering's Search for the Strait*, 107; Chaplin, *Journal of Midshipman Chaplin*, 142, 303.

CHAPTER 3. THE BEST-LAID PLANS

53 **"Let me see everything"**: Jacob von Staehlin, *Original Anecdotes of Peter the Great*, 140.

55 **"with no considerable future"**: Mini Curtiss, *A Forgotten Empress: Anna Ivanovna and Her Era*, 232.

57 **"since these regions are under Russian jurisdiction"**: Bering's Proposal, in Golder, *Bering's Voyages*, 1:25. See also "A Statement from the Admiralty College to the Senate Concerning the Purpose of the Bering Expedition," in Dmytryshyn, Crownhart-Vaughan, and Vaughan, *Russian Penetration of the North Pacific*, 97–99.

58 **"genuine benefit to Your Majesty and to the glory of the Russian Empire"**: Instructions from the empress, in ibid., 108.

59 **officially signed the order authorizing the Second Kamchatka Expedition:** See Golder, *Bering's Voyages*, 1:28–29; and Dmytryshyn, Crownhart-Vaughan, and Vaughan, *Russian Penetration of the North Pacific*, 96–125.

59 **"act in mutual agreement with Captain-Lieutenant Chirikov":** Instructions from the Admiralty College, in Dmytryshyn, Crownhart-Vaughan, and Vaughan, *Russian Penetration of the North Pacific*, 102.

62 **infrastructure to accommodate him and his entourage:** See James R. Gibson, "Supplying the Kamchatka Expedition, 1725–30 and 1742," 101.

62 **"noteworthy in the manner of plants, animals and minerals":** Gerhard Friedrich Müller, *Bering's Voyages: The Reports from Russia*, 79.

63 **"considerably more prudence and thought":** Sven Waxell, *The American Expedition*, 65.

63 **"the story of the journey":** Müller, *Bering's Voyages*, 79.

66 **Golovin proposed something radical to the empress:** See "A Proposal from Count Nikolai Golovin to Empress Anna Ivanovna," in *Russian Penetration of the North Pacific*, edited and translated by Dmytryshyn, Crownhart-Vaughan, and Vaughan, 90–95.

67 **"everything will be ready for him":** "A Statement from the Admiralty College to the Senate," in ibid., 100.

Part Two. Asia

CHAPTER 4. ST. PETERSBURG TO SIBERIA

74 **"deported persons who were to work on board our vessels":** Waxell, *The American Expedition*, 50.

76 **"for after that had been done we had only very few run aways":** Ibid., 51.

77 **they were above the local Siberian hierarchy:** See Peter Ulf Møller and Natasha Okhotina Lind, *Until Death Do Us Part: The Letters and Travel of Anna and Vitus Bering*, 109–123.

79   **the ultimate objective of the entire expedition:** See T. E. Armstrong, "Siberian and Arctic Exploration," in *Bering and Chirikov*, edited by Frost, 117.

79   **Such were the arbitrary decrees:** See ibid., 117–126.

80   **"fallen to death's sickle":** Waxell, *The American Expedition*, 55.

80   **"it must be anticipated that most of them will succumb":** Ibid., 59.

81   **"Yudoma Cross and Okhotsk is a complete wilderness":** Ibid., 66.

81   **"If a packhorse becomes mired there is no way to pull it out":** Stephen Petrovich Krasheninnikov, *Explorations of Kamchatka: Report of a Journey Made to Explore Eastern Siberia in 1735–1741, by Order of the Russian Imperial Government*, 351.

83   **"when large quantities of fish come into the river from the sea":** Waxell, *The American Expedition*, 70.

83   **"has a particularly pleasant taste":** Ibid., 71.

83   **"To put it briefly, this is an emergency harbour":** Ibid., 74.

84   **"a lying and malicious gossip":** Leonhard Stejneger, *Georg Wilhelm Steller: The Pioneer of Alaskan Natural History*, 207.

CHAPTER 5. QUARRELING FACTIONS

87   **cut short by his desire to understand the world:** See ibid., 39.

87   **"an insatiable desire to visit foreign lands":** Steller, *Steller's Journal*, 15.

88   **"I have entirely forgotten her and fallen in love with Nature":** Stejneger, *Georg Wilhelm Steller*, 135.

89   **"accomplish something advantageous to science":** Ibid., 147.

89   **Artists were to sketch buildings, landscapes, and peoples:** See "Instructions from Johann Georg Gmelin," in *Russian Penetration of the North Pacific*, edited and translated by Dmytryshyn, Crownhart-Vaughan, and Vaughan, 104.

92   **"we have had to learn all these things by experience":** Stejneger, *Georg Wilhelm Steller*, 110.

92   **"and there was no way of stopping the madness":** Ibid., 109.

94 **"He bears only malice toward me for them"**: Vasilli A. Divin, *The Great Russian Navigator, A. I. Chirikov*, 109.

94 **"Just what proportion of truth and falsehood these charges contain"**: Golder, *Russian Expansion on the Pacific*, 177.

95 **"and a delay in accomplishing the work assigned"**: Directive from the Admiralty College, quoted in ibid., 174.

96 **"they have to live on charity or by hiring themselves out"**: An eyewitness account of hardships, as reported by Heinrich Von Fuch, in Dmytryshyn, Crownhart-Vaughan, and Vaughan, *Russian Penetration of the North Pacific*, 168. Von Fuch's account runs to twenty-one pages and is an instructive window into the conditions in Siberia, specifically how the general corruption and hardships were exacerbated by the demands of the Great Northern Expedition.

97 **"burden the Iakuts in every possible way to enrich themselves"**: Ibid.

97 **"prevent them from completely ruining the local population"**: Ibid., 169.

97 **"22 men were very sick, and all became emaciated"**: Gibson, "Supplying the Kamchatka Expedition," 108–109.

97 **"It is very necessary to find a way of transporting provisions"**: Ibid., 114.

99 **"they could also have been used as projectiles"**: Waxell, *The American Expedition*, 79.

99 **"None were seen with trousers and all went barefoot"**: Ibid., 83.

100 **"Some of them had silver rings in their ears"**: Ibid., 87.

101 **"the treasury should not be emptied in vain"**: Golder, *Russian Expansion on the Pacific*, 178.

CHAPTER 6. PHANTOM ISLANDS

103 **"to assist in transporting our supplies from those two places"**: Waxell, *The American Expedition*, 91.

104 **"shot to pieces in the first flush of youth"**: Anna Bering to her son Jonas, in Møller and Lind, *Until Death Do Us Part*, 69.

104 **"I live like a nomad"**: Gibson, "Supplying the Kamchatka Expedition," 111–112.

106 **"have I ever been exposed to such great danger as then"**: Waxell, *The American Expedition*, 94.

107 **"among those waves there would have been no saving us"**: Ibid.

109 **"Who believes Cossacks?"**: Steller, *Steller's Journal*, 100.

110 **"no idea what money was"**: Waxell, *The American Expedition*, 98.

110 **"given a good dose of the knout to find out the guilty ones"**: Ibid., 99.

111 **"if I should consent to go along with him"**: Steller, *Steller's Journal*, 16.

111 **"a miserable and dangerous sea voyage"**: Ibid.

113 **"a just dispensation exposed their unfortunately too naked vanity"**: Ibid., 17.

114 **"take counsel concerning various routes to America"**: Instructions from Empress Anna Ivanovna, in Dmytryshyn, Crownhart-Vaughan, and Vaughan, *Russian Penetration of the North Pacific*, 114.

115 **"it certainly would have been discovered"**: Waxell, *The American Expedition*, 89.

115 **"on the map of Professor Delisle de la Croyere"**: Chirikov's Report, in Golder, *Bering's Voyages*, 1:312.

115 **"the scandalous deception of which we were the victims"**: Waxell, *The American Expedition*, 89, 103.

116 **gunpowder, firewood, iron, spare sails, rope, tar, and more**: See "The Log of the *St. Peter*," in *Bering's Voyages*, by Golder, 1:48.

117 **"the winds veered back and forth between S and E"**: Ibid.

118 **"navigate in waters which are completely blank"**: Waxell, *The American Expedition*, 104.

118 **"we had sailed over the region where it was supposed to be"**: Chirikov's Report, in Golder, *Bering's Voyages*, 1:313.

118 **"the tide carries them back towards the land"**: Steller, *Steller's Journal*, 22.

119 **"they had also acquired all other science and logic"**: Ibid., 23.

119 **"might have been decisive for the whole enterprise"**: Ibid.

120 **"a bucket of vodka and gave it to Adjunct Steller"**: "Log of the *St. Peter*," in *Bering's Voyages*, by Golder, 1:41.

Part Three. America

CHAPTER 7. BOLSHAYA ZEMLYA, THE GREAT LAND

124 **"separated by a narrow channel from America"**: Steller, *Steller's Journal*, 26.

125 **"know more than was considered advisable"**: Ibid., 24.

125 **"'you have not been in God's council chamber!'"**: Steller, quoting ship's officers, likely Khitrov, ibid., 26.

126 **"when anyone mentioned anything of which they were ignorant"**: Ibid., 27.

126 **"and thus afford them the most abundant food supply"**: Ibid., 32.

127 **"the whole sea was overgrown with weeds"**: Ibid., 29.

127 **"achievements which pay interest on the outlay a thousand fold"**: Ibid., 26.

128 **"the announcement was regarded as one of my peculiarities"**: Ibid., 33.

129 **"among them a high volcano"**: "Log of the *St. Peter*," in *Bering's Voyages*, by Golder, 1:93.

129 **"higher mountains anywhere in Siberia and Kamchatka"**: Steller, *Steller's Journal*, 33.

129 **"huge, high, snow-covered mountains"**: Waxell, *The American Expedition*, 105.

130 **"nor are we provided with supplies for a wintering"**: Steller, quoting Bering, *Steller's Journal*, 34.

131 **"than for no reason at all and only trusting to good luck"**: Ibid., 36.

131 **"flat, level, and as far as we could observe, sandy"**: Ibid., 35.

131 **"a submerged reef of rocks may be seen in low water"**: "Khitrov's Journal," in *Bering's Voyages*, by Golder, 1:99.

133 **"bringing American water to Asia"**: Steller, *Steller's Journal*, 37.

133 **"my principal work, my calling, and my duty"**: Ibid.

133 **"all respect aside and prayed a particular prayer"**: Ibid., 40.

134 **"cooked their meat by means of red-hot stones"**: Ibid., 44.

134 **ethnographers associate with a summer camp**: See editorial note in Georg Wilhelm Steller, *Journal of a Voyage with Bering, 1741–1742*, 194.

135 **"the three kingdoms of nature"**: Steller, *Steller's Journal*, 49.

135 **or the Tlingit from the east in Yakutat Bay**: See editorial note in Steller, *Journal of a Voyage with Bering*, 194.

135 **"the direction of such important matters"**: Steller, *Steller's Journal*, 50.

136 **"was delighted to be able to test out the excellent water for tea"**: Ibid.

136 **"distinguished from the European and Siberian species"**: Ibid., 59.

136 **"they would leave me ashore without waiting for me"**: Ibid., 51.

136 **"returning at sunset with various observations and collections"**: Ibid.

137 **"The island is sheltered from many winds"**: "Log of the *St. Peter*," in *Bering's Voyages*, by Golder, 1:97.

137 **"in summer to catch fish and other sea animals"**: Khitrov's Journal, in ibid.

137 **"left in the cabin for the natives"**: Waxell, *The American Expedition*, 106.

138 **"conclude that we had intended to poison them!"**: Steller, *Steller's Journal*, 52.

138 **"glass beads, tobacco leaves, an iron kettle and something else"**: Martin Sauer, *Account of a Geographical and Astronomical Expedition . . . by Commodore Joseph Billings in the Years 1785 to 1794*, 194.

139 **"nothing but a detached head or a detached nose"**: Steller, *Steller's Journal*, 36.

139 **"satisfied for this year with the discovery already made"**: Steller, quoting Bering, ibid., 61.

139 **"it was our intention to follow the land as it went"**: Waxell, *The American Voyage*, 107.

140 **"ten hours were devoted to the work itself"**: Steller, *Steller's Journal*, 54.

140 **"Stormy, squally, rainy"**: "Log of the *St. Peter*," in *Bering's Voyages*, by Golder, 1:100.

141 **"continuous stormy and wet weather"**: Steller, *Steller's Journal*, 61.

141 **"is notably better than that of the extreme northeastern part of Asia"**: Ibid., 54.

141 **"densely covered to the highest peaks with the finest trees"**: Ibid., 55.

142 **"as a protester I myself took up too much space already"**: Ibid., 57.

142 **"proved to me that we were really in America"**: Ibid., 60.

143 **"to produce anything outside of marcasites and pyrites"**: Ibid., 57.

143 **"sail N and W in order to observe the American coast"**: "Log of the *St. Peter*," in *Bering's Voyages*, by Golder, 1:103.

143 **"we eventually came out into deep water"**: Waxell, *The American Voyage*, 107.

144 **"got into a slight altercation on the subject"**: Steller, *Steller's Journal* 62.

144 **"to let it go at that"**: Ibid.

CHAPTER 8. CURIOUS ENCOUNTERS

147 **"a sea nettle which is washed ashore in large quantities"**: "Journal of the *St. Paul*," in *Bering's Voyages*, by Golder, 1:289.

147 **"parts of America that are well known"**: "Report of the Voyage of the *St. Paul*," in ibid., 314.

147 **"a fine growth of timber and in places were covered with snow"**: Ibid.

148 **"mountains extending to the northward"**: "Journal of the *St. Paul*," in ibid., 293.

148 **"the misfortune of July 18th"**: "Report of the Voyage of the *St. Paul*," in ibid., 314.

148 **now called Takanis Bay:** See Frost, *Bering*, 143.

149 **"a true and good servant of Her Imperial Majesty"**: "Report on the Voyage of the *St. Paul*," in *Bering's Voyages*, by Golder, 1:316.

149 **"owing to the heavy fog we could not identify the landmarks"**: Ibid.

149 **"therefore supposed that the country was uninhabited"**: Ibid.

150 **"the men did not row as we do but paddled"**: Ibid.

150 **"under and above water on which the surf was playing"**: "Journal of the *St. Paul*," in ibid., 295.

150 **"some misfortune had happened to our men"**: "Report on the Voyage of the *St. Paul*," in ibid., 317.

151 **"made us suspect that they had either killed our men or held them"**: Ibid.

151 **"That is how it must have been"**: Waxell, *The American Voyage*, 162.

151 **"perhaps even the intention of taking the ship"**: Ibid., 161.

153 **"scarcely able to manage the ship"**: Waxell, *The American Voyage*, 107.

153 **"now utilized fruitlessly tacking up and down"**: Steller, *Steller's Journal*, 63.

153 **"the more furious was the subsequent gale"**: Ibid., 64.

153 **"in the water, however, the whole animal appeared red, like a cow"**: Ibid.

154 **a full-grown bachelor fur seal or a young northern fur seal**: See Dean Littlepage, *Steller's Island: Adventures of a Pioneer Naturalist in Alaska*.

155 **"'by the shortest road but in the longest way'"**: Steller, *Steller's Journal*, 68.

156 **"drizzly," "wet," "heavy," "rainy," "foggy," and "thick"**: "Log of the *St. Peter*," in *Bering's Voyages*, by Golder, 1:121–127.

156 **"no one should say anything about having seen land"**: Steller, *Steller's Journal*, 69.

156 **"the quantities of kelp floating from that direction"**: Ibid.

157 **"a depth of 90 fathoms at the most"**: Ibid., 75.

157 **"they could see no farther than nature and experience permitted them"**: Ibid., 74.

157 **"in case of head winds we should not suffer extremely"**: "Log of the *St. Peter*," in *Bering's Voyages*, by Golder, 1:138.

158 **"the honor of the expected discovery"**: Steller, *Steller's Journal*, 77.

159 **"finally through standing become salt water"**: Ibid.

159 **"The water is good, fill up with it!"**: Ibid., 78.

160 **"could at any rate use it for cooking"**: Waxell, *The American Expedition*, 109.

160 **"so that we might sail out back into the open sea"**: Ibid.

161 **"answerable in the future for not investigating it"**: Waxell, *The American Expedition*, 110; Müller, *Bering's Voyages*, 106.

161 **"I had been kept away from his company"**: Steller, *Steller's Journal*, 87.

162 **"had gone wrong and had brought misfortune"**: Ibid., 88.

163 **"Americans received with great pleasure"**: "Log of the *St. Peter*," in *Bering's Voyages*, by Golder, 1:148.

163 **"a sacrifice or a sign of good friendship"**: Steller, *Steller's Journal*, 92.

163 **"strong and stocky yet fairly well proportioned"**: Ibid., 96.

164 **"and I am sure the most eminent of them all"**: Waxell, *The American Expedition*, 113.

164 **"Kamchadals, however, consider such delicacies"**: Steller, *Steller's Journal*, 94.

165 **"where it would have been wrecked on the rocks"**: Ibid.

165 **"letting go of everything in their hands"**: Ibid., 95.

166 **"ordered not to use force against them in any way whatever"**: Waxell, *The American Expedition*, 119.

166 **"the nostalgia of the naval men would not permit"**: Steller, *Steller's Journal*, 99.

CHAPTER 9.
THE SCOURGE OF THE SEA

167 **"drifted on the rocks and been wrecked"**: Steller, *Steller's Journal*, 87.

168 **"serviceable against scurvy and asthma, our commonest cases"**: Ibid., 85.

168 **"such quantity of antiscorbutic herbs as would be enough for all"**: Ibid.

168 **"the preservation of my own self without wasting another word"**: Ibid., 86.

170 **"as to draw their limbs close to their Thyghs, and some rotted away"**: George Anson, *A Voyage Round the World in the Years 1740–1744*, 91.

170 **"restoring us to our wonted strength"**: See ibid., 76–83.

171 **"vegetables and fruit his only physic"**: Heaps, *Log of the* Centurion, 132.

172 **"putrid gums, the spots and lassitude, with weakness of their knees"**: James Lind, *A Treatise of the Scurvy*, 191. The discussion of his experiment is contained on pages 191–193.

174 **"do not know whether they are going too quickly or too slowly"**: Waxell, *The American Expedition*, 120.

174 **"any moment something might come to finish us off"**: Ibid.

174 **"altogether exhausted from scurvy"**: See "Log of the *St. Peter*," in *Bering's Voyages*, by Golder, 1:167–194.

174 **"expecting every moment the last stroke and death"**: Steller, *Steller's Journal*, 115.

175 **"very many were heard to complain of hitherto unwonted disorders"**: Ibid., 106.

175 **"unable to move either their hands or their feet, let alone use them"**: Waxell, *The American Expedition*, 121.

175 **"that it could be greater or that we should be able to stand it out"**: Steller, *Steller's Journal*, 115.

176 **"often from opposite directions"**: Ibid., 116.

176 **"the curses piled up during ten years in Siberia prevented any response"**: Ibid.

176 **"always in danger and uncertainty"**: Waxell, *The American Voyage*, 120.

176 **"kept the men in fairly good fettle"**: Ibid., 121.

177 **"rather die than let life drag on in that wretched fashion"**: Ibid., 123.

177 **"died of scurvy the grenadier Andrei Tretyakov"**: "Log of the *St. Peter*," in *Bering's Voyages*, by Golder, 1:167.

177 **"the cold, dampness, nakedness, vermin, fright, and terror":** Steller, *Steller's Journal*, 121.

178 **"which we may have sailed past at night and in foggy weather":** Ibid., 124.

178 **"would assuredly all together have found our graves in the waves":** Ibid., 125.

178 **"hither and thither at the whim of the winds and waves":** Waxell, *The American Expedition*, 123.

179 **"he had to be replaced by another in no better case than he":** Ibid., 122.

179 **"always been scorned before the disaster":** Steller, *Steller's Journal*, 125.

179 **"find the means to continue our voyage":** Waxell, *The American Voyage*, 123.

179 **"we were utterly wretched":** Ibid.

180 **"the tar bitterness cured them of scurvy":** "Report on the Voyage of the *St. Paul*," in *Bering's Voyages*, by Golder, 1:319.

180 **"the crew should have daily two cups of wine":** Ibid.

181 **"so much noise that we could not make out what was said":** Ibid., 320.

181 **"no harm might come to them from us":** "Journal of the *St. Paul*," in ibid., 303.

181 **"they were afraid we might attack them":** Ibid., 304.

182 **"holding them up, I invited them to come near":** Ibid.

182 **"the third man, who equally insisted on a knife":** Ibid., 305.

183 **"proves that their conscience is not highly developed":** Ibid.

183 **"we attempted to get away from where we stood":** "Report on the Voyage of the *St. Paul*," in ibid., 320.

183 **"It was a narrow escape":** Ibid.

183 **"the color of the water was green":** "Journal of the *St. Paul*," in ibid., 306.

183 **"my mind did not leave me":** "Report on the Voyage of the *St. Paul*," in ibid., 322.

184 **"For that purpose a larger crew is necessary":** Ibid., 326.

185 **"as the officers are dead":** Ibid., 323.

185 **"my teeth are loose in my gums":** Ibid.

185 **no means to replace or repair any of the deficiencies:** See ibid.

Part Four. Nowhere

CHAPTER 10. ISLAND OF THE BLUE FOXES

193 **"scarcely possible to manage the ship":** Steller, *Steller's Journal*, 129.

193 **Siberian soldier Ivan Davidov perished:** See "Log of the *St. Peter*," in *Bering's Voyages*, by Golder, 1:208.

193 **"we think this land is Kamchatka":** Ibid.

193 **"all thanked God heartily for this great mercy":** Steller, *Steller's Journal*, 129.

194 **"they were going to care for their health and take a rest":** Ibid.

194 **"we are not half a mile off":** Ibid., 230.

194 **"while Avacha is two degrees farther south":** Ibid., 131.

194 **"[W]e have little fresh water":** "Log of the *St. Peter*," in *Bering's Voyages*, by Golder, 1:209.

194 **"our provisions and water were gone":** Ibid., 210.

195 **"he would let his head be cut off":** Steller, *Steller's Journal*, 133.

195 **"therefore I would rather not say anything":** Ibid., 134.

195 **"in order to save the ship and men":** "Log of the *St. Peter*," in *Bering's Voyages*, by Golder, 1:210.

196 **"Perhaps God would also help us to keep the ship":** Waxell, *The American Expedition*, 125.

196 **"not knowing whither their fumbling will lead them":** Ibid., 124.

197 **"threatened to strike against the bottom":** Steller, *Steller's Journal*, 135.

197 **"[T]wice the ship bumped on rocks":** Waxell, *The American Expedition*, 125.

197 **"seized with the fear of death":** Steller, *Steller's Journal*, 135.

197 **"A disaster has befallen our ship!":** Ibid., 136.

197 **"without ceremony, neck and heels into the sea":** Ibid., 137.

198 **"as if death in fresh water would be more delightful!":** Ibid., 135.

198   **"all at once quiet and delivered from all fear of stranding"**: Ibid., 137.

198   **"he himself was as pale as a corpse"**: Ibid., 136.

199   **"God's miraculous, merciful assistance"**: Waxell, *The American Expedition*, 126.

200   **"most important thing now is to save the men"**: Steller, *Steller's Journal*, 137.

201   **"even do something to help our own recovery"**: Waxell, *The American Expedition*, 200.

202   **"we were on an island surrounded by the sea"**: Steller, *Steller's Journal*, 140.

202   **"the unjust conduct of various persons"**: Ibid., 141.

202   **"not one of us would have escaped"**: Waxell, *The American Expedition*, 126.

203   **"they were not shy astonished me exceedingly"**: Steller, *Steller's Journal*, 139.

203   **"lairs up in the mountains or on the edges of the mountains"**: Ibid., 213.

204   **"because they wanted to tear the meat from our hands"**: Ibid., 210.

204   **"and they immediately ate up the excrement as eagerly as pigs"**: Ibid., 211.

204   **"ate the hands and feet of the corpses"**: Waxell, *The American Expedition*, 127.

204   **"Some were singed, others flogged to death"**: Steller, *Steller's Journal*, 212.

205   **"Copulation itself takes place amid much caterwauling like cats"**: Ibid., 213.

205   **"necessity of eating the stinking, disgusting, and hated foxes"**: Ibid., 148.

206   **"a tower of strength when we were in trouble"**: "Report of the Voyage of the *St. Peter*," in *Bering's Voyages*, by Golder, 1:281.

206   **"I will divide with you equally until God helps"**: Steller, *Steller's Journal*, 141.

206   **"You do not know what might have happened to you at home"**: Ibid., 142.

207 **"so as not to be laughed at afterward or wait until we were ordered"**: Ibid., 148.

207 **"miserable existence"**: Ibid., 149.

208 **"God's judgement for revenge on the authors of their misfortune"**: Ibid., 151.

208 **"reproaches and threats for past doings"**: Ibid.

209 **"may God at least spare our longboat"**: Ibid., 144.

209 **crashing over the deck and pouring into the hold**: See "Log of the *St. Peter*," in *Bering's Voyages*, by Golder, 1:220–221.

210 **"died like mice as soon as their heads had topped the hatch"**: Waxell, *The American Expedition*, 128.

210 **"attending to the needs of nature where they lay"**: Ibid., 129.

210 **"we abandoned all hope for his life"**: Steller, *Steller's Journal*, 153.

211 **"the enterprises necessary for our deliverance"**: Ibid., 152.

211 **"the ship would be driven out to sea"**: "Log of the *St. Peter*," in *Bering's Voyages*, by Golder, 1:228.

212 **"on the spot where we had planned to lay her up"**: Ibid., 230.

212 **"might ever have been done by human effort"**: Steller, *Steller's Journal*, 152.

213 **"our bodies became distended like drums from flatulence"**: Ibid., 160.

213 **"alike in both regard to standing and work, food and clothing"**: Waxell, *The American Expedition*, 207.

CHAPTER 11. DEATH AND PLAYING CARDS

215 **"brown-black, grown over the teeth and covering them"**: Steller, *Steller's Journal*, 146.

215 **"moving away from the dead"**: Waxell, *The American Expedition*, 134.

215 **"but becomes so depressed that he would far rather die than live"**: Ibid., 200.

215 **"even the bravest might lose courage"**: Steller, *Steller's Journal*, 151.

216 **"men scarcely half his age and one-third his skill"**: Ibid., 155.

217 **"his lively and agreeable company"**: Müller, *Bering's Voyages*, 115.

218   **"where there was no sign of fuel"**: Waxell, *The American Expedition*, 131.

218   **"I wonder at your taste"**: Steller, *Steller's Journal*, 150.

219   **"out of his hands and put into those of a young and active man"**: Ibid., 156.

220   **"suffers from the cold"**: Waxell, *The American Expedition*, 135.

220   **"an earnest preparation for death"**: Steller, *Steller's Journal*, 156.

220   **"died miserably under the open sky"**: Steller letter to Gmelin, in Golder, *Bering's Voyages*, 1:243.

220   **"He died like a rich man"**: Steller, *Steller's Journal*, 157.

221   **"they leaned so heavily on him that he himself must sink"**: Ibid.

221   **"by their too impetuous and often thoughtless action"**: Ibid., 156.

221   **"after Bering's death his greatest accuser"**: Ibid., 157.

222   **"universally liked by the whole command"**: Ibid., 155.

222   **"leaving us lying under the open sky"**: Waxell, *The American Expedition*, 139.

223   **"clung to a stone or anything else that they were able to seize"**: Ibid., 140.

223   **"were the daily guests"**: Steller, *Steller's Journal*, 153.

223   **"Severity would have been quite pointless"**: Waxell, *The American Expedition*, 135.

225   **"a special paragraph giving permission for all suitable pastimes"**: Ibid., 136.

225   **"my successors could deal with matters as they liked"**: Ibid.

225   **"that one has lost so and so much"**: Steller, *Steller's Journal*, 161.

226   **"hate, quarrels and strife were disseminated through all the quarters"**: Ibid.

227   **"the fine sea otters had to offer up their costly skins"**: Ibid.

227   **"their skins, their meat being thrown away"**: Ibid.

227   **"raging among the animals, without discipline and order"**: Ibid.

228   **"cooked for the sick to eat"**: Waxell, *The American Expedition*, 137.

228   **"you have to swallow it in large lumps"**: Ibid., 205.

229   **"as we were never able to get all the oil out of them"**: Ibid., 137.

229   **"the meat almost like veal"**: Steller, *Steller's Journal*, 168.

230 **"were in the proper place and home"**: Ibid., 167.

230 **"resulted in cheerfulness and good feeling among us"**: Ibid.

232 **"for He helps all who help themselves"**: Waxell, *The American Expedition*, 143.

232 **"was not fit for a continuation of our voyage"**: "Log of the St. Peter," in *Bering's Voyages*, by Golder, 1:231.

233 **"To His Highness Lieutenant Waxell"**: Ibid.

233 **"it is difficult to say how badly damaged the bottom is"**: Ibid., 232.

233 **"they had examined the ship and found it unseaworthy"**: Ibid.

234 **"small vessel should be made to take us to Kamchatka"**: Ibid.

234 **"if only we had acted upon this or that"**: Waxell, *The American Expedition*, 146.

234 **"violent northwest gale and a very high tide"**: Steller, *Steller's Journal*, 168.

235 **"ever stronger the closer it came to us"**: Ibid., 205.

CHAPTER 12. A NEW *ST. PETER*

236 **"none of us became well or recovered his strength completely"**: Waxell, *The American Expedition*, 142.

237 **"to make a careful observation of the country"**: "Log of the St. Peter," in *Bering's Voyages*, by Golder, 1:232.

238 **"some mainland or the end of the island"**: Steller, *Steller's Journal*, 169.

238 **"like immovable machines, they could hardly move their feet"**: Ibid., 171.

238 **"God, however, pulled him through without harm"**: Ibid.

239 **"tried to keep myself warm and banish the bitterness of death"**: Ibid., 172.

239 **"safe from the thievish and malicious foxes"**: Ibid.

240 **"The fat is yellow, the flesh hard and sinewy"**: Waxell, *The American Expedition*, 141.

240 **"snow dashing down from the mountains"**: Steller, *Steller's Journal*, 173.

240   **"doubled the northern cape on the other side"**: "Log of the
        St. Peter," in *Bering's Voyages*, by Golder, 1:233.

241   **"escape from this wretched spot"**: Waxell, *The American Expedi-
        tion*, 142.

241   **"therefore we should all stand together as one man"**: Ibid., 143.

241   **"digging for all eternity without making any progress"**: Ibid.,
        145.

242   **"all aboard her would be lost"**: Ibid., 143.

242   **"should find consolation together"**: Ibid., 145.

242   **"Decision Made on Determination That Land Is an Island"**:
        "Log of the *St. Peter*," in *Bering's Voyages*, by Golder, 1:233.

243   **"on the beach directly in front of the ship"**: Ibid.

243   **"crowbars, iron wedges and large hammers"**: Steller, *Steller's
        Journal*, 176.

244   **"we should be able to put to sea in her without risk"**: Waxell, *The
        American Expedition*, 148.

244   **"I used my authority to force them to work"**: Ibid., 147.

245   **"erecting of the stern and the sternpost"**: "Log of the *St. Peter*,"
        in *Bering's Voyages*, by Golder, 1:234.

245   **"crakeberry plants instead of tea"**: Waxell, *The American Expedi-
        tion*, 148.

245   **"We enjoyed ourselves pretty well"**: Steller, *Steller's Journal*, 180.

246   **"quite savage and attack people"**: "Log of the *St. Peter*," in *Ber-
        ing's Voyages*, by Golder, 1:238.

246   **"attacks the men with his flippers and keeps on fighting"**: Georg
        Wilhelm Steller, *De Bestiis Marinis; or, The Beasts of the Sea*, 60.

247   **"without danger to life and limb"**: Steller, *Steller's Journal*, 225.

247   **"white ring around the eyes and red skin about the beak"**: Ibid.,
        237.

247   **"was sufficient for three starving men"**: Stejneger, *Georg Wilhelm
        Steller*, 351.

248   **"among the animals without discipline or order"**: Steller, *Steller's
        Journal*, 161.

248   **"it lies like a person, with the front feet crossed over the breast"**:
        Ibid., 221.

249 **"become sick and feeble, and will not leave the shore"**: Ibid., 220.

251 **"the blood gushed forth anew"**: Ibid., 228.

251 **"surpasses in sweetness and taste the best beef fat"**: Ibid., 234.

251 **"defiled by the blowflies as to be covered with worms all over"**: Ibid., 235.

251 **"we felt considerably better and became quite active"**: Waxell, *The American Expedition*, 151.

252 **"when I went there myself"**: Steller, *Steller's Journal*, 233.

253 **"prospected the island for metals and minerals and had found none"**: Ibid., 196.

253 **"a capstan we had had on the old ship"**: Waxell, *The American Expedition*, 152.

253 **"much splintered and cracked from being wrenched loose"**: Ibid.

254 **"Our ship with God's help will be soon finished"**: "Log of the *St. Peter*," in *Bering's Voyages*, by Golder, 1:236.

254 **"and there is great danger in wrecking the vessel"**: Ibid.

255 **"deliverance from this desert island"**: Steller, *Steller's Journal*, 181.

256 **"much inner emotion"**: Ibid., 182.

257 **"clear with passing clouds"**: "Log of the Hooker *St. Peter*," in *Bering's Voyages*, by Golder, 1:242.

257 **"God's wonderful and loving guidance"**: Steller, *Steller's Journal*, 184.

258 **"fallen into the hands of strangers"**: Ibid., 186.

258 **"regarded the present circumstances as in a dream"**: Ibid., 187.

258 **"plunged into veritable superabundance"**: Waxell, *The American Expedition*, 158.

259 **"it just cannot be expressed in words"**: Ibid.

EPILOGUE: RUSSIAN AMERICA

263 **"reveal the pitiable state in which they then were"**: Ibid., 203.

263 **"[W]hen you have to eat them it requires a great effort"**: Ibid., 205.

265 **"lazy and pompous conduct of the officers"**: Steller, letter to Gmelin, in Golder, *Bering's Voyages*, 1:243.

268 **Bering was never celebrated in his time**: See Müller, *Bering's Voyages: The Reports from Russia*, 3–68, for a detailed background and discussion, written by scholar Carol Urness, of the long list of leaked publications about the voyage and a discussion of the sources, possible authors, and their impact. Further academic study of the historiography of the Bering expedition should begin here.

269 **Their work helped to tell the tale of the survivors**: An account of the excavations is contained in Albrethsen, "Bering's Second Kamchatka Expedition," in *Vitus Bering*, edited by Jacobsen.

271 **observe such violence or to enforce such a law**: See Lydia Black, *Russians in Alaska, 1732–1867*, for a good overview of the history of the early Russian colonial period and the era of the Russian American Company.

273 **"deep waters and exposed anchorages"**: George Davidson, *The Tracks and Landfalls of Bering and Chirikov on the Northwest Coast of America*, 42.

A Note on Sources and Further Reading

There were several publications that were invaluable in creating the narrative account of Russia's great expeditions.

Russian Penetration of the North Pacific Ocean: A Documentary Record, edited and translated by Basil Dmytryshyn, E. A. P. Crownhart-Vaughan, and Thomas Vaughan, is a collection of instructions, orders, journals, and reports of the expedition, select letters mostly to do with the Siberian part of the expedition, and the overall government directive of the enterprise. It is an invaluable source for primary documents relating to the official Russian activities in Siberia and Alaska.

Volume 1 of F. A. Golder's *Bering's Voyages* is a collection of the logbooks of the *St. Peter* and *St. Paul,* official reports, and letters relating to the Pacific voyage. Anyone who wants to know the exact compass or wind directions or precise location of the ship on each day should consult the logs, which provide the exact hourly log entries for each ship and separate supplementary information such as additional letters signed by the officers or journal entries by the officers. It is a wealth of precise information on pragmatic actions of the crew, weather, location, and passing thoughts or suppositions.

Volume 2 of *Bering's Voyages* is an edited, annotated, and translated edition of *Steller's Journal.* I quoted extensively from this translation because I preferred the older archaic English and the less perfected turn of phrase for no other reason than it suited the style of how I felt Steller must have been writing while onboard ship or shipwrecked. For anyone wanting to read Steller's journal for themselves, I would recommend *Journal of a Voyage with Bering, 1741–1742*, edited by O. W. Frost. This translation is more smooth, modern, and fluid and contains numerous interesting annotations and asides.

Sven Waxell's journal manuscript of the expedition, including the crossing of Siberia, was published posthumously as *The American Voyage* and represents, along with *Steller's Journal*, the bulk of the firsthand accounts of the voyage. It is unvarnished and entertaining rather than precise or technical, a window into how things actually were.

Only a small portion of the available documentary material related to the Great Northern Expedition in Russian archives, or published in Russian, is available in English translation. However, in recent years, Peter Ulf Møller and Natasha Okhotina Lind have published *Under Vitus Bering's Command: New Perspectives on the Russian Kamchatka Expeditions*, essays by prominent specialists on various topics deriving from the latest documentary evidence relating to the First and Second Kamchatka Expeditions. This would be the place to start for further reading, with essays on cartography, navigation, surveying, and natural history. These essays are focused on the more academic information collected by the scientific component of the expeditions.

Perhaps the most interesting recent publication on Bering and the Second Kamchatka Expedition is *Until Death Do Us Part: The Letters and Travels of Anna and Vitus Bering* by Møller and Lind, a collection of the personal correspondence of the Berings that sheds previously unknown light on their relationship and personalities that is distinct from official correspondence and reports. It also contains a detailed accounting of the extensive possessions they brought with them to Siberia.

Bering and Chirikov: The American Voyages and Their Impact, edited by O. W. Frost, is a collection of essays by Bering scholars. Particularly useful to me in creating a narrative account of this remarkable expedition was James Gibson's "Supplying the Kamchatka Expedition, 1725–30 and 1742," which included some translations of Russian documents not otherwise available in English.

The only full biography of Steller is *Georg Wilhelm Steller*, by Leonhard Stejneger. Published in 1936 it is thorough and balanced. *Steller's Island*, by Dean Littlepage, is a good more recent account of Steller's explorations in Alaska and on Bering Island.

Vasilli Divin's *The Great Russian Navigator, A. I. Chirikov*, while nearly a hagiography of the Russian mariner, contains a wealth of information about the First and Second Kamchatka Expeditions.

See also *The Journal of Midshipman Chaplin*, the annotated journal of a junior officer who accompanied Bering and Chirikov on the first expedition. It also has some interesting articles on navigation, surveying, and mapmaking in the period that would be of interest to anyone furthering their study of those topics.

Much detail of the work of the scientific component of the expedition in Siberia (weather, flora, fauna and observations of customs, languages, and culture of native peoples) has not been properly published in English. Recently, much more information, correspondence, reports, and the like is being translated and published by scholars associated with the Carlsberg Foundation. See http://www.carlsbergfondet.dk/en /Research-Activities/Research-Projects/Postdoctoral Fellowships /Peter-Ulf-Moeller_Vitus-Berings-Kamchatka-Expeditions.

For further reading on the history of the Russian conquest and government of Alaska, consult Lydia Black's *Russians in Alaska, 1732–1867*.

Selected Bibliography

Andreyev, A. I., ed. *Russian Discoveries in the Pacific and in North America in the Eighteenth and Nineteenth Centuries: A Collection of Materials*. Translated from the Russian by Carl Ginsburg, U.S. Department of State. Ann Arbor, MI: American Council of Learned Societies, 1952.

Anson, George. *A Voyage Round the World in the Years 1740–1744*. London: Ingram, Cooke, 1853.

Black, Lydia. *Russians in Alaska, 1732–1867*. Fairbanks: University of Alaska Press, 2004.

Bown, Stephen R. *Scurvy: How a Surgeon, a Mariner, and a Gentleman Solved the Greatest Medical Mystery of the Age of Sail*. New York: Thomas Dunne Books, 2004.

Chaplin, Piotr. *The Journal of Midshipman Chaplin: A Record of Bering's First Kamchatka Expedition*. Edited by Carol L. Urness et al. Aarhus, Denmark: Aarhus University Press, 2010.

Coxe, William. *Account of the Russian Discoveries Between Asia and America*. Ann Arbor, MI: Ann Arbor University Microfilms, 1966.

Curtiss, Mini. *A Forgotten Empress: Anna Ivanovna and Her Era*. New York: Frederick Unga, 1974.

Davidson, George. *The Tracks and Landfalls of Bering and Chirikof on the Northwest Coast of America*. San Francisco: Geographical Society of the Pacific, 1901.

Divin, Vasilli A. *The Great Russian Navigator, A. I. Chirikov.* Translated by Raymond H. Fisher. Fairbanks: University of Alaska Press, 1993.

Dmytryshyn, Basil, E. A. P. Crownhart-Vaughan, and Thomas Vaughan, eds. and trans. *Russian Penetration of the North Pacific Ocean, 1700–1799: A Documentary Record.* Vol. 2, *To Siberia and Russian America: Three Centuries of Russian Eastward Expansion.* Portland: Oregon Historical Society Press, 1988.

Dobell, Peter. *Travels in Kamchatka and Siberia.* London: Henry Colburn and Richard Bentley, 1830.

Fisher, Raymond H. *Bering's Voyages: Whither and Why.* Seattle: University of Washington Press, 1977.

Frost, Orcutt. *Bering: The Russian Discovery of America.* New Haven, CT: Yale University Press, 2003.

————, ed. *Bering and Chirikov: The American Voyages and Their Impact.* Anchorage: Alaska Historical Society, 1992.

Gibson, James R. "Supplying the Kamchatka Expedition, 1725–30 and 1742." In *Bering and Chirikov: The American Voyages and Their Impact,* edited by Orcutt Frost. Anchorage: Alaska Historical Society, 1992.

Golder, Frank Alfred. *Bering's Voyages: An Account of the Efforts of the Russians to Determine the Relation of Asia and America.* Vol. 1, *The Log Books and Official Reports of the First and Second Expeditions, 1725–1730 and 1733–1742.* 1922. Reprint, New York: American Geographical Society, 2015.

————. *Bering's Voyages: An Account of the Efforts of the Russians to Determine the Relation of Asia and America.* Vol. 2, *Steller's Journal of the Sea Voyage from Kamchatka to America and Return on the Second Expedition, 1741–1742.* Translated and edited by Leonhard Stejneger. 1922. Reprint, New York: American Geographical Society, 1968.

————. *Russian Expansion on the Pacific, 1641–1850.* New York: Paragon Book, 1971.

Heaps, Leo, ed. *Log of the* Centurion: *Based on the Original Papers of Captain Philip Saumarez on Board HMS* Centurion, *Lord Anson's Flagship During His Circumnavigation, 1740–1744.* London: Macmillan, 1973.

Hingley, Ronald. *The Tsars: Russian Autocrats, 1533–1917.* London: Weidenfeld and Nicolson, 1968.

Hughes, Lindsey. *Peter the Great: A Biography.* New Haven, CT: Yale University Press, 2002.

Jacobsen, N. Kingo, ed. *Vitus Bering, 1741–1991: Bicentennial Remembrance Lectures.* Translated by Richard Barnes. Copenhagen: C. A. Reitzels Forlag, 1993.

Korb, Johann Georg. *Diary of an Austrian Secretary of Legation at the Court of Tsar Peter the Great.* Translated and edited by Count MacDonnel. London: Frank Cass, 1968.

Krasheninnikov, Stephen Petrovich. *Explorations of Kamchatka: Report of a Journey Made to Explore Eastern Siberia in 1735–1741, by Order of the Russian Imperial Government.* Translated by E. A. P. Crownhart-Vaughan. Portland: Oregon Historical Society Press, 1972.

Kushnarev, Evgenii G. *Bering's Search for the Strait: The First Kamchatka Expedition, 1725–1730.* Edited and translated by E. A. P. Crownhart-Vaughan. Portland: Oregon Historical Society Press, 1990.

Lauridsen, Peter. *Vitus Bering: The Discoverer of Bering Strait.* Translated by Julius E. Olsen. Chicago: S. C. Griggs, 1889.

Lincoln, Bruce. *The Conquest of a Continent: Siberia and the Russians.* New York: Random House, 1993.

Lind, James. *A Treatise of the Scurvy.* 1753. Reprint, Birmingham, AL: Classics of Medicine Library, 1980.

Littlepage, Dean. *Steller's Island: Adventures of a Pioneer Naturalist in Alaska.* Seattle: Mountaineers Books, 2006.

Longworth, Philip. *The Three Empresses: Catherine I, Anne & Elizabeth of Russia.* New York: Holt, Reinhart, and Winston, 1973.

Massie, Robert, K. *Peter the Great: His Life and World.* New York: Alfred A. Knopf, 1980.

Møller, Peter Ulf, and Natasha Okhotina Lind, eds. *Under Vitus Bering's Command: New Perspectives on the Russian Kamchatka Expeditions.* Aarhus, Denmark: Aarhus University Press, 2003.

———, eds. *Until Death Do Us Part: The Letters and Travels of Anna and Vitus Bering.* Translated by Anna Halager. Fairbanks: University of Alaska Press, 2008.

Montefiore, Simon Sebag. *The Romanovs, 1613–1918*. New York: Alfred A. Knopf, 2016.

Müller, Gerhard Friedrich. *Bering's Voyages: The Reports from Russia*. Translated by Carol Urness. Fairbanks: University of Alaska Press, 1986.

Sauer, Martin. *Account of a Geographical and Astronomical Expedition . . . by Commodore Joseph Billings in the Years 1785 to 1794*. London: A. Strahan, 1806.

Schuyler, Eugene. *Peter the Great*. 2 vols. New York: Charles Scribner's Sons, 1884.

Smeeton, Miles. *Once Is Enough*. 1959. Reprint, New York: International Marine, 2003.

Stejneger, Leonhard. *Georg Wilhelm Steller: The Pioneer of Alaskan Natural History*. Cambridge, MA: Harvard University Press, 1936.

Steller, Georg Wilhelm. *De Bestiis Marinis; or, The Beasts of the Sea* [1751]. Translated by Walter Miller and Jennie Emerson Miller. Transcribed and edited by Paul Royster. Faculty Publications, University of Nebraska–Lincoln Libraries. Paper 17.

———. *Journal of a Voyage with Bering, 1741–1742*. Edited by O. W. Frost. Translated by Margritt A. Engel and O. W. Frost. Stanford, CA: Stanford University Press, 1988.

———. *Steller's History of Kamchatka: Collected Information Concerning the History of Kamchatka, Its Peoples, Their Manners, Names, Lifestyle, and Various Customary Practices*. Edited by Marvin W. Falk. Translated by Margritt Engel and Karen Willmore. Fairbanks: University of Alaska Press, 2003.

———. *Steller's Journal of the Sea Voyage from Kamchatka to America and Return on the Second Expedition, 1741–1742*. Translated and edited by Leonhard Stejneger. New York: Octagon Books, 1968. Vol. 2 of *Bering's Voyages: An Account of the Efforts of the Russians to Determine the Relation of Asia and America*, by F. A. Golder. New York: American Geographical Society, 1922.

von Staehlin, Jacob. *Original Anecdotes of Peter the Great*. London: J. Murray, 1788.

Waxell, Sven. *The American Expedition*. London: William Hodge, 1952.

Williams, Glyndwr. *Naturalists at Sea*. New Haven, CT: Yale University Press, 2013.

———. *The Prize of All the Oceans: Commodore Anson's Daring Voyage and Triumphant Capture of the Spanish Treasure Galleon*. New York: Penguin Viking, 1999.

Zviagin, V. N. "A Reconstruction of Vitus Bering Based on Skeletal Remains." In *Bering and Chirikov: The American Voyages and Their Impact*, edited by Orcutt Frost. Anchorage: Alaska Historical Society, 1992.

Acknowledgments

As usual, a team of people combined their skills and talents to transform an idea into a manuscript, and then a manuscript into a book. I'd like to acknowledge most importantly my editor, Merloyd Lawrence, for helping to define and focus the project and for coming up with a great title. At Da Capo Press I'd like to acknowledge Lissa Warren and all the publicity and marketing team for their energetic efforts, Amber Morris, Annette Wenda, Trish Wilkinson, and cover designer Kerry Rubenstein. At Douglas and McIntyre I'd like to acknowledge Anna Comfort O'Keeffe, Howard White, and Kathy Vanderlinden. Also, thanks to Peter Schledermann for reading an early draft and giving me thoughtful comments and to mapmaker Scott Manktelow for again creating interesting maps. Thanks to the Alberta Foundation for the Arts and Canada Council for the Arts for writer's grants. And last but never least, my wife, Nicky Brink, for listening to endless talks on the latest chapters and for reading the first chapter drafts before the manuscript was even compiled into a single document, long before I dared show anything to anyone else. May you all be ever free of scurvy!

Image Sources

Peter the Great, page 8, Library of Congress
Anna Ivanovna, page 8, Wikimedia Commons
Catherine I, page 8, Wikimedia Commons
The Kremlin, page 9, NYPL
St. Petersburg, page 9, Wikimedia Commons
Packhorse road, page 70, NYPL
Avacha Bay, page 70, NYPL
Yakut woman, page 71, NYPL
Dogsleds, page 71, NYPL
Cook Inlet, page 122, George Vancouver's *Voyage of Discovery*
Waxell meeting Aleutians, page 122, Wikimedia Commons
Steller's sea bear, page 123, NYPL
Steller measuring, page 123, Wikimedia Commons
Khitrov sketch, page 123, Wikimedia Commons
Steller's sea lions, sea cows, and sea otters, page 188, Wikimedia Commons
Bering's ship wrecked, page 188, Wikimedia Commons
US Russian stamp, page 189, Wikimedia Commons
Bering found dead, page 189, Wikimedia Commons
Bering Island, page 189, Sergey Krasnoshchokov, Shutterstock

Index

About the Author

Stephen R. Bown is author of *The Last Viking: The Life of Roald Amundsen* and *White Eskimo: Knud Rasmussen's Fearless Journey into the Heart of the Arctic*, which won the William Mills Award for the best book on the Arctic in 2016. His award-winning books, including *Scurvy* and *Madness, Betrayal, and the Lash*, have led to him being called "Canada's Simon Winchester." He lives near Banff in the Canadian Rockies.